The Liar's Bible

A Good Book for Fiction Writers

LAWRENCE BLOCK

BOOKS FOR WRITERS
WRITING THE NOVEL FROM PLOT TO PRINT TO PIXEL • TELLING LIES FOR FUN & PROFIT • SPIDER, SPIN ME A WEB • WRITE FOR YOUR LIFE • THE LIAR'S BIBLE • THE LIAR'S COMPANION • AFTERTHOUGHTS

ANTHOLOGIES EDITED
DEATH CRUISE • MASTER'S CHOICE • OPENING SHOTS • MASTER'S CHOICE 2 • SPEAKING OF LUST • OPENING SHOTS 2 • SPEAKING OF GREED • BLOOD ON THEIR HANDS • GANGSTERS, SWINDLERS, KILLERS, & THIEVES • MANHATTAN NOIR • MANHATTAN NOIR 2 • DARK CITY LIGHTS • IN SUNLIGHT OR IN SHADOW

WRITING AS JILL EMERSON
SHADOWS • WARM AND WILLING • ENOUGH OF SORROW • THIRTY • THREESOME • A MADWOMAN'S DIARY • THE TROUBLE WITH EDEN • A WEEK AS ANDREA BENSTOCK • GETTING OFF

THE CLASSIC CRIME LIBRARY
AFTER THE FIRST DEATH • DEADLY HONEYMOON • GRIFTER'S GAME • THE GIRL WITH THE LONG GREEN HEART • THE SPECIALISTS • THE TRIUMPH OF EVIL • SUCH MEN ARE DANGEROUS • NOT COMIN' HOME TO YOU • LUCKY AT CARDS • KILLING CASTRO • A DIET OF TREACLE • YOU COULD CALL IT MURDER • COWARD'S KISS • STRANGE EMBRACE • CINDERELLA SIMS • PASSPORT TO PERIL • ARIEL

THE COLLECTION OF CLASSIC EROTICA
21 GAY STREET • CANDY • GIGOLO JOHNNY WELLS • APRIL NORTH • CARLA • A STRANGE KIND OF LOVE • CAMPUS TRAMP • COMMUNITY OF WOMEN • BORN TO BE BAD • COLLEGE FOR SINNERS • OF SHAME AND JOY • A WOMAN MUST LOVE • THE ADULTERERS • KEPT • THE TWISTED ONES • HIGH SCHOOL SEX CLUB • I SELL LOVE • 69 BARROW STREET • FOUR LIVES AT THE CROSSROADS • CIRCLE OF SINNERS • A GIRL CALLED HONEY • SIN HELLCAT • SO WILLING

THE MATTHEW SCUDDER NOVELS
THE SINS OF THE FATHERS • TIME TO MURDER AND CREATE • IN THE MIDST OF DEATH • A STAB IN THE DARK • EIGHT MILLION WAYS TO DIE • WHEN THE SACRED GINMILL CLOSES • OUT ON THE CUTTING EDGE • A TICKET TO THE BONEYARD • A DANCE AT THE SLAUGHTERHOUSE • A WALK AMONG THE TOMBSTONES • THE DEVIL KNOWS YOU'RE DEAD • A LONG LINE OF DEAD MEN • EVEN THE WICKED • EVERYBODY DIES •

HOPE TO DIE • ALL THE FLOWERS ARE DYING • A DROP OF THE HARD STUFF • THE NIGHT AND THE MUSIC

THE BERNIE RHODENBARR MYSTERIES

BURGLARS CAN'T BE CHOOSERS • THE BURGLAR IN THE CLOSET • THE BURGLAR WHO LIKED TO QUOTE KIPLING • THE BURGLAR WHO STUDIED SPINOZA • THE BURGLAR WHO PAINTED LIKE MONDRIAN • THE BURGLAR WHO TRADED TED WILLIAMS • THE BURGLAR WHO THOUGHT HE WAS BOGART • THE BURGLAR IN THE LIBRARY • THE BURGLAR IN THE RYE • THE BURGLAR ON THE PROWL • THE BURGLAR WHO COUNTED THE SPOONS

KELLER'S GREATEST HITS

HIT MAN • HIT LIST • HIT PARADE • HIT & RUN • HIT ME • KELLER'S FEDORA

THE ADVENTURES OF EVAN TANNER

THE THIEF WHO COULDN'T SLEEP • THE CANCELED CZECH • TANNER'S TWELVE SWINGERS • TWO FOR TANNER • TANNER'S TIGER • TANNER'S VIRGIN • ME TANNER, YOU JANE • TANNER ON ICE

THE AFFAIRS OF CHIP HARRISON

NO SCORE • CHIP HARRISON SCORES AGAIN • MAKE OUT WITH MURDER • THE TOPLESS TULIP CAPER

NOVELS

BORDERLINE • GETTING OFF • RANDOM WALK • RESUME SPEED • RONALD RABBIT IS A DIRTY OLD MAN • SINNER MAN • SMALL TOWN • THE GIRL WITH THE DEEP BLUE EYES

COLLECTED SHORT STORIES

SOMETIMES THEY BITE • LIKE A LAMB TO SLAUGHTER • SOME DAYS YOU GET THE BEAR • ONE NIGHT STANDS AND LOST WEEKENDS • ENOUGH ROPE • CATCH AND RELEASE • DEFENDER OF THE INNOCENT

NON-FICTION

STEP BY STEP • GENERALLY SPEAKING • THE CRIME OF OUR LIVES • AFTERTHOUGHTS

WRITTEN FOR PERFORMANCE

TILT! (EPISODIC TELEVISION) • HOW FAR? (ONE-ACT PLAY) • MY BLUEBERRY NIGHTS (FILM)

Grateful acknowledgement is made to *Writer's Digest*, in which the articles contained in this book were originally published.

THE LIAR'S BIBLE
Copyright © 2011 by Lawrence Block
All Rights Reserved.
Production: QA Productions
A LAWRENCE BLOCK PRODUCTION

The Liar's Bible
A Good Book for Fiction Writers

LAWRENCE BLOCK

The Liar's Bible

Introduction . . . 1

1: Make No Misteak . . . 7
2: A Writer's Library . . . 13
3: Getting by on a Writer's Income . . . 19
4: Travelin' Man . . . 33
5: Who It May Concern . . . 38
6: Craven Images . . . 43
7: Who's in Charge . . . 49
8: Huffing and Puffing . . . 54
9: Sticks and Stones . . . 60
10: Crockpot Macramé . . . 66
11: View Finder . . . 71
12: Shifting Gears . . . 77
13: Tune in to Your Creativity . . . and Let the Ideas Come to You . . . 82
14: Applying the Breaks . . . 95
15: Plotting, Plodding . . . 101
16: Secondhand Pros . . . 107
17: So Don't Do That! . . . 113
18: Reflection Slips . . . 119
19. Call Him Ishmael . . . 125

A Good Book for Fiction Writers

20: Eye Strain . . . 131

21: Overcoming the Ultimate Writer's Block . . . 136

22: Self-Analysis . . . 151

23: Nonstop Writing . . . 157

24: Gone Shopping . . . 163

25: Fear of Writing . . . 169

26: Character Studies . . . 175

27: The Guts of the Fiction Writer . . . 181

28: Length Wise . . . 193

29: Spilling the Beans . . . 199

30: Opus 100 . . . 205

31: No Message . . . 211

32: Hands Off! . . . 217

33: First Blood . . . 223

34: Buckling Down . . . 229

35: Are You Sure Alfred Knopf Started This Way? . . . 236

36: Do It Until You Need Glasses . . . 251

37: Dare to be Bad . . . 257

38: Looking for Madame Bovary . . . 263

39: Turnabout is Fair Play . . . 269

40: Pieces of String too Small to Save . . . 276

Introduction

In the fall of 1975 I spent a month on North Carolina's Outer Banks. Every day I fished off the Rodanthe pier, and every night I ate what I caught. It was a full life.

When I wasn't fishing, I sat in my room and wrote. Along with several short stories, I turned out an essay that attempted to answer the perennial (and perennially annoying) question of the non-writer to the writer: Where do you get your ideas? I discussed the way ideas crop up and how they turn into stories, and I mailed the piece off to *Writer's Digest* and forgot about it.

Six months later I remembered, when I learned that the magazine wanted to buy the article. I was in Los Angeles by then, living at the Magic Hotel, and my daughters would be flying out at the end of June to spend the summer with me. I figured they could keep me company at the hotel for July and we could spend August seeing something of the country on the way back to New York. And one of the places we'd stop en route would be Cincinnati, where *WD*'s editor, John Brady, could take me to lunch.

I had an agenda, and I shared it with him over bowls of the chili for which the city is famous. The magazine had several monthly columns, I pointed out, but what it didn't have was a column on the writing of fiction, and that seemed to be the chief interest of the greater portion of its subscribers. Surely they needed a fiction column, and surely I was the very person to write it.

Remarkably enough, Brady agreed with me. Maybe it was the chili. I wound up with an assignment to deliver 1,500 to 2,000 words every other month; they'd cut their cartoon columnist back to six issues a year, to alternate with *Fiction*.

I'd planned on returning to L.A. after I dropped off the kids, but wound up staying in New York. I rented a place on Bleecker Street and went to work. After I'd delivered three columns, Brady bumped the cartoon guy altogether and put me on a monthly schedule. I wrote that column, year in and year out, for fourteen years.

The piece that started it all, the essay I knocked out in Rodanthe when I wasn't hauling spot and croaker out of the Atlantic, wasn't the first I'd written about writing. Seventeen years earlier, in early 1958, I was a college student who'd dropped out to hang on to a summer job at a New York literary agency, quite the perfect learning experience for a wannabe writer. I spent eight hours a day reading fee scripts, the submissions of other wannabes who paid my boss to read their work. I was the one who read it, and it was my task to write letters over his signature detailing why their stories were unsalable, but assuring them that they were talented, and that they were best advised to write another story, and send it in. Uh, with another check, of course.

The moral and ethical aspects of all of this notwithstanding, it was a wonderful job. You learn more reading inept work than you could ever learn from a master. You see what's wrong. That's easier than trying to see what's right.

A couple of months into the job, I noticed one obvious error that a surprising number of my earnest hopefuls were committing. They used unwieldy verbs in dialogue, whipping out *Roget's Thesaurus* to avoid saying "said" all the time, and then wedding the verb to a cumbersome adverb. I wrote a piece about this, called it "Gloomily Asserted Smith," and gave it to Henry Morrison, who occupied the rung directly above mine on the Scott Meredith ladder. He sent it to a magazine called *Author and Journalist*, and, *mirabile dictu*, they bought it. I think they paid $25, but it might have been as much as $35; whatever it was, that's what I got . . . minus 10 percent for Scott, needless to say.

"Gloomily Asserted Smith" never led anywhere, unless you want to see it as a forerunner of my column. But the column itself led to four books.

The first, *Writing the Novel: From Plot to Print*, was the suggestion of Brady and his fellows in *WD*'s book division; by that time I'd been doing the column for a little over a year. It's been in print ever since.

The second and fourth were *Telling Lies for Fun and Profit* and *Spider, Spin Me a Web*. Both were composed of columns I'd written for the magazine, collected and arranged in some semblance of order. *Telling Lies* was published by Arbor House in hardcover and trade paperback, was a Book-of-the-Month Club alternate selection, and has been in print in one edition or another almost continuously since its 1981 publication.

Spider, Spin Me a Web was the same idea, but with columns written after those in *Telling Lies*. It came out from Writer's Digest Books in 1988, and I've always felt it was the better book, but it's never sold nearly as well. The only obvious difference between the two books is the title, and if you think a title doesn't matter, well, you might want to rethink that one.

In 1983, I dreamed up an interactive seminar that would adapt some of the principles and techniques of the Human Potential Movement specifically for writers. I called it Write for Your Life, and for a couple of years my wife Lynne and I flew around the country with it. I realized there ought to be a book version and decided it was a natural for self-publishing, since I could sell it at seminars and promote it in the advertising for the seminar. And if I published it myself I could have copies right away, not a year later. In 1985 I printed 5,000 copies and sold them all; the book's available again, but in ebook form only.

In 1990 I came to a parting of the ways with the folks in Cincinnati. There was a change in the editorship, and the new boy felt a need to assert himself, and that was the end of my column. It was a shabby windup to fourteen good years, and it felt odd not to have a column due every month, but on balance I decided it was just as well. By then I'd long since exhausted everything I ever knew about writing. Time to hang it up and go on to other things.

So here, two decades later, is my fifth book on the subject. How on earth did that happen?

Well, it's not really all that hard to explain. *Telling Lies* gathered columns from my first four years at *WD*, *Spider* from the four or so years after that. That left a lot of columns uncollected, and in the ordinary course of things I would very likely have sorted through them and looked around for a publisher.

But when I rather abruptly stopped writing the column, I quit thinking about the subject. Lynne and I had just returned to New York after a couple of years in Florida and a couple more without a fixed address, and my career as a novelist was blossoming, which meant not only more books to write but more ancillary duties—book tours, promotional efforts, and the like.

Time passed. It'll do that.

And then, a couple of years ago, I heard from a fellow I know named Terry Zobeck. He's a fan and a collector, and his particular collecting interest is centered on the initial magazine appearance of works by those writers he most esteems. Toward this end he had compiled a great number of issues of *WD*, and by purchasing bulk lots he'd wound up with duplicate copies of many of those issues.

He'd checked them against his copies of my books, and established that he had a host of columns and articles of mine that had not appeared in either *Telling Lies* or *Spider*. That was more than enough uncollected material for a new book, and would I like him to send me his duplicate issues?

I could hardly say no. In addition to the duplicates, he went to the trouble of photocopying those columns of mine for which he had only a single copy. In all, I now had in hand 77 pieces that had never previously been published in book form, an ample amount for not one but two books.

So I thanked him profusely and put the box in the corner of my office and forgot about it for a couple of years.

Well, not exactly. I mean, I remembered just where it was, and sometimes I stared balefully at it. But I wasn't ready to do anything about it. I knew the material was worth publishing, but the whole process of getting it into shape for a traditional print publisher felt daunting, and I couldn't make myself believe that my own print publisher would be all that enthusiastic about it, or put forth much of an effort on its behalf.

Then Open Road came along, and set about publishing forty-plus backlist books of mine as ebooks. Whereupon one of those little lightbulbs took form over my head. (It was left over from the cartoon column, the one my own column displaced in *Writer's Digest*. See? Nothing's ever wasted.)

Print publication would have meant more work than I was prepared to undertake, and would have taken more time than I was willing to wait. And I don't know that the resultant book would have flown off shelves and out of stores. Publishing it as an Open Road E-Riginal has entailed hardly any work at all, and just look how little time it's required. I mean, here it is, right? Now that didn't take very long, did it?

If it's been wonderfully simple publishing this way, I've kept it every bit as simple so far as the volume's organization is concerned. In *Telling Lies* and *Spider*, I made an effort to group the columns by subject matter.

This time, I'm presenting everything in chronological order.

And I have to think that's not only the simplest and easiest way to do it, but the best as well. This way you'll be reading them in the order they were written. Which isn't to say that you can't skip around as the spirit moves you.

I am, as you may imagine, profoundly grateful to Terry Zobeck, but for whom this book would not exist. And I'm grateful as well to all my friends at Open Road, similarly indispensable; they made the book possible, and made my role in the process easy and pleasurable.

My publishing arrangement with Open Road was a richly gratifying one for its five years duration. When it had run its course, I knew it was time to take the training wheels off the bicycle and put my own hands on the handlebars. I've been able to take over publishing my backlist titles, and am thus pleased to present this new edition of *The Liar's Bible*. I am, as you might imagine, grateful to everyone who has supported me in this endeavor, and especially to Jaye W. Manus, who has throughout been my Goddess of Design and Production.

Finlly, I'm grateful to you, Dear Reader, as all of us who write can only be grateful to those who read our work. Isn't it remarkable, when one thinks of it, that the binary electronic blips and blops of e-publication can take something ephemeral by definition—words printed in magazines—and fix them in cyber-permanence?

Who knew?

Lawrence Block
Greenwich Village

• 1 •

Make No Misteak
August 1981

A couple of summers ago, while one of my mysteries was wending its way through the editorial process, my editor gave me some incidental good and bad news. A fellow in one of the other departments had read my book and loved it. That was the good news. But, she went on, he had pointed out that there are no buses on West End Avenue. Early on I had my lead character take a bus down West End from around 87th Street to around 71st, and it seemed that no corresponding bus existed in what we persist in calling the real world.

Some years back I had lived at West End and 71st, and I used to see buses proceeding down the avenue before turning east at 72nd Street. I hadn't realized they'd only come from a couple of blocks north of there. I digested this information, looked at the manuscript and contemplated the aggravation involved in changing it in line with this unwanted bit of information, and decided the hell with it.

As is my frequent custom, I had several rationalizations. Manhattan buses, I pointed out, are by no means as fixed and intransigent as the stars in their courses. For all any of us knew, there might be a bus on West End Avenue by the time the book reached the stores. In any event, only those readers intimately familiar with Manhattan's Upper West Side would know the difference, and only the nitpickers among them would care.

"Besides," I concluded, "my book, like all fiction, takes place in an alternate universe. In Bernie Rhodenbarr's world, there are indeed buses on West End Avenue. After all, I'm not writing a New York guidebook here, you know. This is a mystery, a light one, a diversion, an entertainment. Who gives a damn where the buses go?"

I don't know if my editor was convinced, but she rather liked the line about the alternate universe. The book went to press with the bus on West End Avenue, and reviewers neglected to take me to task for it. Two readers did ask me about it, but they didn't seem awfully bothered, nor was I. The book did have two rather more serious minor errors—a typo had transformed the titular hero of a book of Smollett's from Launcelot Greaves to Laurence, and some other gremlin had reversed the death dates of Rudyard Kipling and King George V. (One reader apiece wrote in to apprise me of those errors, and I was grateful to both of them.)

I've thought about that bus route since then. And I've reached an astonishing conclusion.

I was wrong.

A Perforated Ulster

I was driven to this thoroughly unpleasant realization not by its results but by my own observations. Much of what I've learned about writing has been acquired by reading other people's work, and this revelation came about as I made my way a while ago through what may charitably be described as an indifferent thriller. One of the characters was from Ireland. "I was born in the County Ulster," he proclaimed.

Well, the hell he was. Because there is no County Ulster. Historically, Ireland is composed of four ancient kingdoms, Ulster, Munster, Leinster and Connaught. Nowadays journalists have made Ulster synonymous with the six-county political entity of Northern Ireland, but this is not strictly correct; Ulster properly includes as well three counties that were incorporated with Southern Ireland at the time of partition. But that's minor. What's more important is the incontrovertible fact that no one born in Ireland would refer to the County Ulster.

This doesn't mean the author's an idiot, or even an ignoramus. It's an easy mistake to make, and just unfortunate that no one caught it in the course of copy editing. What's more to the point is the effect it had on me as a reader.

My immediate reaction was twofold. First of all, I was at once shaken loose from my belief in the story. "Hey, wait a minute," an inner voice said. "There's no County Ulster for him to have been born in, which means none of this ever happened; it's not real; it's just a made-up story." Well, of course. They're all stories. But fiction works because a part of the mind forgets that it's fiction while we're reading it.

Another part of self, the detached observer, had another reaction. "This writer doesn't know spit from shoe polish," I thought, approximately. "If he can be that ignorant and that sloppy about such an obvious point, how can I take anything he says seriously?"

I don't know that I stopped reading the book at that point. But I certainly ceased to be a receptive audience for it, and I began at once to regret that West End Avenue bus.

I don't think the two errors are of equal moment. Bus routes *do* change while the counties of Ireland remain more or less constant. (Although a couple did have nomenclatural changes earlier this century, as a matter of fact.) All the same, it struck me that any departure from reality that could easily be avoided ought to be avoided. Why do anything that might provoke a reader into the reaction I've just described?

OK. Cut, as they say in the movie business, or Fast Forward, as they put it on tape recorders. My next book about Bernie Rhodenbarr had a couple of discussions of the price of silver, which at the time of initial writing was somewhere stratospheric, up around $40 or $50 an ounce. By copy-editing time, silver had plummeted. My editor asked me if I'd like to change the book's mathematics.

I thought about it and decided against it. For one thing, the price of silver, like that of any commodity, is very much subject to change, and substantially more so than even the scheme of New York bus routes. For another, the high price I cited had indeed existed, and reflected reality at the time the book was written. I concluded that I was comfortable with the book as it stood, despite its not jibing with current reality. After all, in years to come the price of silver will unquestionably fluctuate, and I would hardly respond by making corresponding changes in future editions.

The more I think about this whole area, the more confused I get. On the one hand, it is not fiction's job to hold a hand-mirror to reality. I've written more than a few books set in areas I haven't visited, and I'm sure my Yugoslavia has precious little in common with Tito's Yugoslavia, and I don't care. On the other hand, I have a certain horror of committing any County Ulsters of my own.

A common out is through the use of a fictional terrain, whether it be Faulkner's Yoknapatawpha County or Wolfe's Catawba or Ed McBain's Isola. I trust every reader of McBain's 87th Precinct novels knows the city in question is New York, but by changing the names of the streets and neighborhoods, by creating a fictional equivalent of New York, McBain is able to write eloquently about the city without wasting hours poring over maps and street guides, and without taking innumerable research trips to determine just where the hospitals and precinct houses are and what they look like. He can depict them as he wants them and put them where he wants them and not worry that some reader will straighten up in his chair and say: "Wait a minute! That's *wrong!*"

I set most of my own books in New York, and have not as yet been tempted to rename the city. It seems to me that the gains are offset by the loss in reader identification. I've noticed that one of the things readers particularly respond to in my recent novels is the city in which they are set, and those readers specifically acquainted with the neighborhoods in question seem to respond most strongly. I find this interesting, and I might do a column on this aspect of reader identification if I ever sort out my thoughts on the subject. For one reason or another, many of us evidently get a special kick out of reading fiction set in areas we know well. "That's it," we say. "He's got that right. I know that candy store. I passed that bar just the other day. He knows his stuff, all right."

Of course, you have to pay for this kind of identification. If you're going to make it work, the candy store had best be on the right corner, the bar correctly described. And yet one doesn't want to pay too much attention to trivia.

On the other hand—and aren't you beginning to feel like one of those eight-armed Hindu idols, with all of these other hands all over the place? On yet another hand, a book I may write one of these days may be set in a town in the west of England, and if that's the case I may well change the town's name and let geography go hang so that I don't have to pay slavish attention to reality. I think it would be too much trouble to be accurate, and that there would be relatively little payoff in increased reader identification; how many readers, after all, would be familiar with the town? Easier to make up my own town, lay it out to my own purposes, and concentrate on characters and story.

John O'Hara laid particular stress on getting things right in his fiction, and his research was prodigious. Here's his foreword to *Ten North Frederick*, one of several novels set in the fictional terrain of Gibbsville, Pennsylvania:

> This, of course, is a work of fiction, but I have also taken liberties with those facts that sometimes help to give truth to fiction. To name one: the office of Lieutenant Governor was created by the 1873 Constitution, so it would have been impossible for Joe Chapin's grandfather to have been Lieutenant Governor at the time I state. There are one or two other deliberate errors of that kind, but I hope they will be pardoned by the alert attorneys who are sure to spot them. If this were straight history, and not fiction, I would not ask to be pardoned.

Well, I wonder. The word that gives me pause is *deliberate*. I can't banish the suspicion that it came to O'Hara's attention after the book was written that the lieutenant governorship existed only after 1873, and that he decided reasonably enough that making the change would be more trouble than it could possibly be worth. The foreword serves its purpose, though, don't you think? Should someone steeped in Pennsylvania history encounter an error, even one that O'Hara didn't know about when he wrote the foreword, he's prepared to overlook it. "Oh, yes," he'll say to himself. "This is one of those deliberate errors of O'Hara's. It's not a real mistake."

Ah, well. "There's tricks to every trade but mine," said the carpenter, hammering a screw.

• 2 •

A Writer's Library
October 1981

Virtually every writer I know is a reader. Most of us were readers first, and our enjoyment of the printed word was often one of the factors that led us to find this silly business attractive in the first place. I've known a few people who came to writing without a prior addiction to reading, and they invariably got the habit in due course. Perhaps they started reading heavily to find out how other people were handling problems of craft. In any event, they're readers now. Accordingly, just about every writer I've known has tended to live in the presence of books. We put up shelves and surround ourselves with books, spending immense tax-deductible sums acquiring more and more of them, spending still more money and incalculable time and effort packing and shipping the little devils when we move from hither to yon and back again. We won't take possession of new quarters unless they afford ample space for our books, and we don't consider ourselves moved in until the books are out of their boxes and placed in orderly fashion upon our shelves.

More often than not, we don't even think of this as a matter of choice. Their enrichment of our leisure hours aside, books are tools of our trade. Ours, after all, is a profession that requires little in the way of capital investment. It's possible, to be sure, to spend thousands for one of those word processors that does everything for you but get your lead character out of the doldrums, but in a pinch any of us can get by with a battered manual portable and a stack of yellow sheets—or, come to that, a few sharpened pencils and a lined pad. Why, a college kid doing odd jobs has more dough tied up in a power mower and other tools than it costs us to set up shop.

For a whole lot of years, I was a positively compulsive acquirer and retainer of books. I operated under a stunningly simple rule: to wit, no book that entered my possession (except through borrowing) was permitted to leave it. If I bought a book, I kept it forever. No matter if it turned out to be unreadable. No matter, indeed, if it turned out that I already had a copy of the damned thing. If I owned a book, it was going to be mine for life.

Sometime in the late '60s, my bibliomania began to change. I came to the realization that I owned too many books to too little purpose. Perhaps a third of my library consisted of books I had read once and would not read again under any circumstances. Another third, say, was composed of books I had bought for some reason I could no longer recall, books I had not read and had no intention of reading, ever. These two classes of books, I had to recognize, constituted not an asset but a liability. They kept me from finding the book I was looking for. They got in the way.

Packing and Pruning

So I began reducing the size of my library. I gave away innumerable books to libraries, to the Salvation Army, to other institutions. Next time I moved, I reduced my library further. I got rid of several thousand paperbacks that time around (including, I blush to recall, a few dozen copies of my own works left behind by mistake). Each move since then has seen my stock of books further reduced, until I reached a point a few years ago of setting aside only a small area for books and pruning them as they accumulate.

Not long ago I once again prepared to move from an apartment and went through the process of packing some books and carting others to bookstores and thrift shops. I find this liberating, but then I find divesting myself of possessions a freeing experience in general. At the same time, I find it helps me to focus on what books are genuinely and enduringly important to me, as tools for living and tools of the trade. A timely note advising me that *WD* was planning a reference books issue further centered my attention on the topic, and led me to consider just how books are useful to me, and just what ones I find indispensable for the production of my own fiction.

The most useful single book I own is *Bartlett's Familiar Quotations.* There's a copy on my desk right now—there's always a copy on my desk—and I suppose if I had to be stranded on a desert island with only one book for company, that's the one I'd take. I couldn't begin to guess how often I pick it up to check something, wander from one entry to another, and surface an hour later, having lost track entirely of what sent me to the book in the first place. You would think that by now, after all these years, I would have read every blessed word in *Bartlett's*, and perhaps I have. All the same, it seems to me that I never open the book without finding something new, and I'm not sure it's hyperbole to argue that a thorough familiarity with its contents is as good as a college education.

How does it help me in my writing? It's especially useful in my mysteries about burglar Bernie Rhodenbarr, which so teem with literary allusions as to suggest I'm better read than I am. But I think it enriches my writing in less obvious ways as well. I seem to find things in its pages that tend to stimulate the flow of fictional ideas, and any book that has that effect can sit on my desk forever.

I also keep an atlas close at hand, and my filing cabinet contains a sheaf of maps of all sorts—road maps, city maps, everything. I hang onto guidebooks, too. I have a slightly out-of-date set of Mobil Travel Guides and a variety of individual guides for foreign countries and various sections of this country. Sometimes I'll set a book or part of a book in a region with which I'm unfamiliar, and I want to be able to provide a couple of specific touches to make the background convincing. This is handy, too, when you've got a character, say, who's described as hailing from Hartford. Perhaps you want to mention that he used to lift weights at the YMCA on Jewell Street. Somewhere out there is a reader from Hartford who knows the Y is indeed on Jewell Street. "Gee," he'll say, "this guy knows

Hartford. He must know what he's talking about." Well, I don't know Hartford, and I hardly ever know what I'm talking about, but a good geographic library not only helps me to appear knowledgeable but also helps stimulate the fiction factory in my head.

Purges and Poetry

Some of the books I keep through purge after purge have no direct relationship to my writing. I hang onto poetry, for example. Now, I must spend 20 times as many hours reading fiction as I do poetry, but novels pass in and out of my hands while volumes of poetry are mine for life. I guess it's because I want to be able to put my hands on a poem when the impulse strikes. Most of the poems I read these days are poems I've read before, or at least are the work of poets I've read before, and I want to be able to return to these old friends indefinitely.

Speaking of old friends, I'm similarly incapable of parting with books written by friends of mine. In an instance or two, I've gone on owning the book after the friendship has long since withered. Happily, these books aren't excess baggage. My friends are good writers, and I tend to find their books rereadable.

There are other books I cling to for reasons I would be very hard put to explain. I'm glancing right now at a shelf of books that I've decided, after some soul-searching, to hang onto for the time being. Three of them, standing one next to the other, are *America's Garden Book*, by James and Louise Bush-Brown, *Mushrooms of the World*, by Lucius von Frieden, and *Handbook of Turtles*, by Archie Carr. I have owned these three books for a dozen years, and I guess I'll own them for a little while longer, and I'll be damned if I can tell you why.

I don't have a garden, and I don't expect to have one in the foreseeable future, and if I did, it wouldn't be any great problem to pick up a basic text on the subject. I suppose I hang onto the Bush-Brown book because it's a good reference work on the subject, although I've never referred to it while writing fiction. Still, perhaps I will. Someday.

The mushrooms book is a nice one, with beautiful color plates. I must admit, though, that when I flipped through the book to weigh the merits of keeping it, I was seeing those color plates for the first time in at least five years. I have no interest in mushrooms. I don't expect to write a book in which someone gathers wild mushrooms, or gets poisoned by them, or anything of the sort. If that should happen, a couple of hours at the library would provide me with all the mycological lore I could possibly need.

In the late '60s, I got into turtles in an intense way, as the kiddies might put it. I kept more than a dozen species in various fish tanks and terraria, became a member of the International Turtle and Tortoise Society (I swear I'm not making this up) and went to great lengths to acquire a copy of Archie Carr's book. God knows why I still have it. Perhaps because it was so hard to find in the first place. I certainly never read the whole thing, and as I recall, my interest in turtles (and the turtles themselves) had largely died out by the time the book arrived.

Never mind. I've got the book and I don't intend to part with it.

For the past four years I've had access to an *Oxford Universal Dictionary*, it being the property of my erstwhile consort. As soon as I relocate I'm going to replace it, because it's a wonderful dictionary.

The dictionary I own, and the one I always keep atop my desk, is the *Thorndike Barnhart Comprehensive Desk Dictionary*. I use it to check spelling. It's an awful dictionary, but that's just as well; I don't want to get sidetracked when I'm just checking spelling.

I own a dictionary of American slang, and that's just plain fun. I browse in it now and then and store things up for the future. But I don't use it as a direct reference work. I think that would lead to some very stilted dialogue. Slang has to become a part of my own personal language before I can start stuffing it into the mouths of my characters.

I've recently divested myself of several hundred books, and I'm sure I'll miss a couple of them sooner or later. That's OK. I can always buy new copies if I really want them. There are a couple books I've bought three or four times now. It still beats schlepping all of those cartons, and building all of those bookshelves. The first time I liquidated a part of my library I felt as though I'd had a limb amputated, but it hurts a little bit less each time.

Somewhere, though, at this very moment, someone is putting a book of mine on the pile for donation to the Goodwill. Know something? The thought drives me crazy.

· 3 ·

Getting By on a Writer's Income
October 1981

A LESSON IN HOW TO DEAL WITH SLOW PAY, LACK OF A WEEKLY PAYCHECK AND OTHER "OCCUPATIONAL HAZARDS" THAT CREATE PROBLEMS BEYOND SIMPLE FINANCIAL INSECURITY.

A writer, James Michener has said, can make a fortune in America. But he can't make a living.

I think the point is good. It's hardly a secret that a few people get rich every year at their typewriters. The same media attention that 50 years ago lionized a handful of writers as important cultural leaders now trumpets the income of a comparable handful. The tabloid reader knows nowadays about paperback auctions and movie tie-ins and multi-volume book contracts with sky-high advances and elevator clauses.

Balanced against this image of the writer as fortune's darling is a similarly glamorous picture of the unsuccessful writer starving in an airless garret, eating baked beans out of the can and pawning his overcoat to buy carbon paper. The poor blighter's starving for his art, and he'll either go on starving in pursuit of his pure artistic vision until they lay his bones in potter's field, or else he'll suddenly break through to literary superstardom, and the next we'll see of him he'll be at poolside sipping champagne and snorting lines with the Beautiful People.

The validity of both of these images notwithstanding, most of the writers I know have never gotten rich but have always gotten by. This has certainly been the case with me. I have, to be sure, had good years and bad years. I had a couple of years when I made more money than I knew what to do with—although I always thought of something—and I had other years, and rather more of them, when I might have switched to another line of work had there been anything else for which I was qualified.

I did live in a garret once, in a rather pleasant area under a sloping roof atop a barbershop in Hyannis, Massachusetts. For a couple of weeks I subsisted solely on peanut butter sandwiches and Maine sardines, and I wrote a short story every day, one of which ultimately became my first sale. (The room was $8 a week, the sardines were 15¢ a can, and I got a hundred bucks for the story.)

"I've been rich and I've been poor," Sophie Tucker said, "and believe me, rich is better." I suppose I believe her, but I also believed showman Mike Todd when he said he'd been broke innumerable times, but he'd never been poor.

I think the distinction is useful. The writing life has had me broke any number of times, and I suspect it will continue to do so as long as I pursue it. I won't be poor, though, not so long as I'm able to recognize that being broke is a temporary thing, that it's part of the business, and that it doesn't have to interfere with either my writing or my living.

There are several reasons why being broke is inevitable now and then. Sometimes the fault is my own. My ability to produce marketable material varies with the ups and downs of my own emotional life. Writers are not machines, and even machines do break down from time to time. Like most writers I've known and known of, I have occasional periods when I can't get anything written and other stretches when what I write just doesn't work.

Other times my writing goes along just fine, but I can't seem to be able to get money to come into my house. Sometimes changes in the market leave me in the position of a dress manufacturer with a warehouse full of mini skirts. Other times the entire publishing industry seems to have gone on hold, and manuscripts sit on editors' desks for months without being either accepted or rejected. Sometimes I get slow-paid by publishers intent on solving their entire cash flow problems at my personal expense. Sometimes a publisher decides his inventory is too large and elects not to publish dozens of books he's already bought and paid for; I get to keep the advance, but I can forget about royalties, foreign sales, and all of the subsidiary income that make the difference between profit and loss.

Any number of things can happen to render a freelance writer insolvent, and if you stay in the game long enough, all of them will happen to you sooner or later. But the point of this piece is not that dire events will occur, but that you can survive them. You may decide it's not worth it—some of us are not temperamentally suited to the financial ups and downs of fulltime freelancing. If you can't stand that kind of heat, then you should probably stay out of this particular kitchen.

If you can stand it, and would like to survive as gracefully as possible, here are some survival tips.

1. Don't Run Scared

While fear may not be the only thing we have to be afraid of, it's certainly up there at the top of the list. It can be an absolutely paralyzing emotion, utterly undercutting the self-confidence it takes in order to put words on paper in the expectation that someone will be eager to read them.

Fear keeps a lot of writers from freelancing in the first place. Some people are never comfortable with the financial insecurity of freelance writing, and do better emotionally if they remain employed and write on the side. Those of us who do choose to write fulltime must balance fear with faith—in ourselves, in Providence, or in both.

Just about the time I was starting to write stories, Richard S. Prather published an article in *Writer's Digest* explaining how he'd become a fulltime writer. He'd begun with the revelation that nobody starves in America; accordingly he'd decided to quit his job and invest a year in the process of establishing himself. It was, of course, the best investment he ever made, and before the year was out he had sold novels about private eye Shell Scott and had launched what was to be an extremely successful career.

Prather's piece must have impressed me; not only do I remember it after all these years, but also my own first published story began with the line, "Anybody who starves in this country deserves it," an observation of dubious socioeconomic validity, perhaps, but a not-bad opening shot for a suspense story.

In any event, it was easy enough for me to decide to freelance. My salary and expenses were so low at the time that I didn't have to sit down and write *Forever Amber* to make ends meet. Some years later, when I returned to freelancing after a year and a half's gainful employment, I had a wife and two children and a somewhat higher standard of living. But I also had the knowledge based on previous experience that writing was something I could make a living at, and I made the move without thinking to be afraid of the outcome.

2. Watch Out for Sure Money

There are more ways than one to run scared. In my own case, fear has tended to manifest itself more in terms of an inability to take chances *at the typewriter*. For a few too many years I wrote pulp novels on regular assignment for sure money rather than risk failure by attempting something more ambitious.

This is even more of a hazard for writers who are rather better established than I was. Not long ago, for example, I was talking with a successful Hollywood screenwriter. He had had some success with a novel some years ago and was talking about wanting to write another novel—and did a pretty good job of talking himself out of it.

"It would take a minimum of six months and probably more like a year," he explained, "and then what could I expect to see out of it? A $10,000 advance? A couple grand more in royalties if it gets lucky? Maybe a few thousand in foreign sales? You write one half-hour sitcom script and you make more than that by the time you're done with the residuals.

And what does that take—a week of real work? I'd love to write a novel, but I don't see how I can afford it."

It's hard to fault his dollars-and-cents logic. But when I start thinking along these lines, I try to take a step back and remind myself that I never got into this business for the money in the first place. I became a writer so that I could do what I wanted, and if I reach a point where my "success" as a writer keeps me from doing what I want to do, there would seem to be something seriously wrong with the turn my career has taken.

In my friend's case, it may be close to impossible for him to gamble the six months or year required for that novel's production. If he's used to living on a six-figure income, how can he survive the drop in income that writing that novel will almost inevitably entail? Prather may be right, and perhaps nobody does starve around here, but mortgages get foreclosed and cars get repossessed. Should a simple urge to write a novel leave a family living in Griffith Park on nuts and berries?

Which brings up another point.

3. Keep the Nut Down

However good we are at what we do, however much acclaim we win for our efforts, we are not working for the government or IBM. We do not have that kind of job security. We have security of another sort, the knowledge that we possess a marketable skill that no one can take away from us and that will ultimately carry us through adversity. But the operative word there is *ultimately*. We can't count on a weekly check the way others can.

For this reason, and to keep from painting myself into a financial corner where I can't afford to take professional chances, I find it worthwhile to keep my fixed costs as low as possible. I don't buy things on time, and my rent is relatively low in proportion to my income. (I did buy a house on time, there being no other way for most of us to purchase real property, but when a Hollywood windfall came along, I paid off the mortgage rather than spend the money upgrading the property or enhancing my standard of living, or investing for future gain. Paying off the mortgage, several people assured me, was not a sound move economically. I knew what they meant, and I knew they were right, but I knew the best thing I as a self-employed writer could do with that windfall was knock out that monthly payment, and I never regretted doing it.)

I don't want to give the impression that I live like a church mouse: I very likely spend as high a percentage of my income as the next wastrel. But I try to squander it on luxuries rather than saddle myself with a heavy burden of ongoing necessities. I'll spend money on travel, blow it on high living, or otherwise find a way to divest myself of it without increasing my day-to-day expenditures. Thus, when the money supply dries up and I have to cut back, I simply go without. I don't own a car; I take cabs when I'm flush and use the subway when I'm not. I treat myself to a lot of good dinners when there's money on hand, and I stay home and eat rice when it's gone.

4. Don't Take Income for Granted

When pests asked J.P. Morgan what the stock market was going to do, he always gave the same answer: "It will fluctuate."

So will a writer's income. If anything, my income seems more subject to fluctuation now than it ever did, and seems concurrently to depend less on how hard I work than ever before. When I started out, I wrote a book a month for one publisher, working on regular assignment and knowing that I was going to get a certain check every month. I would write the book and I would get the check. Nowadays I'll work hard and produce a lot and make next to nothing, and then the next year I'll goof off and get little done and earn a lot.

Just recently, for example, a book of mine was published and sold to a paperback house. The publisher was as certain as he'd ever been that he was going to get a six-figure advance for this property, and his track record shows he doesn't make many mistakes along these lines. Well, there was no book club sale, and no paperback publisher submitted a floor bid, and they finally had the auction and he got the six-figure price, all right, but two of those figures came after the decimal point.

Well, these things happen, and I'm glad I've been in the business long enough to roll with the punches. The real heartache comes when you take the big money for granted and act accordingly.

Friend of mine writes mysteries. For quite a few years he had a movie sale every year, regular as clockwork. Sometimes two books sold in a year, but there was always one that came through for him, and that was half his income.

Not surprisingly, he learned to count on it. If you make, say, $60,000 a year, year in and year out, and half of that comes from film sales, it's not too long before you're living on $60,000 a year, and in the expectation of $60,000 a year. It would be hard to do otherwise.

Then the well ran dry. Nobody bought movie rights to his books, and he sat around wondering what he was doing wrong. Well, he wasn't doing anything wrong, any more than he'd been doing anything especially right previously. You just can't take windfalls for granted, and when they come regularly, it's an easy mistake to make.

There are other ways to take income for granted. When I write a mystery, my income is realized from several sources. There's the advance my hardcover publisher pays me. There's the royalties the book earns over and above the advance—they don't amount to an awful lot—and there's the paperback money. There's another small chunk from a book club specializing in mysteries, and there are checks from the six or eight foreign countries where my books are regularly published.

Every now and then, these sources of subsidiary income dry up. There was a two-year stretch, for instance, when my French publisher didn't buy a single American mystery. There was another point when the Scandinavians suddenly ceased buying foreign books. It's important—but almost impossible—for me to remember that the only thing I can take for granted when I write a book is the initial advance. Other sources of income may be probable, but they're a long way from certain.

Fortunately, there are so many diverse sources of subsidiary income that I can survive when one or two of them dries up. Which leads us to our next point.

5. Don't Put All Your Eggs in One Basket

As I said, when I was first in the business, I wrote a book a month for one publisher. Then I had a falling out with my agent and we parted company, and the publisher in question turned out to be a closed shop, dealing only through that particular agent. Although I liked writing for him and he very much liked publishing my work, we both had to live without each other. This was manifestly easier for him than it was for me.

Well, I survived, and in the long run the experience was enormously beneficial for me. I was forced to grow as a writer. But I had made a mistake. I had grown far too dependent upon a single market, and when it was closed to me I found it extremely difficult to make a living.

This happens to lots of people. You can take a market for granted just as you can take certain income for granted, and an abrupt change in that market can be devastating. Sometimes there's not much you can do about it. In the '50s the market for pulp westerns dropped absolutely dead. A whole slew of writers had done all their writing for these magazines for a couple of decades. They didn't know how to write anything else. Some of them managed to write western novels for the paperbacks, but that market couldn't absorb all of them, nor could all of them produce novel-length stories successfully. Others switched and wrote mysteries, or got into television work, or somehow adapted.

But some of them stopped being writers.

Now, you can say with some justification that these fellows should have seen the scribbling on the side of the building. The pulps didn't all die on the same afternoon. There was a point where some western writers realized they were going to have to develop new markets while others missed the boat—or stagecoach, if you prefer.

Any market can dry up. While it's hard to guard against the collapse of a whole genre, a writer can avoid being too dependent upon a single publisher. If too much of your income comes from a single source, you might as well be on that man's payroll. You're working for him and he can fire you at will. Or he can go out of business.

Or the editor who likes your work can move elsewhere. This is almost certain to happen repeatedly in the course of a writing career, and it has its good and bad aspects. While it can mean the end of a relationship with one publisher, it can also mean the beginning with another. And that's one way to . . .

6. Make Friends in the Business

I haven't heard of a business yet, with the possible exception of the undertaking trade, where people wouldn't prefer to deal with people they know. Some writers use this fact of life to explain their own lack of success, muttering darkly that a conspiracy of old friends is keeping their work from getting published.

That's paranoia. Editors don't keep their jobs and publishers don't remain in business by buying inferior work from their buddies. (And yes, I have known an editor or two who bought garbage and took kickbacks, and another who published his old pals out of friendship even when their work was no good, and none of these people is working today.) What a good relationship with an editor or publisher will do is assure you that they will use you if they can. They would rather work with you than work with an unknown quantity. They know you're reliable. They know you can deliver. They know you won't make a nuisance of yourself over some minor point. And, all things being equal, they'll do business with you rather than take a chance on some yo-yo they've never laid eyes on.

Publishing is an extremely small business in relation to its importance and influence. Editors commonly change jobs many times in the course of a career, even as writers commonly change publishers. One happy result of this—there are unhappy results, too—is that sooner or later you wind up knowing a whole lot of people at a whole lot of publishing houses.

It's worthwhile to cultivate these friendships. This doesn't mean sending out a ton of Christmas presents. It means becoming as genuinely friendly as your nature permits with the people you do business with. If you don't live near New York, it means budgeting for one or two trips a year just to allow yourself the chance to know personally some of the people with whom you've been corresponding.

It means, too, that you must get past thinking of the relationship between writer and editor or writer and publisher as on a par with that of tenant and landlord. It's hard not to regard it as essentially an adversary relationship, especially during the early years when the chief function of an editor seems to be that of spilling coffee on your story prefatory to returning it to you with a form rejection slip. But we are all of us in this silly business together, and working for the same ends, and it's useful to remember this.

7. Be Careful with Advances

William Faulkner once wrote a friend that the best way to get published was to secure an advance from a publisher. Then, he explained, the only way the publisher can get his money back is by publishing your book.

Faulkner's point is not altogether off the mark. There's a definite advantage in getting a publisher to make a commitment in advance. While he still may elect not to publish a book if it falls short of his expectations, he at least has a vested interest in publishing it and this can make him more receptive to the final product.

There are dangers, though, in living on advances. You find yourself trying to come up with an idea that will lead to two chapters and an outline and a fast contract, not something that will evolve into the best possible book. Some years ago, when I was more prolific than I am now and landed virtually all of my contracts on the basis of an outline or a brief proposal, I could hardly avoid the realization that I was writing a couple of hundred words for half the money and then had to write an entire book just to get the other half. It seemed economically sensible to stick to outlines—I could write dozens of them in the course of a year far more easily than I could produce half a dozen actual books. But sooner or later, I found, you have to deliver the book, or after a while they won't make more deals with you.

Years ago I knew a writer who was always living on advances. His agent operated as sort of a banker; whenever my acquaintance sold a story, the agent would advance him the sum due him, reimbursing himself when the check ultimately arrived from the publisher. At other times, when the writer needed money and had not sold anything, the agent would extend an advance against future sales, which is really nothing more than a polite term for a loan. On one such occasion, the writer turned up to collect a $50 advance, and received a check for $45; the agent was so accustomed to taking 10% out of everything, he'd even done so with the loan.

If you live on advances, you're always behind, working to get even. You're like a coal miner in debt to the company store. I think it's sound business sense to contract for one's work in advance rather than write all the time on speculation, and it's undeniably true that the greater a publisher's cash commitment to a book, the more likely he is to promote it effectively. Still, living on advances has its dangers.

8. Have a Way to Make the Rent

My grandfather started out as a plumber. He saved a few dollars and bought a couple of buildings, and he ultimately made his living in real estate. But he never let his card in the plumbers' union expire. He paid his dues every year, just in case.

Writing's the only trade I know, so I can't go down to the union hall if the rent's due and the wolf is at the door. I've often wished I could. I think a writer should know how to do something, preferably the sort of thing that enables him to pick up day work when the going gets tough. I know writers, for example, who are experienced bartenders. They can get work whenever they need it. Experience as a fry cook is probably more useful to a writer than experience writing ad copy or selling insurance, because it's the sort of thing you can walk into on the spur of the moment and keep as long as the financial shoe pinches.

While I don't have that sort of fallback skill, I do have some things I can do to bring in small sums on a steady basis while my main business of book-writing blows hot and cold. I write my *WD* column, for example; it provides a steady monthly check and gives me a regular task to perform. I do occasional reviewing for a book club. I teach a course at a university.

Occasionally I've thought about getting a hack license, or doing office temp work, but I haven't had to yet. When the time comes that I do, I hope I won't let pride stand in the way. Having to do something else to make a few bucks doesn't mean that one has failed as a writer. It just means you've got a case of the shorts, and that, as we've seen, is part of the game.

9. Remember the Difference Between Poor and Broke

And act accordingly. Being broke is not a crime, nor is it proof of one's inadequacy as a writer or as a human being. If you go around with an attitude of implicit apology for being temporarily without funds, it's going to do you more harm than good.

Conversely, an air of confidence can get you through some tight spots. Some years ago I bought a house in New Jersey. I made the deal and set the closing date with the intent of making the down payment with a chunk of movie dough that was coming my way.

Now, this didn't seem unrealistic at the time. The deal with the movie company was already made when I arranged to buy the house. It was just a question of drawing up the contract and getting the cash.

Terrific. Various lawyers dragged their feet on the contract, and then, when it was finally signed, the producer found a way to stall. He kept being out of town and unreachable by phone, and the closing date on the house kept approaching, and I didn't have any money. My then-wife asked if I didn't think I should tell the seller. "No," I said. "I can't see how it will help me to give him that information in advance." Well, then, didn't

I think I ought to engage a lawyer? "No," I said, "because if I have a lawyer and he has a lawyer, the two lawyers'll fight." Then what did I intend to do? "I'll just play it by ear," I said. "Maybe the money will come in by then." And if it doesn't? "Maybe I'll think of something."

Well, I went to the closing and explained the situation. I offered to pay the down payment with a post-dated check, which would enable the sellers to sue me if I couldn't cover it but which wouldn't really get them their property back, since title would have passed to me by then. Still, they were eager to sell, and they knew I wasn't going to put the house on wheels and truck it across the state line, and I knew the money was going to come in from Hollywood sooner or later, and because I didn't have a lawyer their lawyer didn't have anybody to fight with, and I bought the house. I think the fact that I was really quite confident about the whole thing had a lot to do with its outcome.

10. Let Financial Need Be a Spur, Not a Sledgehammer

Mickey Spillane has told of the time when he was living on an offshore island, spending a lot of time on the beach and generally taking life easy. "I decided it would be fun to write a story," he recalls, "but I couldn't get an idea. I took long walks, I sat at the typewriter, but I couldn't seem to come up with an idea. Then one day I got a call from my accountant. He said the money was starting to run short. And you know what? All of a sudden I started getting one idea after the other."

I love that story, and I can believe it. Financial need can very well be necessary to goad the unconscious to come up with story ideas. But when the need is too great, when it weighs too heavily upon the mind, it can have the opposite effect, serving not as a spur in the horse's flank but as a sledgehammer blow between his eyes that stops him dead in his tracks.

I try to avoid this by divorcing myself from financial matters as far as I possibly can. I have an accountant, and for a couple of years now all my income has gone directly from my agent to him. Similarly, all my bills go straight to him as well. Sometimes there's a lot of money in my account and sometimes there's not, but unless matters are very urgent, I don't know how high the stack of bills is, and that's fine with me. I can forget all that and concentrate on writing.

Not everyone would be comfortable turning over financial management to another party. Sometimes I wonder if I shouldn't handle this aspect of my life myself. But all in all I like things as they are.

11. Remember, It's Only Money

According to Dr. Johnson, no man but a blockhead ever wrote except for money. Now, you can read that line in more than one way, and I prefer to believe that Johnson meant that one is not justified in writing in the *expectation* of anything but financial gain, that he who writes hoping to be rewarded by fame, or to change the world, is unrealistic in his expectations.

I write for money, and if I struck oil in my backyard I can't be certain I'd ever write another line. All the same, I try to remember that it's only money and that money is just not all that important. I didn't get into this business for money and I don't stay in it for money. If I write something I don't want to write, I'm giving up some personal freedom. Perhaps more important, if financial considerations induce me to forego writing something I would really like to write, I'm giving up a large measure of freedom and defeating my own purpose in having become a writer in the first place.

I have come to believe that freedom is ultimately the chief attraction of the writing life. I believe, too, that we are about as free as we recognize ourselves to be. The more I realize that material possessions have little to do with my happiness and that money is accordingly of rather little importance, the freer I am to enjoy this life and to fulfill whatever potential I have.

And that's as much as I have to say on the subject of living on a writer's income. Now that I've said it, they'd better pay me for it. And fast.

• 4 •

Travelin' Man
December 1981

You don't have to travel to be a writer. You can, certainly, spend a lifetime on the top floor of a house in Massachusetts, or in a cork-lined bedroom in France. For many of us, there is no frigate like a book, especially one we write ourselves, to take us lands away in space, in time, in way of life. We do our traveling at our typewriters, and in the relative privacy of our minds.

Others of us find that travel plays an important role in the process of generating fiction. Somerset Maugham found plots in the South Seas, even as Alec Waugh found them in the Caribbean. Many writers find that a new location stimulates the creative process, serving as background for a story, getting ideas in motion. New experiences and new perceptions in unknown lands serve to prime the pump, to recharge the batteries, to—well, choose your own metaphor. Somehow, travel helps to keep us fresh.

I know that our freedom to travel is one of the things non-writers tend to envy about us. "Oh, you're a writer," a housebound chap will say, often with a barely perceptible curl to the old lip. "That means you can write anywhere, can't you? Just go anyplace and knock the stuff out."

What it as often means, during those weeks and months in the trenches of the Slough of Despond, is that I *can't* write anywhere, that my inability to produce anything publishable exists irrespective of location. But it's true that, as a freelance writer, I can live just about anywhere (although I'll almost certainly earn less if I don't live in or near New York City). And it's similarly true that I can incorporate a considerable amount of travel time into my schedule, and justify it for any number of professional reasons.

I can also continue to do my work *while* I'm traveling.

Doesn't that have a seductive sound to it? The writer, solid and reliable pro, is In Transit. Holed up in a hotel room in Rabat, let us say, or in his stateroom on a transpacific freighter. Or legging it along the Appalachian Trail, or driving cross-country in a camper, or on a beach blanket at St. Tropez. But is he merely kinging it in slothful leisure until the dollars run out? Not a chance. Clever little devil that he is, he's letting his trip pay for itself, writing as he goes along. While he catches the rays on the Riviera, he's blocking out an outline for his next book. While his freighter is island-hopping, he's typing away in his cabin. Even as the sunset stains the western sky, his trusty ballpoint—

Well, you get the idea, and what a charming one it is. Cost-effective travel, after all, is the best kind, and blissfully free of guilt. If I'm working in Rome, I don't have to listen to that inner Jiminy Cricket telling me I should be home working.

Sounds good. But how well does it work out in practice?

The Write Way to Travel

The answer, of course, is that It Depends, and on several things. On the particular temperament of the writer, for one. Some of us are only comfortable working in familiar surroundings. It depends, too, on the nature of the trip, on our mind-set of the moment, and on what sort of writing we're trying to do. Sometimes it works out very well indeed, and a trip does pay for itself. Other times it does not work out at all, and a trip is spoiled by our having tried to get some writing done under unfavorable circumstances.

The late John Creasey, a super-prolific mystery writer, did not allow his work habits to vary. They remained the same wherever he happened to be. He wrote, he once told me, 2,000 words every day before breakfast. He wrote in longhand, and it did not matter whether he was at home, abroad, or on a ship. He got his day's work done before he allowed the rest of his day to begin.

Some years ago a television documentary disclosed the writing methods of Georges Simenon, another extremely productive mystery novelist whose approach was more that of the hare than the tortoise. After a period of gestation at home during which a plot would take form in his mind, the French writer would pack his bags and typewriter and hie himself to Geneva or Vienna or wherever. There, locked in a hotel room, Simenon would work 12 or 14 hours a day until, in 11 or 12 days' time, his book was finished. After each day's stint at the typewriter, he would compulsively follow whatever routine he had established on the first day, ambling through town according to precisely the same route, buying his tobacco at the same kiosk, ordering the same meal at the same restaurant, doing all this presumably to eliminate the need to make decisions and to maintain the same turn of mind, insofar as possible, throughout the writing of the novel.

For my own part, I have done and continue to do as much traveling as I possibly can. I have on occasion traveled for the express purpose of writing. I have written in transit out of need, and occasionally out of impulse. I have turned out fiction and nonfiction, books and short stuff, and with about the same proportion of success and failure that I've enjoyed generally.

Ariel, I suppose, was the most peripatetic book I ever wrote. I began it at a fishing lodge on the Outer Banks of North Carolina, kept at it in motel rooms in the Carolinas and a down-and-out rooming house in Charleston, reached the two-thirds mark on Jekyll Island, Georgia, then started over and pushed through to the finish in St. Augustine, ultimately doing a full rewrite back in Manhattan. *Burglars Can't Be Choosers* was begun in Los Angeles, continued in Wyoming and Eastern Pennsylvania and Tidewater, Virginia, then rewritten in Greenville, South Carolina. A Tanner book was begun in New Jersey and completed on a rented typewriter in Dublin.

Behind the Wheel

I've found it generally easier to write short pieces than books while on the move. While I can write a novel as well in an unfamiliar setting as at my own desk, I prefer to write it all in one place, and I can readily understand Simenon's same-thing-every-day routine.

At times I've found traveling particularly conducive to the production of short stories and articles. There was one stretch during which I woke up every morning, had breakfast, and drove a couple of hundred miles, during which time my mind played around with a story idea. Around noon I would check into a motel, set up my typewriter, and write what I'd plotted behind the wheel. I wouldn't want to count on being able to do this, but it worked surprisingly well for a while there.

With rare exceptions, my own writing in transit has been limited by my dependence on a typewriter. If I intend to write on a trip I bring a machine along; if I leave it home, I make the trip a vacation. Brian Garfield had similar experiences until one holiday when the writing impulse took him unawares. He went down to the beach with a yellow pad and a pen and found, much to his surprise, that he was perfectly capable of writing in longhand and that he could thus produce a short story while working on his suntan. In the process he discovered that there were certain satisfactions in producing handwritten copy. Other writers I've known have taken to using small cassette recorders on their travels.

Drawing a Blank

Because I do virtually all my work at the typewriter, I've learned to examine hotel and motel rooms before checking in. I make sure that there's a suitable desk or table and that it's near, or can be positioned near, an electric outlet. (A manual typewriter would eliminate this last requirement, just as a truly lightweight portable would make writing in-transit a simpler matter for the bus or train traveler, or the backpacker.)

Somebody—it may have been Balzac—is supposed to have said that the ideal view for the working writer is a blank wall. The view with which

I've been most frequently confronted in my on-the-road writing has been, I submit, the furthest possible from ideal, in that motel desks are almost invariably positioned right in front of motel mirrors. I tend to do my writing first thing in the morning, and at such times—indeed, at most times—the last thing I want to do is look up from the typewriter and meet my own despairing eyes in some unhappy looking glass. Sometimes I have been able to slip the mirror from the wall, or shove the desk to some other part of the room. There have been times when I have torn a sheet from the bed and covered the offending mirror. When the work goes well, of course, I don't look up, or don't notice what I'm looking at if I do. But it is when the work is not going well that I least desire to examine my reflection, and am most apt to find myself so doing.

I'm handicapped in certain ways when I try writing in transit. My files aren't at hand. My reference library is not available to me. I can't reach over my typewriter and lay my hand on my dictionary, or my copy of *Bartlett's Familiar Quotations.*

Nor, on the other hand, am I as likely to be distracted by certain things that distract me at home. My phone's less likely to ring. I won't find myself breaking automatically from my work around noon to run downstairs and check the mail. I've left my New York routine in New York, and I'm freed to work at whatever hours I want. Several times, when I've had difficulty with a piece of work, I've gone to some other city for the express purpose of going ahead full steam with it, and if my ritual has been less compulsive than Simenon's, it has taken much the same form. The results have been positive.

Other times, when I've simply sought to incorporate writing into a trip, I've had less success. And it's important, I think, to give oneself permission *not* to write on a trip. I've ruined some trips out of an inability to accept a slight touch of traveling writer's block. Far better, I think, to regard the trip as sufficient unto itself, and any writing that happens to be produced in its course as a bonus.

· 5 ·

Who It May Concern
January 1982

A few years ago, science fiction writer Samuel R. Delaney was teaching creative writing at the State University of New York at Buffalo. He responded to one exercise by a graduate student with the suggestion that the writer pay a modicum of attention to the rules of grammar, and took particular exception to his habit of using "who" as the object of a preposition.

"Well," the young man said, "I thought I would try experimenting with the 'to who' form."

"The 'to-who' form," Delaney fumed, recounting the incident. "What, pray tell, is the to-who form? And what makes people think they can write stories when they can't write a sentence?"

What indeed? It would seem, certainly, that a writer ungrounded in English grammar would find himself in the approximate position of a one-legged man in an ass-kicking contest. I know that I, as a reader, frequently find myself clucking and tssing over the sins other writers have perpetrated in print. And, almost as frequently, I find myself bridling when some keen-eyed copyreader calls my own grammatical lapses into question. In such matters, as indeed in most matters, I employ a useful double standard. When other writers make grammatical errors, they're sloppy. When my own usage is challenged, that's nit-picking.

I think it's interesting to consider just what sort of obligation we owe to the gods of grammar. As fiction writers, we would seem to have a little more leeway in grammatical matters than our fact-bound fellows. Our words, after all, are designed to do more than merely convey information. While we may not be writing poetry, we are allowed to claim a certain amount of poetic license, which might perhaps be defined as the right to suspend the rules in favor of what sounds good.

In *American Tongue and Cheek*, Jim Quinn questions innumerable rules on the grounds that various great writers broke them with impunity. I'm not sure I buy this argument—does the Law of Gravity no longer bind the rest of us simply because Baryshnikov can defy it? What, after all, is proved by the successful breaking of a rule? Some decades ago, a mystery writer—it may have been S.S. Van Dine—drew up a list of rules by which all writers ought to be bound in constructing a detective story. Craig Rice promptly countered by writing a story that broke every single one of those rules—and still succeeded admirably as a story. Were the rules perforce invalidated?

> Let us go then, you and I, When the evening is spread out against the sky . . .

So wrote T.S. Eliot in *The Love Song of J. Alfred Prufrock*. Any sixth-grade English teacher ought to be able to point out that it ought to be "you and *me*." But it sounds better the way Eliot wrote it. Even if *I* didn't have to be there to rhyme with *sky*, it would still sound better the way Eliot wrote it. (Or do I just think so because I've grown so used to it as it is, so much so that I have read and reread the poem for 25 years and never once noticed the grammatical error?)

No Rules in Dialogue

The allegiance writers of fiction must pay to rules of grammar and usage would seem to me to vary from one work to another and within a particular work. There are, for example, no grammatical rules in dialogue. Not all people in the real world speak grammatically, and thus neither do all characters in fiction. Indeed, a character's approach to the language as displayed in dialogue often tells us more than any descriptive or narrative material the author might supply about that character's fundamental nature.

You'd think this would be obvious, and yet I've had copy editors who yearned to make proper grammarians out of some of my semi-literate characters. But this doesn't happen very often, and such persons can be readily shouted down.

Does this mean that characters have infinite grammatical latitude in dialogue? I think not. It's worth remembering that dialogue must be somewhat selective in echoing reality. Human conversation reproduced precisely as it is spoken becomes very nearly incomprehensible on the printed page, since so many of us speak not in sentences but in fragments, depending upon inflection and gestures to fill in the gaps. It is the writer's job to convey the flavor of that sort of conversation without letting verisimilitude get in the way of communication.

Similarly, grammatic lapses ought not to be overdone. An accent is best suggested not by spelling every word phonetically but by highlighting an occasional word, and departures from orthodox usage can be suggested in much the same way.

In first-person narration, the rules are not quite so relaxed as in dialogue, but neither are they as hard and fast as in third-person narrative. The narrator, after all, is engaged in a lengthy dialogue with the reader, and how he elects to express himself is very much a part of who he is. At the same time, the narrator's loose approach to the language can grate on the reader's ear, while he might accept the same sort of thing in actual dialogue. There are things that bother me in first-person narration—the misuse of *like* for *as*, for instance—and I can only suppose that other departures bother others in the same fashion.

In my own writing, my narrators tend to be no more slipshod in their prose than is their creator; i.e., I don't consciously play fast and loose with the language, but let them make only those errors that I myself make unwittingly. During the editing of a recent book of mine about burglar Bernie Rhodenbarr, a copy editor questioned a sentence with the observation that Bernie didn't usually make that sort of error. "It's not Bernie's error," I said, agreeing to the suggested change. "It's mine."

Gray Areas

It is probably worth remembering that English, unlike Latin and Sanskrit, is a living language, constantly changing, constantly evolving. New words keep entering it. Old words keep shedding meanings and acquiring new ones. Nouns turn into verbs. Rules of grammar bend in evident obedience to some higher authority.

This vitality of the language, like poetic license, can be employed to rationalize whatever one wants to do. Humpty Dumpty told Alice that when he uses a word, it means exactly what he wants it to mean, neither more nor less, that it's a question of who's to be master. He might as cavalierly have assured her that he was building a living language. While I would agree that writers are obliged to reflect the realities of contemporary English rather than sit around sounding like Fielding and Smollett, I'm not sure we have to rush to enlist as shock troops in the linguistic revolution.

And there are great gray areas. I never know, for instance, just how I feel about the business of single-subject-plural-predicate. The rules, when I learned them as a lad, were quite clear. Agreement between subject and verb was taken for granted and violation of this principle was an error. But now it would seem that everybody, so to speak, has a right to their own opinion.

Yecchhh! I hate typing sentences like that. "A person can do what they want." Double yecchhh!

And yet consider the alternatives. "A person can do what he wants" is not only considered objectionably sexist by a sizable portion of the population, but this charge of linguistic sexism has also been around long enough and penetrated our consciousness enough so that it's begun to *sound* wrong in and of itself. Witless substitutes along the lines of "A person can do what s/he wants" have not caught on, and, God willing, never will. "A person can do what he or she wants" is fine, if the problem comes up only once every couple of pages or so. But inevitably one finds oneself confronted by something along the lines of "A person can do whatever he or she wants with his or her own possessions, insofar as they concern him or her." Now I don't know anybody who talks like that, and I don't ever want to.

Sometimes, to avoid the issue altogether, I find myself deliberately looking for other ways to write or speak. Perhaps I switch to a plural subject so that it can come into agreement with the sexually neutral *they*. "People can do what they want"—well, there's nothing wrong with that sentence, but that may not be what I want to say. Perhaps I had it in mind to write not about people collectively but about a person, individually. You'd think I ought to be able to do that. If a person can do what they want, why can't I?

Ah, well. This, I submit, will straighten itself out in the course of time. In England, collective nouns have been taking plural verbs in public print for quite some time now. One may read that a flock of sheep are grazing, for example. More often than not, it sounds better that way to me. And I suspect the time is not far off when "Everybody can do what they want" will sound right in much the same fashion.

For language is ultimately a tool, not a god. We whose vocation it is to use it tend to revere it, and I suppose it is fitting and proper for us to do so. I trust my gorge will never fail to rise when some witling prattles about experimenting with the to-who form. But when some ink-stained wretch changes *who* to *whom* in my copy, or *that* to *which*, or whatever, I trust I will be as indignant as was Winston Churchill when called to account for ending a sentence with a preposition. "This," he thundered, "is the sort of errant pedantry up with which I will not put."

Craven Images
February 1982

The telephone clicked in his ear. Derek stood for a moment, the receiver in his hand. Then he released it. It fell to within a few inches of the floor and swung to and fro like a pendulum.

He walked slowly, heavily, out of the room. As he cleared the doorway he could just hear the recorded voice of an operator advising him that the receiver was off the hook. He closed the door, shutting her off in mid-sentence.

Outside, he looked off into the distance. Storm clouds, darker than death, loomed menacingly on the far horizon. Far off to the west, a lonely train whistle sounded once, twice, and then was still.

Somewhere a dog was barking.

Wait a minute—I can explain everything, even the nauseating passage above. What we have just suffered through is an onslaught of imagery. The telephone receiver, dangling like a participle, the interrupted recording, the storm clouds, the train whistle, even the inescapable barking dog, all serve as images to highlight or underscore or otherwise reinforce what's going on in the story.

These particular images are banal and obvious, and deliberately so; I exaggerated to make a point. Their triteness is exacerbated by the author's editorializing. Storm clouds gathering on a far horizon are image enough. When I say they're darker than death, and have them loom menacingly, I'm telling the reader how he's supposed to feel about them.

I got to thinking about images when I came across a particularly effective use of imagery in *A Married Man*, a recent novel by Piers Paul Read. The lead character, John Strickland, is a fortyish London barrister who has been engaging in a flirtation with a 17-year-old girl. His infatuation is sufficient to move him to write her a compromising note proposing an assignation. She does not respond to the note, and he subsequently learns that she showed it to some of her friends, and that the group sat around having a laugh at his expense. Enraged, he drives to her flat, demanding an explanation. She won't let him in, and after an awkward conversation he turns to leave, whereupon Read ends the chapter with this paragraph:

> . . . *He turned away from the row of buttons and the aluminum box, and went back down the steps into the square. He stood for a moment looking up—not at the flat but at the orange London sky. Then, suddenly, every electric light in that section of the city was simultaneously extinguished and he saw above the black trees a muted yellow moon. He stood for some time watching the moon; then he went to his car and drove home through the chaos caused by the power cut.*

When I read the passage I was immediately struck by the effectiveness of the blackout as a way of ringing down the curtain on that particular phase of John Strickland's life. Once those lights go out and we are left with that muted yellow moon, we are prepared for the next chapter to introduce a new stage in his evolving mid-life crisis. We know that the 17-year-old won't be back.

But there's more to it than that. The story takes place in 1973, during a time when a coal strike had substantial repercussions throughout England. Intermittent power outages and cutbacks were a fact of London life during the period of the novel, and the socio-economic context of the story is very much a part of Strickland's turning toward political activity as a way of affirming his personal worth and vigor. The strike, the power outages, the day-to-day political realities, had to be introduced into the novel somewhere or other, and how better to manage the trick than by switching all the lights out just as Strickland's flirtation comes to an abrupt halt?

I wonder, as I'm often inclined to wonder, to what extent the author's use of the blackout image was deliberate and calculated. Read is very much a craftsman, so I'm perfectly willing to believe he knew exactly what he was doing. At the same time, I know how often creative decisions of this sort are made intuitively. In my own experience, I've found that most of the images I use, and almost all of the ones I wind up even halfway pleased with, creep into my writing simply because they seem like a good idea at the time.

In *The Triumph of Evil*, which I published under the pen name of Paul Kavanagh, birds serve as an ongoing image. The book opens with the lead, Miles Dorn, watching the baby robins in the nest in the eaves over his kitchen window:

> *The eggs had hatched a week ago, and since then he had found himself spending hours at a time watching them. There was little drama in it, no cuckoo egg in the robins' nest, no cats to be warded off, only the constant feeding and attendance by the parent birds and the steady growth and development of the young.*

His watching is interrupted when two visitors from the past enlist him for the mission of intrigue and political assassination which is to be the plot of the novel. They leave, and a pupil of Dorn's—with whom he is to have a love affair—arrives. They have an extended conversation. Then she leaves, and we have this passage:

> *Twice more before the sky darkened he went to the kitchen window to watch the robins. The amount of work required of the parent birds was prodigious. They were constantly flying off and returning with worms to be thrust into gaping mouths.*
>
> *He wondered why they bothered. Because they were robins, he thought, and that was what robins did.*
>
> *Could they think, he wondered. Could they in any sense muse on the instinct, the irresistible urge to fill up the planet with copies of themselves? He decided they could not. The musers, the ponderers, would miss too many worms. They would build shaky nests. Cats would stalk them and pounce upon their reveries. And their seed would die, while less intellectual birds killed off the more thoughtful worms.*
>
> *A wave of wholly unreal sadness enveloped him. "What shall I wish you?"*

> he asked the birds, speaking aloud in English. "A long fruitful stupid life? Or fatal insight into the avian condition? Eh?"

A few chapters further, Dorn is in New York. In Central Park he sees a woman feeding bread crumbs to pigeons. Dorn muses on this, and on something he has read about a program to exterminate pigeons by feeding them a chemical that makes them lay eggs without shells. The eradication program is characterized as humane, and Dorn wonders why. It also occurs to him that the woman might be feeding the pigeons such a chemical, or that she might be poisoning them. The act he observes, in other words, tells him nothing of either its motive or its probable result—and this can be said as well for what Dorn is doing in his political intrigues and manipulations.

Not long after this, Dorn is in New Orleans.

> One of the places he visited was a wildlife museum, where he examined row after row of glass cases filled with dead birds. Several of them were specimens of extinct species. He got halfway through the display when he was overcome by a feeling of utter revulsion. He left the building as quickly as he could, certain that the sight of one more dead bird would make him vomit.

The next chapter begins with Dorn's return to his home, and newspaper items for the next several weeks are summarized, with a paragraph for each. The final paragraph advises that

> The baby robins, still uncertain fliers, began leaving their nest for longer periods of time.

Then Jocelyn, his young pupil, visits him. She has brought her cat along, and while Dorn and Jocelyn are talking, the cat slips outside and kills one of the baby robins. Jocelyn, upset, hits the cat, and it runs off. The scene is emotional, and there is a discussion of the killing of birds being in the nature of cats. In an interior monologue, Dorn compares himself as a killer of men to the cat's role as a killer of birds.

This whole business with birds seems very deliberate, and yet I can remember when I wrote it that I never intentionally decided to use birds as an image. The robins made their first appearance in the book's first paragraph, before I had much of an idea where the book was going, let alone how it would get there. The business with the pigeons in the park echoed a similar musing I'd had not long before when I'd read a similar news item in the paper. The wildlife museum got into the book because I'd gone to that very museum in New Orleans a year or two previously, although I had not had a reaction like Dorn's.

Does this mean the recurring bird imagery was coincidental? I think not; I'm more inclined to say it represents choice, but not conscious or deliberate choice. Many of the choices we make in our writing are unconscious ones. Once I had those baby birds in the nest, a portion of my mind was aware of birds, and was ready to slip them into the matrix of the story whenever it seemed appropriate. The business with the cat was purposeful enough; it helped in defining the relationship of Jocelyn and Dorn, in addition to serving as a good dramatic incident.

In the Midst of Death, one of my detective novels about Matthew Scudder, includes a few images here and there. Scudder's client is a corrupt cop accused of murder, and Scudder has an affair with the man's wife; the cop has been maintaining a clandestine apartment in Greenwich Village, and Scudder spends a drunken night alone there, even donning a pair of the man's pajamas. The image of his trying on the other man's life is, I suppose, obvious enough. At the book's end Scudder calls the wife but no one answers. He hangs up and dials another number, that of a woman murdered early on in the story, and gets her machine with its recorded message in her voice. I did this because I liked the image of a leftover voice and message, and of someone deliberately calling to hear that voice. A few years later my stepfather died, and just recently my mother told me how she had on several occasions called his office just to hear his voice on tape. Neither of us had gotten the idea from the other.

I don't know that there's a point to all this, but if there is it may well have something to do with the value in letting one's literary images flow out of the story and one's own relationship to the material rather than grabbing images out of the air and slapping them relentlessly onto the page. The old advice about style—i.e., that you cross out whatever turns of phrase you're most proud of—may apply as well to imagery. If you know something's an image, maybe you ought to strike it out, or at least cast a coldly critical eye on it.

· 7 ·

Who's in Charge?
April 1982

Let me tell you about a couple of reviews. Reviews are part of the game, and one of the nice parts that come after publication. In the course of time, most of us learn to deal with them, just as we learn to roll with the punches of rejection in other areas of the business. Whoever you are and whatever you've written, some reviewers will miss the point and others will detest the book out of hand. You get so you can shrug this off while basking in the glow of the occasional brilliant critic who catches onto the fact that your book represents the first real advance in the print medium since movable type. What the hell, at least the negative reviews are publicizing your work. If nothing else, they're spelling your name right.

OK. Back in October, Arbor House brought out *A Stab in the Dark*, a detective novel of mine featuring a private eye named Matthew Scudder. The reviews, happily, have ranged from great to terrific, but of course there have been the stray exceptions. One mixed notice began by stating that Scudder was described as "charismatic," and went on to take dogged exception to this adjective. There's such a thing as negative charisma—i.e., when you walk into a room, it's as if someone has just left—and while this chap didn't quite accuse Scudder of possessing it, he seemed on the verge. Charisma? Scudder? Ha!

Thing is, I never mentioned charisma and Scudder in the same paragraph. I looked at the publisher's blurb and sure enough, there it was, right there on the flap. "Investigator Matthew Scudder, Lawrence Block's relentless and charismatic plainclothesman extraordinaire . . . ." Well, gee, fella, *I* didn't write that. There are 70,000 words that I *did* write, and why can't you concentrate on them?

Oh, well. These things happen. As counterpoint, though, consider a review *The Burglar in the Closet* received in the *Minneapolis Tribune* a few years ago. The reviewer began by quoting the flap copy at surprising length, and with considerable approval. Then he went on to bemoan the fact that the same person hadn't written both blurb and book, that the book itself couldn't hold a candle to the blurb, and that Random House ought to get rid of this clown Block and start publishing books by the blurb writer.

Well, that's cute, I suppose, but the fact of the matter is that *I* wrote that blurb, as I've written the flap copy for all the Burglar books since the inception of the series. There is something about getting upstaged by one's own advertisement for oneself that beggars description. I couldn't even write the reviewer a note and upbraid him for preferring the blurb to the book. All I could do was shake my head and make clucking sounds, and there's but limited satisfaction in those two pursuits.

What I'm getting at is the notion that there are variables rather far removed from the actual book you write which will have an effect upon its reception—by critics, by store owners, by potential buyers. Once the book has been written and rewritten and edited and sent down for typesetting, several decisions have to be made which play a role in the book's success or failure and which may well be made without your participation. The title, the blurbs, the jacket design, the nature and amount of advertising—these are all areas of some importance, and ones over which you will very likely have little or no control.

The writer generally has a certain amount of control over the title. While he cannot demand unequivocally that his own title be used if everybody else hates it, it probably won't be changed without consulting him, or to a title he finds absolutely unacceptable. What most often happens is that the publisher expresses a dislike for the author's own title and that everyone involved comes up with ideas until somebody supplies something that everybody can live with.

A Stab in the Dark was originally entitled *Deep with the First Dead*. I had a certain attachment to the title; it fit the book perfectly, and it came from the same Dylan Thomas poem that had supplied me with a title years ago, *After the First Death*. I liked the cadence of it, too, but when people at Arbor House objected I didn't argue, because I could agree that it didn't work all that well as a title. An editor offered a list of possibilities, none of which quite worked, and I went into a huddle and came back with *A Stab in the Dark*, and everybody liked it.

Often a title represents a compromise, or an attempt to make the best of a bad situation. I just recently read Donald E. Westlake's new novel, *Kahawa*, and called him to tell him how much I enjoyed it, adding that I liked the book almost as much as I hated the title. "Oh, *that*," he said. "It's Swahili for We-couldn't-come-up-with-a-title. Believe me, everything else we thought of was worse."

Paperback publishers are more likely to change a title without consulting the author. My first Gold Medal suspense novel appeared as *Mona* because the editor had recently bought some cover art featuring a woman's face, and later on I was asked to provide a female character in another novel with a tigerskin coat so that the book could be retitled *Tanner's Tiger*. In the course of a continuing relationship with a paperback publisher, one can so arrange things that one is at least consulted about title changes, but these decisions are still often made quite arbitrarily.

The cover has a great deal to do with a book's commercial success or failure. This makes it a matter of concern to author and publisher alike. It also touches the author's ego; he wants his book to look like a classy article and hopes too that the cover will accurately reflect the book's contents.

I think the cover is the publisher's business, and I think it's unrealistic for most of us to expect cover approval. On the other hand, it's fair to expect to be shown proofs of the cover before it's printed, and to be able to jump up and down and scream if the proposed cover is a disaster. It's at times like this that an agent can be enormously helpful, not only because he's better at shouting than the average author but also because his opinion is acknowledged to be more dispassionate and based on broader professional experience than that of the author. I've known of innumerable instances in which the combined protests of author and agent have resulted in the publishers' springing for a new cover.

While the writer can't properly *control* the cover, he may be able to make a useful contribution. I've been enormously happy with the cover art Emanuel Schongut has supplied for the four Burglar books. In each case I suggested an illustration, and for three of the books Mr. Schongut followed my lead. I think it's worthwhile for a writer to make suggestions of this sort, and I also think it's essential to remember that the cover artist knows more about graphics and the publisher more about the commercial impact of covers than the writer knows about either. You can offer suggestions, but you shouldn't feel rejected if your ideas don't get used. I had a cute notion for *Telling Lies for Fun and Profit*—Pinocchio at the typewriter, his nose grown long from lying. I'm sure it would have worked, but it couldn't have had the impact of the all-type cover Antler & Baldwin designed, and when I saw a proof I was glad my suggestion had been dismissed.

Blurbs are important enough, and close enough to the writer's job, that I think more of us ought to take more of a role in their creation. The job of writing blurb copy often falls to an overworked editor who may or may not have a knack for that sort of thing. In some houses, somebody has to read the manuscript specifically and solely in order to produce a blurb; it's not uncommon for such a cursory reading to yield an inaccurate chunk of copy. Far too many blurbs give away far too much of the plot. I can recall a Bantam paperback of a Ross Macdonald novel which unmistakably revealed the killer, a bit of information the writer himself had reserved for the book's final page.

Some editors will ask the writer to take a shot at the blurb while reserving the right to redo it if necessary. In the absence of such an invitation, it is perfectly in order for a writer to offer to prepare a draft of the blurb, or to do so out of hand. Again, you have to recognize and accept the fact that your copy may be rewritten or replaced.

If you become a superstar, a veritable legend in the biz, you have the option of exerting considerably more control over these aspects of the publishing process. Some top writers get things like cover approval written into their contracts, and even in the absence of such a clause the publisher is unlikely to use a cover to which the author takes violent exception. Some writers, I understand, even have the contractual right to approve advertising copy.

All of which, I suppose, amounts to yet another reason to become a top writer. And that's a process that starts, not with blurbs and covers and titles, but with the unavoidable process of putting one word after another.

So hop to it.

Huffing and Puffing
August 1982

Couple of weeks ago my search for a place to live led me to a part of Brooklyn that was new to me. I found, wonder of wonders, a commodious apartment at an affordable rental. I checked out the neighborhood, spending a couple of hours walking up one street and down another. There was, I noted, a sizable park half a dozen blocks away. There was a YMCA around the corner. The streets were remarkably traffic-free.

I went back to the landlord's office and signed a lease.

Afterward, I realized what a high priority I had automatically assigned to exercise. I was charmed by the apartment and had quite fallen in love with the neighborhood, but I wasn't ready to commit myself to it until I'd investigated the opportunities for runners and swimmers and weight-lifters. Long before I bothered figuring out where I'd stick the typewriter, I was planning running routes and wondering which room would house my exercise bicycle.

This may not be as wacky as it seems. I can, after all, write almost anywhere, and under almost any conditions. I've proved that in attics and basements and motel rooms. I'm proving it right now in my new kitchen—new to me, that is; untold generations of immigrant housewives have boiled cabbage on this stove. My typewriter is perched on a little walnut end table, once the property of my grandmother. Its keys are consequently six inches closer to the floor than I'm used to their being. My typing paper and carbon paper is on the little shelf below, and the pages I've finished—few of them right now, but there'll be more—are resting atop the wastebasket, which in turn rests on the scarred linoleum in front of my left foot. (The table's so positioned that my knees wrap around it.) If I screw up a sheet and want to throw it away, I have to move the finished pages in order to chuck the discarded page in the wastebasket. This gives me a nice incentive to proceed with care, or may lead me to crumple the rejected page into a ball and flip it at the sink, which is just over my left shoulder.

Now, this is no way to write, but the point is that I can do it if I have to. But I can't swim without a pool, or work out without a weight room. I can run anywhere and could, if pressed, circle a single city block repeatedly, or jog on a treadmill like a caged squirrel. But I can't do that for any length of time without souring on it and abandoning running altogether.

All well and good, but what does all this have to do with writing?

I submit that it has everything to do with writing. I've been writing professionally for a quarter of a century, and for the past three years or so I've been getting a daily dose of strenuous exercise, and I can only wish I'd discovered this twenty-some years earlier than I did.

You see, it was not ever thus. I've a hunch that one of the earliest attractions of writing as a profession was that it demanded no more in the way of athletic ability than the manual coordination to hit the right keys, the sheer brute strength necessary to operate the carriage return, and the stamina it takes to sit in one place for long periods of time. There would be no huffing and puffing, no unseemly sweating. For one who was born out of shape and out of breath only to blossom into a fat and ungainly youth, it sounded like heaven. I could drink and smoke and eat and sleep, and, as long as I got the right words in the right order, no one would give a damn.

Now, curiously enough, one of writing's attractions is that it affords so much opportunity for exercise. Even when I'm working on a book at maximum intensity, I can't spend more than four or five hours at the typewriter without producing gibberish. More often, two hours of writing is my daily dose, and there are weeks or months between books when I barely look at the typewriter. I can, in the ordinary course of things, fit a long run and a session at the gym into my schedule with no great difficulty. And my schedule's flexible; even if I give writing first priority, I can juggle my time so that everything fits.

Accordingly, I completed five full marathons last year, and I can think of nothing more likely to astonish anyone who knew me way back when. I don't know what the information would do to my grammar school gym teacher. Give him a heart attack, I suppose.

I'm not going to bore you with a recital of the health benefits of all this athletic excess. They're probably considerable, but I suspect that what I gain at the cardiologist I lose to the podiatrist. I'm more concerned for the moment with the value of exercise to me as a writer. While it's arguably true that I'll write more and better books if I'm alive and well, I submit that there's a more direct link between physical exercise and the mental work of writing.

First of all, I've found out that physical exercise is the best tool available for relaxing and refreshing a mind and spirit that writing has tired. Writing is hard work, and it seems to me that every year it gets harder. The concentration required for me to do my best work leaves me drained and enervated after a few intense hours.

I always assumed that simple rest was the best cure for this exhaustion. But such rest was hard to come by. I frequently found that I couldn't get my head out of my work. The process of writing would degenerate into a form of mental wheel-spinning.

I generally coped with this by unwinding with the aid of a few drinks or an oddly scented cigarette, and these tools seemed to do the job. I've since come to see that drugs and alcohol didn't restore me as much as they numbed me to the fact that I was depleted. They didn't help me to relax, but merely kept me from feeling the tension.

Exercise is a different matter. It takes me out of my head and puts me into my body. As a writer, I spend too much time involved in mental activity, and I tend to get locked in there. A half hour of running or swimming or lifting heavy metal objects turns the body on and the mind off.

I'm often tired after a workout, but I'm also generally refreshed in a way I couldn't be otherwise.

Puff Puff

When I first started working out with weights a few years ago, I did so because of the physical benefits such activity was said to provide. I found, much to my surprise, that I felt an enormous sensation of well-being after a workout and sauna, a sort of muscular high unlike anything in my experience. I got into the habit of going to the gym as soon as I finished my stint at the typewriter, and before long I discovered that I was counting on my workout to straighten me out and settle me down.

I found out, too, that exercise helps to keep me in a state of mental equilibrium, or as close to such a state as I'm ever likely to get. I'm subject to depression—as are a considerable number of other writers, and, it would appear, a great many Real People as well. (Something like 85% of persons seeking psychotherapy do so because of problems with depression.) Exercise alleviates depression. I know this on the basis of my own experience, and I've learned that there is a real physical basis for the results I've observed, that the body produces its own natural antidepressants during extended aerobic exercise.

I get depressed when my writing isn't going well, and when I'm depressed I can't write, and so on. If I can make myself continue with my regular exercise routine at such times—even though depression makes me inclined to say the hell with it—my depressions aren't as severe and don't last as long.

Exercise also uses up a lot of energy, and writing requires a lot of energy, and you would think one would exist only at the expense of the other. There's a point where this becomes true. I wouldn't want to attempt working full steam on a novel and simultaneously building my mileage toward a marathon.

However, writing and exercise tend to be more complementary than mutually competitive as far as energy is concerned. Consider the experience of my friend John J. McAleer, who is writing two novels and a biography of Emerson and is editing two journals while teaching fulltime and presiding over a large household. "It's only by a miracle of scheduling that I keep these writing projects moving forward," he wrote me recently. "But I jump up every morning at 6:30 and swim two miles before breakfast, and that gears up my metabolism enough to get me through till 1 a.m. next morning. I find that for every hour I swim I need two hours less sleep—a convenient exchange."

Some writers, like McAleer and Joe Henderson, who does most of his writing about running, like to make exercise the first thing they do each morning. I've tried that, and my writing suffers for it. Things work better for me if I write first and then work out as soon as I get up from the typewriter. There don't seem to be any universal rules.

Nor is there any single ideal exercise. I think there are certain requirements, however. Our exercise of choice ought to be something we can do on our own, something that doesn't depend upon the availability of a partner or access to a tennis court. And it ought to be something we can enjoy doing. We don't have to become obsessive about it—nobody has to run marathons, or indeed any races at all, in order to get a lot out of running. But if we find it boring or actively unpleasant we won't stick with it, and if we don't stick with it, what good is it?

I mentioned an exercise bicycle earlier. I bought one this past winter when a stress fracture made running temporarily impossible, and I'll continue to use it when the weather's awful, and to tone muscles that running neglects. But if the bike were the only exercise available to me, I'm sure I'd drop it before long. It's too monotonous and unenjoyable, even for someone with my high boredom threshold.

You might find running similarly boring. But the chances are you can find *something* that works for you. I tend to embrace athletic activity with the fervor of the middle-aged jock, compensating no doubt for a youth of indolence and a young manhood of sloth. You might not find it quite that fulfilling, but you'll very likely find it an asset to your writing. Give it a fair trial—three months, say, long enough for the novelty to wear off and for it to become a part of your routine. You may find, as I have, that exercise helps create a climate for the solution of writing problems. You may find only that it makes you feel better. On the other hand, it may be that all you get for your troubles is better health and longer life.

Listen, you can't win 'em all.

Sticks and Stones

September 1982

A few years ago I did a column on pen names. It appeared in March of 1980 as "Altered Egos"; later, as a chapter in *Telling Lies for Fun and Profit*, I changed the title to "Bic, Scripto, Parker and Cross." (I am, I blush to admit, immoderately pleased with that title change.)

And I figured that was the end of it. One inevitably returns to topics over a period of years as a columnist, but I didn't expect to return to this one. I figured I'd said what there was to say, and, while it had made a reasonably interesting column, I certainly didn't suppose it added up to anything very substantial. More to the point, I didn't think anyone cared all that much about the subject.

And why should they? It would seem to me that the least important aspect of a manuscript is the name beneath the title. How much weight could it possibly carry with the editor, the reader, or with the writer in the first place?

(I just realized something. In the first sentence of the preceding paragraph, *they* is wrong. Its antecedent is *anyone*, so instead of *they* it should be *he*. Or *he or she*. But this column is about pen names, not about grammar, so what do you say we let it pass?)

Where were we? Ah, yes. Pen names. The column in question generated more than the usual amount of reader mail, not because it touched a nerve or struck a chord so much as it dealt with a subject with which many of you were concerned and upon which some of you had some very interesting things to say. Since then, enough letters have continued to trickle in to convince me that pseudonyms, aliases, noms de plume, and other forms of nomenclatural flummery are of more concern than I'd realized.

Consider the experiences of Susan C. Feldhake, whose book *How to Write and Sell Confessions* I'm pleased to recommend to you. In a letter to me she related how she'd offered second rights to an article to a wildlife publisher.

"The editor who bought first rights cared not a whit that I'm a femme," she explained. "The second editor sent me a scorching letter of rejection. My feminine instincts told me he was reacting to me, not my writing. I waited a decent length of time, submitted the same article under a macho moniker, and it was purchased promptly."

Ms. Feldhake has continued writing for this editor under her butch pen name and has fantasies of sidling into his editorial offices and introducing herself. When she cashes checks from him, she's careful to use a masculine scrawl.

This sort of subterfuge can take on a life of its own. "The editor thinks this guy Norm DePloom is a real he-man who knows his way around the woods," Ms. Feldhake reports. "I don't—I get chiggers. Anyway, he has this macho image of Norm. So for the fun of it I wrote a humor piece about the wife's viewpoint of helping to train a coon dog. I submitted it as Mrs. DePloom, Norm's wife, and this editor bought it. I suppose the next step is for Norm and the missus to hatch a baby pen name."

Editors, she points out, can become rejectors out of habit, conditioned like a drooling dog to respond negatively to a writer they've turned down in the past. "I decided to make my own little experiment," Feldhake writes. "I retyped a story previously submitted—and rejected—under my own name. I submitted it to a rejecting editor under a pen name. She bought it."

In this case, I'm not positive the pen name is what turned the trick. It's an unfortunate truth in this business that not all submissions get a fair reading. Indeed, many don't get read at all. Reading unsolicited submissions is far down the list of editorial priorities, and there are days when editors send everything back virtually unread. There are other days when their state of mind is such that they can't respond favorably to anything, under any name. Perhaps resubmission under any name would have smelled as sweet.

Competing with Yourself

Ivan B. Berger wrote in response to my column to advise me that I'd left out a reason to use a pen name, one that's more a problem for magazine article writers than for book writers or fiction writers generally. "It's hard to make a living writing for any given magazine that excludes you from writing for its competition," he explains. "At the moment I'm writing for two competing pairs of publications, using my own name on one and a pen name on the other of each pair. All four publishers know and approve, but if I had only my own name to fall back on, one publisher of each pair would dump me for writing for the competition. Once upon a time, in fact, I was writing regularly for the three major competing books in one field, using a separate name in each."

I know that some publishers expect this sort of exclusivity and I suppose I can understand why. From the writer's viewpoint, I think it's regrettable. It's very difficult building any sort of following in this business. *WD* readers are exceptional in that they pay more attention to bylines than most people do; writers themselves, they recognize that some human intelligence put the words in the order in which they appear. Most readers barely note a byline, especially in a magazine, and they have to see it over and over again before it makes a lasting impression.

We dilute our impact in this area when we use pen names. Consequently, when we bow to editorial whims of the sort Mr. Berger describes, we do our careers a disservice and, paradoxically, make ourselves less valuable to the very publishers who insist upon the pen names.

I haven't written for any other writer's magazines since I started my hitch at *WD*. I've no intention of so doing, but if I did I suppose I would have to use a pen name.

Many magazines also insist on a pen name when an author has more than one story or article in a single issue, and I have no quarrel with this practice. When the same byline appears more than once, it looks as though one person wrote the whole magazine, and the overall effect is vaguely unprofessional. In the pulp days, magazines often had "house names" that they slapped on second stories by a particular author; John D. MacDonald's only pseudonymous efforts, for example, were of this sort. The house name practice has always struck me as a bit high-handed. An author ought to have the right to pick his own alias, I would think.

Suppose one is writing not on the same subject for different publishers but on different subjects? Or, as a writer of fiction, suppose one is writing different kinds of stories? Isn't a pen name in order?

In a word, no. In two words, Isaac Asimov.

The good Dr. Asimov has written more books than most of us have read, and his range is literally encyclopedic. The man is a brilliant generalist, driven by an evident need to explain everything to everyone. He can write about Shakespeare, about music, about all of the sciences. He can write mystery stories, science fiction, limericks. He does all of this under his own widely recognized name, and he does it all supremely well.

The conventional wisdom would seem to hold that he has made a mistake. Readers, presumably unwilling to believe that one small head could contain all that knowledge, will distrust him. Critics, sure that no one that prolific could be good, will scorn him. His books will be remaindered. His unpublished manuscripts will turn the color of Nero Wolfe's pajamas.

Don't bet on it. Quite the reverse happens. Readers with no particular interest in a subject will read what Dr. Asimov has to say about it—because they've grown interested in the author himself.

In my own case, I write several different sorts of books. My mysteries about burglar Bernie Rhodenbarr are light-hearted and breezy. My novels about ex-cop Matthew Scudder are more serious in mood and tone. *Ariel* is a novel of psychological suspense with supernatural elements. *Ronald Rabbit Is a Dirty Old Man* is a pornographic comedy.

Perhaps this harms me commercially, in that some readers surely prefer authors to be brand names, so that they'll know exactly what to expect. But I think this is offset by what we might call the Asimov effect, in that I've heard from quite a few readers who read—and professed to enjoy—books of mine that they would have passed up under a pseudonym. Some of Bernie's fans bought *Ariel* although they usually don't like occult stuff. Some Scudder followers discovered Bernie in spite of their disaffection for comic mysteries.

When I find an author whose work engages me, I want to read everything he's written. I may not like all his auctorial personae, but I'd as soon have the opportunity to determine as much for myself. As a writer, I want to extend this opportunity to my readers.

Call Me Ishmael

How do you pick a pen name? However you wish, I should think, and I wouldn't raise the question if several readers hadn't raised it themselves in letters over the years. A fiction writer, obliged to come up with names for his characters, shouldn't have a great deal of trouble doing as much for himself. Perhaps the nonfiction writer, harnessed in his work to the cumbersome machinery of reality, is less accustomed to this sort of invention.

Ivan Berger suggests a few ways to devise a pen name that disguises the writer while growing out of his name or family history. "Of the four pen names I've used," he offers, "one is a translation of my name into another language, a second is a translation of my nickname into its historical equivalent in another tongue, another is a switch on my first and middle names, and yet another is my father's and grandfather's first names."

Two of my pen names were the names of characters in the books concerned. In *Such Men Are Dangerous*, Paul Kavanagh was both the pen name and the narrator; I used the byline on two other books which were not about that character. Four books "by Chip Harrison" all concerned Chip Harrison. Two of them, I'm happy to report, will be reissued next spring by the Countryman Press. They'll appear together in a double volume under the joint title *A/k/a Chip Harrison*, with my own byline. I find myself pleased at the prospect of having my own name on the books after lo these many years.

If one is of a playful turn of mind, the anagram pen name may have a certain appeal. My very first pen name, on a letter to the editor of the *Buffalo Evening News* written when I was in high school, was Allor Bryck, which was a rearrangement of the letters in Larry Block, which in turn was how I then signed myself. (I became Lawrence a little later, probably in the hope that people would think I was a grownup. They still haven't fallen for it, either.)

The best anagram pen name I ever heard of was Poul Anderson's. Recalling that A.A. Milne had written of Winnie the Pooh as living under the name of Sanders, he dubbed himself Winston P. Sanders, which is an anagram for P. Anderson's Twins.

I'll tell you, it makes a whole lot more sense than Allor Bryck.

Crockpot Macramé
October 1982

Good morning, class.

Good morning, sir.

I'd like to talk a little this morning about a teaching job I interviewed for last week. I put on a jacket and real shoes and rode the subway and—yes, Rachel?

Did you get the job, sir?

I didn't get it, and neither did it get me. I was coming to that, Rachel. Don't rush me.

Sorry, sir, but the suspense was killing me. I was afraid you'd be disappearing into the halls of ivy and leaving us forever.

I could never leave you, Rachel. And this place didn't have any ivy on its glass and steel walls. I didn't notice any metaphorical ivy, either. I was interviewed by someone in the Continuing Education Department. I'd been recommended as a possible instructor in the writing of mystery and spy fiction, and the interview was designed to determine how I would approach such a course.

I answered by describing the course I'd taught at Hofstra University last season. My students prepared exercises each week, writing a scene or a story on an assigned topic, and class time was devoted to their reading their work aloud and criticizing one another's efforts. This, I allowed, is hardly a revolutionary approach. I don't much like it, but there's this to say for it: every other method I've heard of is even worse.

My interviewer offered some objections. First of all, she said, my students would be paying for my expertise. If they were to get their money's worth, they should be receiving my criticism, not the judgment of their peers. To this I said something about motes and beams, explaining that weaknesses are more apparent in another's work than in one's own, and insight that can be applied to one's own writing comes most often by analyzing somebody else's writing.

She seemed unconvinced, but moved on to another point. What the students were most interested in, she said, was getting published. That's why they would be taking my course, so that they could turn out publishable work and, more important, get it into print. They would want market tips from me. They would want to know how to get an agent. They—

I could have left right then and there. For this I shaved? For this I put on real shoes? For this I changed trains at Queens Plaza?

I explained that I wasn't terribly interested in providing market information. I added that I thought it might be a trifle previous, as they say down home, in that, whether or not you count chickens before they're hatched, you certainly don't run around trying to peddle them. Furthermore, I told her, I felt a course aimed specifically at the production of publishable fiction was unrealistic.

The odds were, I pointed out, that the vast majority of my students—or anybody else's students—would never produce any marketable fiction. No instructor could change that fact. Writing is not computer programming. A school in computer programming can virtually guarantee its students that they will find jobs upon graduation. A writing school cannot begin to guarantee that a single one of its alumni will ever write anything that anyone would read with pleasure. This being the case—yes, Arnold? Did you say something?

I just said, "Here it comes," sir.

Here what comes?

The bit about writing-can-be-learned-but-it-can't-be-taught, sir.

Well, I'm glad you're prepared, Arnold, because here it comes. Writing can be learned but it can't be taught. And talent can't even be learned. It can be developed, but only if it's there. And the absence of talent is never visible, which is to say that, while I can look at one student's work and say for certain that he's talented, I can't look at another's and say for sure that he's not. I can only say that his talent hasn't yet become visible.

What, then, can I as an instructor attempt to accomplish in a classroom? As far as I can see, I can create an environment that will best facilitate the students' own development. I can stimulate students to write regularly and to come up with ideas on a regular basis.

I can direct the discussion of student work. Most students tend to be far too bland and supportive in their analysis of their fellows' stories. "I liked it, it was interesting, I thought the descriptions were good"—that sort of critical pablum doesn't help the writer or anybody else. On the other hand, an occasional student with a sadistic streak can be cruel enough in his comments to hurt his fellow writers and inhibit their future efforts. I can draw his fangs and neutralize some of his venom.

I didn't say all of this to the woman who interviewed me because there wasn't really much point. It had become clear to me that this particular institution was dedicated, at least in its Continuing Ed program, to the Polly Adler principle of giving the paying customer whatever he wants. If 12 people will sign up for a course in Crockpot Macramé, for heaven's sake provide the course and ballyhoo it in the catalog.

"The sort of student we draw," my interviewer went on, "may not have done any writing before. He may have a particular book that he wants to write, and so he's coming to take your course so that he can learn how to write his book and get it published. Now, what are you going to be able to do for him?"

"Wait a minute," I said. "He hasn't written anything?"

"Little or nothing."

"And he has a book in mind that he wants to write?"

"That's right. He has an idea for a novel, a mystery or spy novel, which is why he would select your course. Now, how will you teach him to write that book? What will he get out of your class?"

You know what I think I'll do? I think I'll go to a voice teacher. I'll explain that I've never done any singing, except for belting out "On the Road to Mandalay" in the shower. I've booked Carnegie Hall for a Thursday night in November, and I want to make sure I'll be terrific. What can the voice teacher do, I'll ask, to guarantee that my debut will be a success?

Actually, the analogy is unfair. Shower singers like me don't wind up onstage at Carnegie Hall, while every now and then somebody who never wrote a word, never took a course, never put pen to paper other than to jot down a laundry list, sits down at a typewriter and produces something that gets published. Maybe it turns out to be a bestseller, maybe they make a movie out of it, maybe the author winds up with his picture in *People* magazine. That sort of thing happens just often enough to keep the Crockpot Macramé people in business.

I have no quarrel with writers who achieve instant stardom in this fashion. I may envy them, tempering my envy with the knowledge that overnight success is not without problems of its own. Nor have I any quarrel, really, with people who aspire to this kind of success. I think their expectations are generally unfounded, as I think they'll find out sooner or later, but that's their problem. It's not mine.

I do quarrel, though, with an educator who panders to this lust for overnight success. I expressed my reservations and stopped short of rejecting the job out of hand because I realized that, if they hired me, I could then teach the course my way. I wasn't sure I wanted to, but I have a hard time turning down any money that I can get without writing. After a quarter century at the typewriter, getting paid to stand around and talk is like finding money in the street.

Even so, I decided in the next day or two to leave the filthy lucre in the gutter. Then I got a call informing me they'd found someone else, which made one less high moral stand I've had to take this month.

And it's given me something to write about.

One thing I realized, while arriving at a decision I ultimately didn't have to make, was that I like teaching and that I'm fairly good at it. All of my students at Hofstra improved in the course of a semester. They produced a story every week, they participated in discussion, and both their critical abilities and their writing skills were visibly superior at the term's end. Two of them are talented enough to have realistic expectations of eventual success. Neither has written anything publishable yet, and I don't think that's important.

I found it gratifying to watch my students improve. I've always believed, too, that a writing course is valuable independent of its producing talented writers. Anyone who participates wholeheartedly in a good writing workshop will, at the least, become a better and more perceptive reader for the experience.

I also realized that there were only two things I liked about teaching—the actual interaction with students in the classroom and the money I got for my trouble. Everything else—grades, schedules, faculty memos—I could do without. Accordingly, it struck me that perhaps the most effective way for me to teach a writing workshop and get the most satisfaction out of it lies in doing so without the auspices of Crockpot Macramé U.— or any other institution. Toward that end I—Gwen?

I sense a plug coming, sir.

What makes you say that?

You raised your voice, sir. On television, the commercials are always louder than the programs. Why is that, sir?

To let you know they're the important part. As I was saying, I've decided to explore the possibilities of teaching a 15-week Workshop in Fiction. Classes would be held one night a week during early evening hours, probably in Greenwich Village or SoHo. SASE sent to me c/o *WD* will get a reply when I know more about scheduling and price.

I guess that's all, class. I didn't mean to turn this into a commercial solicitation. It started out as a thoughtful essay into the nature of writing instruction and look where it went. Well, have I covered everything? Are there any questions?

Will you be singing "On the Road to Mandalay" at Carnegie Hall, sir?

Watch it, Rachel. Just watch it.

• 11 •

View Finder
November 1982

The Gantreson living room came alive with the hum of conversation as the party shifted into high gear. Under the Rouault lithograph, Jim Klaiber stirred the punch bowl idly and wondered how he'd made out on his anatomy exam. A second-year medical school student, he was once again supplementing his student loans and summer job savings with a stint of party bartending.

Across the room, red-haired Sue Penobscot weighed the alternate attractions of another cup of punch against walking out onto the terrace and flirting with the piano player. Meanwhile, the object of her deliberations worked his way through "Send in the Clowns" and smiled wryly, thinking that the song's request had been answered in advance. Someone had sent in more clowns than anyone could possibly want; the Gantreson house overflowed with them.

Upstairs, Polly Gantreson sprawled full-length upon her patchwork quilt-covered bed and wept soundlessly into her pillow. She wanted to scream, to break glasses, to throw things. Here it was, her thirtieth birthday, and she . . . .

Well, that's quite enough of that. If I don't stop myself, I might get caught up in the thoughts of all these people and wind up writing a book no one in his right mind would want to read. The point of this exercise, insofar as it has one, is to show how point of view can shift within a scene.

It's not the sort of scene I myself often write. My own books and stories tend to be written each from a single point of view. The reader receives all his information through the eyes of a central character. More often than not, my books are written in the first person, so that the reader knows no more than the narrator elects to tell him. While other characters will express themselves in dialogue and through their actions, it is only the lead character's thoughts to which the reader will be privy.

I write this way because it seems most natural to me. As reader and as writer, I'm most comfortable identifying solidly with a single character and perceiving the fictional world as he perceives it. Then too, most of the books I've written in recent years have been detective stories, and the detective story usually works best when told from a single point of view. The viewpoint character need not be the detective himself—Sherlock Holmes had his Watson, Nero Wolfe his Archie Goodwin—and one could cite no end of examples of multiple-viewpoint novels of detection, but the typical detective story is indeed told from a single point of view.

The advantages of a single viewpoint are fairly clear-cut, in detective stories or any other sort of fiction. Reader and writer identification is facilitated considerably. Similarly, the disadvantages are also quite clear, and I suspect the chief one is tedium.

It can be tiring, for the reader and for the writer, to be locked to a single character's point of view for an entire novel. The longer the novel and the greater its scope, the more exhausting it can be to spend all one's time in the presence of a particular character.

Similarly, a single viewpoint is limiting. It keeps you from describing scenes at which the lead character is not present. It prevents you from recounting the thought processes of other characters, or telling the reader directly about their prior histories without filtering all that information through the lead, with this sort of result:

> *The Gantreson living room came alive with the hum of conversation as the party shifted into high gear. Under the Rouault lithograph, Jim Klaiber stirred the punch bowl idly. Maybe he was wondering how he'd made out in the anatomy exam. I knew he was a second-year medical school student, and once again he was supplementing his student loans and summer job savings with a stint of party bartending.*
>
> *I turned to glance across the room and saw red-haired Sue Penobscot. Her eyes went from the punch bowl to the door that led onto the terrace, as if she was*

weighing the relative charms of the spiked fruit juice against those of the guy who was working his way through "Send in the Clowns."

Out on the terrace, the pianist dropped me a wry wink. Don't bother, it seemed to say, underscoring the tune's lyrics. Don't bother, they're here . . . .

This deathless passage is designed to show that the thoughts and backgrounds of other characters can be conveyed through a viewpoint character, even a first-person narrator. It's even possible for a first-person narrator to describe events at which he is not present, although it requires more than a little skill to bring off this sort of thing. W. Somerset Maugham's *The Moon and Sixpence* is a particularly good example; the narrator presents material by describing it as the work of his own imagination, albeit based upon deduction and inference.

Ariel View

In multiple-viewpoint fiction, different portions of the work are told from the viewpoint of different characters. The general label of multiple-viewpoint covers any number of narrative methods. A multiple-viewpoint novel may have a predominant lead character who is more important than the others and whose story constitutes the basic plot of the book. Other viewpoint characters advance the plot, enlarge the book's scope, provide additional perspectives on the lead, but never really take over the spotlight. John O'Hara's *Ten North Frederick* is a good example; the narrative is multiple-viewpoint, but the book never ceases to be the story of one man, Joe Chapin.

My own novel *Ariel*, concerned an adopted girl whose younger brother died mysteriously. Ariel was the book's most important character, but I don't think I ever seriously considered telling her entire story exclusively through her eyes. For one thing, my plot called for things to be going on within her family of which Ariel could not be entirely aware. For another, I wanted the reader to be uncertain about Ariel, and to see her not only as she perceived herself but also as she was perceived in turn by others. Accordingly, I told a large portion of the book from Ariel's viewpoint but intercut the book with chapters from the viewpoints of her mother, her father, and her mother's lover.

Some multiple-viewpoint novels have no central character, although there is often one person with whom most readers are more likely to identify. In Ed McBain's 87th Precinct police procedurals, there's really no lead character, although Steve Carella is the most important character in the series and the central figure of some of the books. In *Peyton Place* and novels of that ilk, no single character predominates.

In multiple-viewpoint fiction, the writer has choices to make. He must decide who is to be the viewpoint character for a particular scene. Sometimes the selection is obvious, but not always. Now and then he might want to relate a scene from the point of view of a relatively minor character, because of the particular perspective it might afford.

The writer also decides when to switch viewpoint, and whether to remain with the focus fixed upon a particular character for a scene or a chapter or a brace of chapters.

As a writer, I probably tend to demand more of myself in the way of consistency than would matter to me as a reader. If I'm changing point of view with each new chapter, the prospect of telling two consecutive chapters from a single point of view seems disharmonious to me. I don't know that readers care much about this sort of thing, or even notice it.

In *The Triumph of Evil*, a novel I wrote under the pen name of Paul Kavanagh, the entire book was told from the viewpoint of Miles Dorn—except for a single scene. That scene, somewhere past the midpoint of the book, involved an assassination which Dorn arranged by manipulating another man. For plot purposes, Dorn can't be present when the assassination is carried out, yet I wanted to be able to describe the incident directly rather than have Dorn learn about it from a distance.

So I wrote that scene—it runs about a page—from the point of view of the young man who performs the actual assassination. It's the only scene like it in the book, and when I wrote it I had the feeling that everyone who read it would be knocked off balance by the sudden shift in narrative focus. I imagined every copy of the book automatically falling open to the tell-tale page and every reader shaking his head at my structural inconsistency.

But I let it go to the publisher that way. I felt I was doing something dishonorable, but weighed against putting Dorn on the scene or recounting the scene second-hand, it still seemed the least of three evils. I took a deep breath and awaited repercussions.

I'm still waiting. As far as I know, nobody ever even noticed that there's one scene in the book at which Dorn's not present. Certainly nobody's ever said anything. That may not prove much—the book only sold 18 copies, as I recall. But I'll tell you, I went back and read the section just now before writing this column, and I don't think I'd notice the shift myself if I hadn't written the book, and if I didn't remember agonizing over it back then.

View and Far Between

One thing I often have trouble with in multiple-viewpoint books is chronology. It seems to me that the continuous sequence of a book ought to be one straight temporal line. Aside from flashbacks, the time of the book ought to go ahead rather than folding back on itself. But this is frequently impossible when a story is told from more than one point of view, and almost always impossible when a novel contains the stories of several characters interwoven together. The scenes are going to overlap somewhat; George's story won't pick up exactly where Martha's leaves off. Again, this is something that bothers me as a writer but not as a reader.

A reader wrote recently asking if it was possible to have first-person and third-person chapters within a single novel; the first-person chapters were to be the lead's narrative, while other chapters would be told in the third-person from the viewpoints of other characters.

I see no reason why this wouldn't work, and it seems to me that I've read books in which this was done. I know I've read multiple-viewpoint novels written in the first person; different characters took turns narrating the story. (Come to think of it, I wrote one myself once, and while it was tricky moving from one voice to the next, it was fun, and worked out well enough. If you do this sort of thing, chapter headings will help the reader make the transition smoothly from one voice to another.)

Generally speaking, I'm not comfortable with viewpoint shifts within a scene. I don't like it when we bounce back and forth between various characters' minds. This is occasionally all right—as in the example that opened this column, the party scene, where the shifting focus gives us an overview of the scene, much in the manner of a montage of establishing shots in a movie. It's less successful when one leaps back and forth between the minds of two or more characters who are interacting with one another.

Finally, it seems to me that, as with so many aspects of fictional technique, there are really no firm rules. We make our own—and break them when necessity demands it. I would suggest only that you be a little bit more aware of point of view in your reading, so that you notice some of the options other writers have had available and the choices they've made.

· 12 ·

Shifting Gears
December 1982

As I write these lines, Pocket Books is preparing to ship the paperback edition of my book *The Burglar Who Studied Spinoza*. It's a light-hearted mystery featuring a series character of mine, one Bernie Rhodenbarr, a sort of buttoned-down burglar who owns a secondhand bookstore and sort of coasts through life on a cushion of hapless urbanity. While the good people at Pocket are getting their trucks loaded, bookstore shelves are already groaning with Arbor House's hardcover edition of *Eight Million Ways to Die*; it's my latest novel about Matthew Scudder, a guilt-ridden alcoholic ex-cop, and it's all about as light-hearted as a massive coronary.

The two books—and the two series of which they are parts—are very different from one another. It is not merely that their tone is different but that they reflect two disparate worlds. While both are set in New York, Bernie's New York seems another place altogether than Scudder's. Scudder inhabits a city whose criminal justice system has broken down altogether, a city whose inhabitants live in constant peril, a city with, as the title reminds us, innumerable doors to let out life.

Bernie's New York is a happier place. The subways break down and the cops take bribes, and people do indeed get killed, but there's a difference.

Which of these two worlds is real? I would submit that each is as real as the other, that the difference between the two worlds and the two New Yorks is attitudinal, that each reflects reality as the lead character perceives it.

But the perceptions of a lead character are nothing more or less than the perceptions of the writer, are they not? So how can one writer have two so conflicting sets of perceptions and reflect two utterly different realities? Isn't it inevitable that one of these series be dishonest and false, a distorted mirror to its author's own view of the world?

I certainly don't think so. I don't see the world the same way all the time. I don't have the same set of feelings about New York, or about life, or about much of anything, seven days a week and 52 weeks a year. The world according to Bernie Rhodenbarr and the world according to Matthew Scudder represent two different and two equally honest versions of the world according to Yours Truly.

Some readers find this puzzling, even disturbing. They want an author's work to be all of a piece. Some writers allow for this tendency by using different names on different kinds of books.

Some years ago Robert Ludlum wrote a comic caper novel about the kidnaping of a pope. Rather than confuse the audience he was steadily building for his richly plotted suspense novels, he published *The Road to Gandolfo* under a pseudonym. This past year the book was reissued in paperback under its author's own name. Ludlum's reputation had by then been sufficiently established so that an atypical book would not put readers off, and in fact his loyal fans quickly made *Gandolfo* a paperback bestseller; it had had an indifferent sale in its first go-round.

Graham Greene labels his lighter efforts as "entertainments" to distinguish them from his more serious novels. His original intent was to use a pen name on such books; his publisher was agreeable, but told Greene he would pay him a lower advance, since books under another name could not be expected to sell as well. "Well, the hell with that," said Greene, or words to that effect—and the "entertainment" was born, with no discernible adverse effect on the author's sales or critical reputation.

How does one shift gears? How does a writer go from writing one kind of book to turning out something quite different?

In my own case, I sometimes think the process of shifting gears is made somewhat easier by the lengthy periods I spend in neutral. I take a lot of time off between books, so it's not as though I finish writing something bubbly about Bernie on Friday and plunge into Scudder's angst-ridden universe first thing Monday morning.

Switching from one sort of book to another would seem to provide a useful change of pace. A change is allegedly as good as a rest, and while I personally have trouble believing that anything's as good as a rest, I'd say there's some truth to the allegation. When I'm writing something heavy and intense, the prospect of making my next book light and bouncy has a lot of appeal. Similarly, when I'm emerging from the hard work of a book with an elaborately dovetailed plot, I get the urge to make my next one the sort that doesn't require much in the way of plotting, a book where incident follows upon incident without any need for the ends to knit together at the climax.

What this amounts to, I sometimes think, is the simple hope that the next book will be *easy*. But I'm afraid this always turns out to be a false hope. Writing isn't easy for me, and hasn't been easy for years now. I don't think it will ever be easy so long as I try to make everything I write as good as it can possibly be. A book about Bernie may involve the use of different muscles than are exercised in a book about Scudder, but I can't do either to my satisfaction unless I use the respective muscles to the utmost. Light books probably look easier, but in certain respects they're harder, and sometimes the hardest part lies in making it look easy.

In the introduction to *Night Shift*, a collection of his short stories, Stephen King mentions that he's often asked why he writes about the things he does. His frequent reply, he explains, is another question: What makes you think I have any choice?

I'm not sure how much choice I have in what I write. I sometimes like to think of myself as a cool-headed professional writer, but the choices I seem to make sometimes demonstrate precious little commercial sense.

Eight or ten years ago I got an idea for a novel. I was going to have a gang of Arab terrorists lay siege to a Catskills resort during a singles weekend. I sat down to write up a treatment of the idea and found myself describing a Moshe Dayan–type character as Israel's one-eared Minister of Retaliation. Now I had already pitched the notion to a prospective publisher, and he'd made it clear that he could only see the book if it were done straight, but my typewriter seemed to have a will of its own. I could evidently only write the book funny.

I never sold it. I wrote about 120 pages of it. A couple of publishers assured me it wasn't possible to be funny on the subject of Arab terrorism. Maybe they were right. I'd already established to my own satisfaction that it wasn't possible for me to write seriously on the subject either, and the book never got finished.

Looking back, I'm not sure that wasn't the best thing that could have happened to it.

Don Westlake had a similar experience, but with a far happier ending. After having written quite a few books under the name Richard Stark, hard-boiled books about the criminal career of a chap named Parker, Don found himself hung up on a Parker book in which things kept turning funny. Parker had to steal the same damned jewel over and over, and there was no way for him to maintain his dignity while so doing, and he didn't. Don finally realized that his mind was trying to tell him something, started over from the beginning, changed Parker's name to Dortmunder and let the book take the comic turn it had been wanting to take all along. The result was *The Hot Rock*, very successful as book and film and the start of a whole series of books about Dortmunder.

Things reached something of a crest in *Jimmy the Kid*, in which Dortmunder and his friends come to grief carrying out a job inspired by a Richard Stark novel. It's been a while now since a book has come out about either Parker or Dortmunder, and I wish Don would remedy that situation. But maybe he hasn't got much choice.

I didn't seem to have a choice two years ago when I resumed writing about Scudder after a hiatus of quite a few years. The first three Scudder novels were Dell originals, the series did not get good distribution, and I had no reason to believe that I'd have an easy time finding a publisher eager to adopt my orphaned detective. But the book, *A Stab in the Dark*, demanded to be written, and I wrote it with no real regard for commercial considerations. It repaid me not merely by being a joy to write but by doing better commercially than anything I'd written, except for those lucky longshots that sold to Hollywood.

In an introduction to his current book, *Different Seasons*, Stephen King talks about how, at the beginning of his career, his publisher was concerned that he was bringing out successive books in the horror genre. "You'll get typed," King was told. Then, as one book followed another and each was more successful than the last, the publisher was worried that King might depart from the horror genre and alienate his fans.

Go figure.

Some writers never shift gears. They have a particular world and a particular way of looking at it, and everything they write reflects it. Perhaps they never attempt a change of pace. Perhaps they do, with unhappy results, and promptly return to what they do best.

I know that I'm frequently surprised, on reading the biography or a collection of the letters of some novelist, to find that a chap whose every printed utterance was as dour as Schopenhauer on a cloudy day was, in his private life and personal correspondence, as airy as a soufflé out of P.G. Wodehouse. Similarly, I'm now and then astounded to learn that some writer who never produced anything but the bubbliest froth was a depressive, a deep thinker, a man who had to wrestle hard with life. We (most of us) have more than one side to ourselves. How odd that some of us can only express one side in our work.

For my own part, I'm glad I seem to be able to shift gears and change hats with abandon. I may disappoint some readers in the process, but I suspect I'll gain others, the sort who are more interested in experiencing the full range of another person's work than in taking home a reliable Brand Name product, as unvarying from the last one as a box of corn flakes. That, I know, is more the sort of reader I am, and certainly the sort I prefer to cultivate.

Tune In to Your Creativity...
and Let the Ideas Come to You
1983 Yearbook

IDEAS, LIKE RADIO WAVES, ARE EVERYWHERE. CREATIVITY, THEREFORE, IS NOT SO MUCH A MATTER OF FINDING IDEAS AS IT IS ONE OF LEARNING TO BECOME RECEPTIVE TO THEM. HERE'S HOW.

Around the end of February, some three and a half months ago as I write these lines, I finished writing a novel called *Eight Million Ways to Die*. I had never worked longer or harder on anything. It was a demanding book, one that occupied me for more of the day's hours than is usually the case.

When it was done, I knew that I wanted a long rest. I didn't want to think about the next book, let alone commence work on it. I wasn't even sure what the next book would be. *Eight Million Ways* has Matthew Scudder for a lead character, and my publisher had let me know he'd be glad of a new Scudder book in time for the spring list. I had half of a Bernie Rhodenbarr mystery written. I would, I assumed, do one of three things next—finish the Bernie book, write a different Bernie book, or do another book about Scudder. I didn't know which I would do and I didn't much want to think about it.

And that was that. Time passed, as is its wont. I moved from Washington Heights to Brooklyn, where I set about converting a humble railroad flat into a perfect replica of Dresden after the bombing. I unplastered brick walls, I pulled down tacky paneling, I ripped up linoleum. Occasionally I cavorted in the rubble.

I didn't start a novel, or think about starting one. I turned out my monthly *Writer's Digest* column along with a few other short pieces. I kept up with correspondence, or tried to.

And then one evening in May I went into Manhattan to spend an hour or so with some friends, then wandered alone up Broadway to a Chinese restaurant, where I sat by myself with a plate of Hunan-style mixed vegetables and a pot of tea. I had a book with me—I often do—and I was turning the pages with one hand while manipulating the chopsticks with the other, which is not as hard as it sounds.

Somewhere in the course of things I put the book down and gazed off into the middle distance, which was somewhere between the kitchen and the powder room. I had been visited by an idea.

Let me retype that sentence, salting it lightly with capital letters. I had been Visited by an Idea.

That's better.

Because it wasn't just a little idea. It was the whole plot of a novel, and I have not the slightest notion whence it came. It did not turn up piecemeal but popped into my head more or less intact, much as Minerva emerged from the brow of Jupiter. I don't suppose Minerva sprang forth fully clad, and neither did my idea; I was given to know what would happen in my book but I didn't know who the people were or where the book would take place. But the plot was all there, however unformed some of its details might be, and I played with it as I polished off the bean sprouts, the snow pea pods, the baby corn.

I went home, and on the several subway trains I had to ride to get from there to here I intermittently considered and contemplated my idea. It was sound, I decided, and it was more than a little exciting, and it hadn't been done before, certainly not as I would do it, and while there were further things I would have to know about the book before I commenced writing it, I was confident they would turn up when they were needed.

I haven't started the book yet. Idea or no idea, I still don't want to begin work on a book until the fall. Now and then I take out the idea—or it takes itself out—and I look it over and ponder it and embellish it a bit. I think it's the book I'll start work on in September or October, but maybe not; sometimes my ideas sit around for years before I'm ready to make the best use of them.

But I got the idea. And I'm glad of it.

I don't know where it came from. I've discussed the origins of fictional ideas before (viz. "Where Do You Get Your Ideas?" in *Telling Lies for Fun and Profit*) and I don't want to belabor the subject anew. I'd rather have a look at the way ideas come to us, and some of the things a writer can do to make himself accessible to them.

Fredric Brown, who wrote delightful mysteries and science fiction, went through a ritual immediately before starting work on a book. He rode buses all night long. Or at least he said he did, and I heard about his practice at an impressionable age and was duly impressed. At that stage in my development, most advice to writers went right over my head. I didn't understand what the experts were talking about. But this was something I could grab onto. Hell, even I knew how to ride a bus.

Besides, there was an element of the ordeal about it that appealed to me. Here's the hard-bitten novelist, as Snoopy might put it, sitting up all night on a bus, working out the troublesome plot details of his next bestseller. Oh, I loved the idea, and I always wanted to stay up late, anyway.

It didn't take me long to try it. I was 19 years old, working in New York at a literary agency, writing stories for the few remaining pulps and eager to take a crack at a novel. I had the glimmer of an idea—it was, it suddenly strikes me, more than a little in the mode of Brown's *The Fabulous Clipjoint*—and I wanted to get the plot formed before I sat down to write the thing. I set out around 10 one evening, determined to ride the subways until dawn, which I could do for a single 15-cent token.

I suppose I lasted about an hour and a half. By then the drama of what

I was doing had faded and I was thinking about everything but the book. I went home and went to bed.

I did ultimately plunge in and start writing that book, though I can't recall whether I began it the next day or waited a week or two. I ultimately wrote 30 or 40 pages before abandoning the thing. There really wasn't much to the basic premise; I could have crisscrossed the country by Greyhound without hatching a proper plot.

But let me tell you, albeit with some reluctance, how I did plot my first novel.

It was that same year, and I was still working at the agency and living in a hotel on West 103rd Street and spending most of my free time in Greenwich Village. One night I went down to the Village and got drunk. This was not the first time this had happened, nor was it destined to be the last. I drank a staggering amount, and the adjective is particularly apt. Most of the details of the evening are lost to memory, which is probably just as well. Eventually a friend siphoned me into a cab, and the next thing I knew it was morning and I was in my hotel room, feeling every bit as bad as I deserved.

I didn't go to work that day. I'll tell you, if I'd felt that bad without having been drunk the night before I'd have gone to a hospital. Instead, I stayed right there in my room waiting for the hours to pass, and they have never passed with a more measured tread.

And, from a standing start, I wrote out the entire plot of a novel, scene by scene, chapter by chapter.

It was a perfectly sound outline, too. I put it aside for a while until I'd finished my stint at the agency. Then I moved from my hotel to my parents' house in Buffalo, and in two weeks I wrote the book. My agent sent it straight over to Fawcett and the editors bought it. Just like that.

Now, I wrote a great many books in the years that followed, and God knows I had my fair share of hangovers, but I can't think of another instance in which one led to the other in the fashion described above. (Sometimes a book led to a hangover, but that's another story.) It's just as well. I'd hate to be in the position of deliberately courting a hangover in the hope of blossoming creatively, much in the manner of Charles Lamb's legendary Chinese gentleman who burned down the house every time he wanted roast pork. Over far too many years, alcohol cost me a good deal more writing time and creative energy than it ever gave me.

Nevertheless, I can't dismiss the certain conviction that the particular altered state of that particular hangover enabled me to outline that particular book. The hangover didn't give me an idea, but somehow it got me out of my own way and allowed my creativity free rein. Somehow, on that particular dreadful morning, I was able to put it all together.

For the fiction writer, ideas mean several different forms of inspiration. There's the sort of idea that came to me in the Chinese restaurant, the fundamental plot principle, the one-sentence description of a book that gives the writer a handle on it.

"I have an idea," I told an agent of mine once. "A *Peyton Place*-type of novel set in Bucks County, Pennsylvania." That was an idea, and it was ultimately a book, but not without a great many more specific ideas of plot and character along the way. That book, as it happens, was written from a fairly detailed outline, yet every day's writing required the spontaneous generation of any number of fresh ideas—ideas of incident, of scene, of character, of structure.

In *Writing the Novel: From Plot to Print*, I describe a process of outlining which many writers find useful in developing a novel. There are several sound arguments against such a method, and I only occasionally use it myself, but I'm occasionally amused to hear outlining criticized as if it were unfair for the writer to prepare in this fashion, as if he's not really creating anything when he's taken the trouble to plan ahead. But writing—writing that works—is never a matter of filling in blanks, of painting by number. The writer's own creative ingenuity is summoned up on every page and leaves its stamp on every line.

* * *

Mozart, I'm told, said offhandedly that composing was really quite simple, albeit tedious at times. He heard this music in his mind, he explained, and had merely to write it down on paper.

Levitation's easy, too. You just jump up into the air—any fool can do that—and you stay there.

Mozart's remark suggests a nice distinction between genius and talent. The talented composer works out his music theme by theme, note by note. The genius just writes down what he hears in his head.

The only way I get to hear the Jupiter Symphony is by playing the record. Yet, there are moments when I don't have to do much more than write down what I hear whispered by an inner voice.

It's hard to write about this because I don't entirely understand it, nor am I altogether sure anyone does. I'm convinced, though, that there are moments—in writing, but in other areas of my life as well—when I seem to have a clear channel to something larger than myself. Perhaps I'm tapping into my own unconscious, perhaps it's the collective unconscious of the human race, perhaps it's some form of higher power. I don't know what it is, and I don't know that it matters, but I can assure you that there are times when I feel less the source of the words I type than a simple medium for their transmission.

I suspect that everyone is occasionally the beneficiary of this sort of grace. In *The Sweet Spot in Time*, John Jerome discusses this phenomenon in athletics. I haven't read his book, just reviews of it—which is like eating menus—so I can't really discuss the details of his thesis, but I know from my own experience those special moments when the body does everything right in a manner that approaches magic. I had two of those moments. The first came in an intramural basketball game my freshman year in college. I was a hopeless basketball player, but one blessed afternoon I could not do a single wrong thing. Every time I threw the ball at the basket the thing went in. I had the touch, and I never had it again. Fifteen years later, the same thing happened on a pool table. For about an hour and a half I was unbeatable. The experience so delighted me that I went on to buy my own pool table. I practiced often, I developed a certain ability, but I never had what I'd had that one magical night.

I've had a related experience in a far less dramatic fashion when doing crossword puzzles. Every now and then I don't think of the answers because I don't *have* to think of them. They just seem to pop into my mind before I've even registered the definition. They're simply *there*. Sometimes, with one of those cryptic English-style crosswords, I'll know the right answer without knowing *why* it's the answer. It just comes to me.

And of course this sort of thing happens to me at the typewriter. This gift is most frequently given to me in dialogue. Sometimes I'll write down whole conversations almost as fast as I can type, just copying down the voices in my head. It ain't *The Magic Flute*, but I'll settle for it. Other times I'll have to invent, say, a minor character I haven't foreseen in the outline, and out of thin air a whole personality and past history takes form while I'm writing. Part of this is professional skill, to be sure, and part is the exercise of a writer's trained imagination, but another part is most assuredly a gift of some sort, and I needn't know the giver's name to be profoundly grateful.

How can we open ourselves up to the flow of creativity? What can we do to make ourselves available to the ideas that bubble up from within or fall like manna from on high? Or is there nothing specific we can do, and are we merely to take what comes along and be glad of it?

I've come to believe two things—first, that I cannot force this sort of creativity to happen, and second, that I can make myself more or less receptive to it.

It's no great secret that some of us try to give the creative process a chemical assist. Various drugs ingested in various ways can set the mind slightly askew, and the result is occasionally something that can be transmuted into art. My own conviction, based on observation and experience, is that drugs may work for a person at the beginning but always work against him in the end. Anything taken to enhance creativity winds up stifling creativity. The user forgets how to manage without the drug. Then the drug stops working.

Happily, there are drug-free methods to stimulate the flow of one's creative energy. Here, in no particular order, are a few I've found helpful.

1. Bring a Fresh Mind to the Typewriter

Early in my career, I as often as not did my writing at the end of the day and on into the night. Well, there are lots of things you can get away with early on. Since then I've learned to make writing the first thing I do each day. I'm stronger and fresher and possess more energy.

Typically, I get up, eat breakfast, read the paper, have a second cup of tea, then settle down to work. But I amended this routine somewhat while I was writing *Eight Million Ways to Die*, and the change was worthwhile.

Years ago I'd read a novel by Edmund Schiddel, I think it was, in which one character was a writer who rose each morning and went directly to the typewriter. He was very careful not to talk to another human being first. He didn't want anything to dilute his creative energy.

Since I woke up alone, I didn't have anyone around to talk to. But what I did, recalling Schiddel's character, was stop reading at the breakfast table. Indeed, I stopped reading anything, stopped looking at anything with print on it, until I had finished my day's work.

I think this helped in two ways. First, the time between rising and beginning work was a time for the day's work to shape itself in my mind. Outside input of any sort could only impede this process. Similarly, any reading I might do would serve to take me out of the book's fictive reality.

There is one sort of reading I sometimes like to do before I start work, and that's the work I did the day before. Proofreading the previous day's output can help me ease back into the flow of the book. Some writers actually retype the last page or two with this goal in mind, but that always struck me as a little too much like work.

2. Try Meditation

There are innumerable ways to meditate; I was taught one of them half a dozen years ago. I have never managed to make it the regular twice-a-day part of my life its proponents advocate, but I've held onto the technique and haul it out now and then for special occasions.

The writing of *Eight Million Ways to Die* turned out to be such an occasion. The book was the most demanding writing experience I've ever had, and while I knew where the book's overall plot was going, knew generally what was going to happen and who dunnit, the specific events of each chapter had to be determined anew each day.

After my silent print-free breakfast, I would stretch out on the floor for 20 minutes and let my mantra run through my mind. I did not specifically try to think about the book. All I tried to do was concentrate on the meaningless two-syllable mantra. When other thoughts intruded, I let them float away. But, varying from the meditative technique as I was taught it, I did not purposely drive away any thoughts that related to the book I was working on. I let them occupy my mind for as long as they were inclined, then returned to the mantra until more thoughts about the book made themselves known to me. And so on, until my 20 minutes were up.

This always worked. The process was so helpful in furnishing me with ideas for the day's writing that I resolved to continue it when the book was done.

I'm afraid that that went the way of most New Year's resolutions. I hope, though, that I'll at least continue to use it when I'm working on a book.

3. Don't Unplug the Phone

I'm not talking about the real telephone. Unplug that if you will, especially if there's a plague of telephone solicitors in your area.

What I'm getting at, in my cunning metaphoric fashion, is the importance of being available to creative ideas, not only before I sit down at my desk or while I'm there, but also around the clock. We writers often defend our apparent indolence with the airy statement that we're actually working 24 hours a day. Often it seems to me, though, that my hours away from the typewriter are devoted more to turning off the book in my mind than to furthering its development.

Some years ago, during my drinking days, I used booze to turn myself off at the end of the working day. It worked all too well. Drunk, I didn't think about the book, either consciously or unconsciously. The continuity of the writing process was interrupted, much to the detriment of the work at hand. Since then, I've found that following my writing stint with physical exercise will give me the necessary release from my labor without short-circuiting the creative process.

But there are other ways I can get in my own way, and I realized this while writing my most recent book. I generally went downtown of an evening, and I generally took along something to read on the subway, reading being a pleasant alternative to the local sport of trying to guess which of my fellow passengers are muggers and rapists. One night I didn't have a book with me, and in the course of the 30-minute ride I found myself ruminating upon a plot problem and coming up with several possible solutions for it. I hadn't set out to think about the book, and if I'd disconnected the phone by distracting myself with someone else's fiction, I wouldn't have had those ideas.

Sometimes, of course, an idea will break through and cause me to set down what I'm reading, as in the Chinese restaurant. (Do you suppose it was the MSG that did it?) And sometimes distraction is necessary. There are writers who make it a rule not to read anyone's fiction when they are working on fiction of their own, and I can understand the underlying logic, but I'm not inclined to go that far myself.

4. Find an Activity That Unblocks Your Creativity

I have a feeling it's not coincidental that so many men seem to get their best ideas while they're shaving. I suspect that there's something about the act that allows the mind to roam in a peculiarly creative fashion. Shaving demands precision, but it doesn't take a whole lot of thought. Some day, some scientist will no doubt attach electrodes to a safety razor and determine that just the right sort of brainwaves for creative problem-solving are produced while one shaves.

Be that as it may, one can't rush to the sink and lather up whenever inspiration is needed. It's useful, I submit, to seek out another activity that allows the mind to wander freely without getting lost altogether.

For most people, long walks seem to be the best activity of this sort. Household chores sometimes facilitate the production of ideas. For me, they generally demand too much concentration and yield mental wheel-spinning rather than useful ideas. Running works for me, but not if I'm training seriously, building my mileage for a marathon or working on my speed for a race; then the running takes too much of my energy and there's not enough left over for creative rumination.

I can't effectively set out on a long walk, say, with the specific goal in mind of coming up with an idea for a book, or solving a plot problem. What I must do is not so much make it happen as let it happen. Some activities make it easier for me to let it happen, and it's worth experimenting to find out what activities work best for you.

Take a long look backward now and then and pay some attention to what you were doing when an idea just happened to come to mind. If your best ideas tend to come at certain times and under certain conditions, try to re-create those conditions. You can't shave ten times a day, or eat every meal in a Chinese restaurant, and you certainly can't do both at once, but—well, you get the idea.

5. Change the Scene

Travel is helpful in nudging the mind into new directions. Somerset Maugham sailed the South Seas in search of plots, but not all of us have to wander so far afield to get the same effect. The South Seas, the South of France, or South Philadelphia—any change of scene may turn the trick.

Maugham said that the kind of plots he was able to make use of were to be found in those Pacific islands, but I have a hunch it was less what he found there than the increasingly receptive person he became by going there that made his travels so rewarding. Not the least useful element of travel for me is the solitude of it. The lack of companionship is a form of sensory deprivation that forces the mind to turn inward. I always learn something about myself from such journeys. Directly or indirectly, my work ultimately gains from it.

You don't have to travel to change the scene. You can achieve much of the effect of travel by keeping yourself open to new experience. We get into ruts by always taking the same route over the same patch of ground; it's our own relentless footsteps that tread ruts into the earth.

Walk or drive a different way home. Stop at a different coffee shop. Read a different newspaper. Take the road less traveled by—and see if it makes a difference.

6. Seek Out People Who Stimulate Your Idea Production

Companionship can be at least as great a creative stimulant as solitude, if in another way. Over the years I've noticed that certain friends are uncommonly useful to me in this respect. They seem to be forever dropping anecdotes and bits of information I can use. Other people, just as interesting and enjoyable to be with, never trigger an idea. While I don't choose my friends on the basis of their value to my work, I certainly do treasure those who have a strong positive effect on my creativity.

And for Heaven's sake, keep your ears open. A few years ago I was in a restaurant waiting for a friend to show up. At the next table a man said: "The damnedest things happen to me. Just the other night I was in here having a few pops and on the way home it occurred to me that I'd like a bacon, lettuce and tomato sandwich. So I picked one up at the deli and went home, and I'm sitting on the edge of the bed eating it, and I eat half the sandwich and then I set the plate down on the floor and stretch out and go to sleep. So middle of the night, 4, 5 in the morning, I wake up and I gotta go to the bathroom, right? So I stand up, and there's this sharp pain, and there I am with little bits of bacon and tomato oozing out from between my toes, and this toothpick is sticking three quarters of an inch into my foot. Now I'm not sure about this, but I got a hunch that a guy who doesn't drink, this sort of thing never happens to him."

A guy who doesn't keep his ears open, he never hears this kind of stuff.

7. Know When to Stop

There's a point in the course of a day's writing when my mind's tired. If I push on, I'm not going to produce anything good. Any further hours I put in will be counterproductive.

The same thing goes for thinking about writing. There's a difference between creative mental rambling and the kind of obsessive-compulsive wrestling with a problem in which all its negative aspects echo in the mind like a repeating decimal. When that happens, I have to remind myself that it doesn't mean my problem is insoluble and my creativity is zero. It merely means that my mind is tired and I should turn it off and tune in again tomorrow. I just have to know when to stop.

Speaking of which, now's as good a time as any.

• 14 •

Applying the Breaks
August 1983

Every now and then I get a letter from someone who's read in a book or column of mine that I broke into the fiction dodge by writing soft-core sex novels. My correspondent allows as to how that sounds like something right up his or her street, and asks for some specific information on markets and their requirements. Just last week a chap stated that he'd produced just such a novel and couldn't seem to find anyplace to peddle it. Could I help him out?

Alas, I could not. My labors in that particular vineyard took place 20 odd years ago—and *odd* is the word for them, all right. The publishers I toiled for have gone on to other things, or to that Great Peep Show in the Sky. More to the point, that whole category of trashy novel has essentially disappeared. With the easing of censorship regulations, a sort of Gresham's Law operated under which hard-core pornography drove out and replaced the soft-core sex novels. Such hard-core stuff does continue to exist, and people presumably write it just as others appear to publish it, but I would not advise any new writer to try breaking in here.

I have two reasons for this, and prudery is neither of them. First of all, the hard-core garbage found nowadays in adult bookstores and other emporia of sleaze just won't teach anyone very much about writing. Twenty years ago, the sex novel field was a good place to earn while you learned. The requirements were extremely elastic. The books had to be erotic in nature, with a sex scene of one sort or another every 15 or 20 pages, but within that framework you could write almost any kind of novel with almost any kind of background and structure. The sex scenes themselves were not overly long, and one had to display some ingenuity in order to avoid various forbidden words and clinical descriptions.

Today's porn is something rather different. Story and characterization are minimal, and drawn-out explicit description of unlikely sexual activity takes up most of the wordage. You can't learn anything writing this stuff, and once you're over 12 or so, I don't guess you can learn much reading it, either.

A similar decline is observable in the publishers of this sort of material. Without skirting the libel laws, let me say simply that many of the rhinestones in the rough who publish and distribute and otherwise disseminate contemporary porn display bad table manners, drop their final *g*'s, and have close associates who will break your arms and legs on command. You do not want to hang out with these people. Trust me on this one.

They don't pay much, either. I know a pleasant young woman who worked for some months in a porn factory. She spent eight hours a day at a desk where she was expected to turn out 20 or 30 pages of copy, all according to formula, and all for a weekly stipend that, while it kept her in drugs and alcohol, hardly constituted fair market value for her services.

Enough. Porn's no place to break in. The writing's uncreative, the money's lousy, the finished product is something you can't show your mother, and you meet a better class of people on the subway. Rather than belabor the point, let's turn to a more important point.

To wit: Where *do* you break in?

Breaking and Entering

Before addressing that question directly, it seems worth pointing out that not every successful writer does break in, not in the sense of undergoing an apprenticeship writing for more accessible if inferior markets. Some writers know what they want to write and sit down and do what they can to write it. They may indeed serve an apprenticeship in that they write several novels or innumerable stories before producing one that is publishable, but they don't break in at a low level and work their way up.

In my own case, I knew I wanted to be a writer before I knew what I wanted to write. Exercise at the craft of writing was more important to me than exercise at self-expression. Thus it was natural for me to break in, first with stories for the crime pulps, then with sex novels, before eventually finding out what I wanted to write and figuring out how to write it. But whether to break in at the bottom or start at the top is very much an individual matter, and neither way is inherently preferable.

That said, let's ask again. Where does a would-be apprentice fictioneer break in?

Not, I don't think, in magazine fiction. The emergence of paperbacks and the rise of television dealt magazine fiction a one-two punch from which it seems unlikely ever to recover. The markets are too small, too lacking in depth and breadth, to be an ideal starting place for a writer. (They don't pay much, either, but that's a minor consideration in this context.)

Does this mean writing short fiction is a waste of time? No, not if that's what you seem to be geared to write. Nor do I think, having written a short story, that it's a waste of time and postage to submit it to the magazines most likely to be receptive to it. I do think, however, that it's a mistake deliberately to choose the magazine market as an entry point into the world of commercial fiction. It's probably easier to write a novel than a short story, and Lord knows it's easier to publish one.

What kind of novel? Go out and look at the paperback racks. Spend a whole lot of time looking at the paperback racks, and spend a little money while you're at it, because you must become familiar with more than the outsides of these books. Try to find a type of novel that is as ubiquitous as the dandelion and that you can read all the way through without having your stomach turn.

If you can't force yourself through a particular sort of book, you're not going to be able to write it, either. If you enjoy a certain kind of book but find yourself rather in awe of it, unable to fathom how the writer got his ideas or managed to make the plot fall together so brilliantly, you'll probably make a better fan than a writer in this category. (I was like this with science fiction; I liked the stuff well enough but never could figure out how to write it.)

If, finally, your reaction amounts to something along the lines of This-is-probably-junk-but-I-can't-seem-to-put-it-down, you may have found your neophyte's métier. When you're at once able to see through a type of book while still enjoying it, there's a better than average chance that you'll be able to produce something comparable to it, and have a good time while you're doing it.

There's a thin line between confidence and contempt. Not long ago I had a letter from a woman who'd read some romances, I guess it was, and was sure she could do better with one hand tied behind her back and three broken fingers on the other one. Now, maybe she can, and I know how often arrogance is a mask for timidity, but it struck me that her attitude was going to be a handicap to her. It's best, I think, if you have at least a grudging respect for the kind of book you're trying to emulate.

Breaking News

What kind of books are we talking about?

Romances, certainly, whether contemporary or historical. Gothics, surely, although that category seems to have been somewhat supplanted by the tidal wave of romances. Male-oriented adventure epics à la *The Executioner*. Occult novels of suspense. Westerns, most notably the "adult" westerns that are probably the closest thing around to the sex novels of the late '50s and early '60s, solid and reasonably realistic western novels with vivid sex scenes slung in every couple of chapters. Science fiction, of course.

In some of these lines, especially the adult westerns and male action-adventure, most books feature long-running series characters, Longarm or Slocum or Nick Carter or Mack Bolan or whoever. In some instances all the books are the work of the writer whose name or pseudonym appears on the cover. In others, the name's an umbrella beneath which any number of writers may be taking shelter from the storm. If you find a particular series which you enjoy reading and think you would enjoy writing, you can certainly take a shot at it.

Let's say you have this sort of positive response to a series of sexy westerns featuring Seth Saddlesore, purportedly written by one Ruff Diment, and coming out at the rate of one a month. Having read every Saddlesore book you've been able to get your hands on, you write to the editor at Diment's publishing house who edits that particular series. (It's best if you can write directly to that editor and address him by name. If you can't figure out how to obtain this sort of information, I'm not sure you have a sufficiently devious mind to write fiction successfully.)

Explain in your letter that you like the Saddlesore books and would like to try your hand at one. (Assume, in your letter, that the books are a collective effort. If so, you look knowledgeable by so assuming. If not, you'll be so informed.) Offer to supply chapters and an outline on spec. Don't tell the editor you can do a better job than the dummies who've been churning out the latest Saddlesores. The editor probably likes those books—that's why he published them—and you won't win his heart by knocking his wares.

A tip—the earliest books in a series are generally the work of the writer who originated the series, and are thus apt to have the firmest grip on the background and personality of the lead character. Play closest attention to those in developing your plot and characterization—unless all of the most recent books reflect a sharp turn in a particular direction, in which case you can assume someone made a conscious decision to reslant the series, and you may act accordingly.

Categories change frequently, and the latest scuttlebutt suggests that erotica of a sort may be in for a renaissance. There is no shortcut to the process of familiarizing yourself with what's on the newsstands and saturating yourself in it.

Do you have to start out this way? No, of course not. *Gone with the Wind* was a first novel. Every year first novels appear on the bestseller list. (Some of them, admittedly, are the work of writers who've quietly produced a couple dozen pseudonymous paperback novels, but others have never previously written anything longer than a note to the milkman.) There are no rules, no right ways and wrong ways. You may, if you wish, spend eternity writing short stories and submitting them to *The New Yorker*. You may even sustain yourself with the hope that someday they'll buy one.

As my burglar character, Bernie Rhodenbarr, would tell you, just how you break in is your business.

Plotting, Plodding
May 1983

Sometime last fall I taped a half-hour interview for National Public Radio. The interviewer, Walter James Miller, was of the rare sort who actually Reads The Book, in this instance my most recent Scudder novel, *Eight Million Ways to Die*. Mr. Miller asked me a number of incisive and provocative questions, and toward the end of our time together he did it again.

"How do you plot a mystery?" he wanted to know. "Do you start with a villain, or a murder method, or what? How do you work it all out?"

"I don't know," I said. "Sometimes I sort of outline and sometimes I sort of don't. I'm a largely intuitive writer, and I just sort of, uh, do it."

I don't know if the answer satisfied Mr. Miller; he moved courteously on to another area of inquiry. I do know that the answer failed to satisfy me, and I evidently brooded on it for the next several weeks, ultimately recounting the exchange over the telephone to my friend Donald Westlake.

"I don't get it," I said. "Here I've written 20 or 30 of the things, and a man asks me how I plot them, and I have to tell him I haven't a clue. How do *you* plot a mystery?"

Mr. Westlake, who plots them superbly, seemed to shrug over the phone. "Haven't the foggiest," he said.

"You too? The more time I spend in this business, and the more time I spend writing about it, the more I become aware of the extent of my ignorance. All I seem to do is get an idea and write until I get in trouble, and then lower my head and write my way out of the trouble. Can you imagine standing up in front of a class and telling them to do it that way?"

"No."

"Neither can I. I got a letter from a reader the other day asking about subplots. I didn't tell him this, but I'll tell you. I've been writing since the touchdown at Ararat and I don't know what a subplot is."

"Nobody does," said Mr. Westlake.

"Honestly?"

"Well, I have an idea," he admitted. "A subplot is what goes on in the story while your hero's taking a shower."

"Now that makes sense," I said. "When I'm taking a shower, what happens is somebody in America flushes a toilet and I get scalded. Would you call that a subplot?"

"I'd call it a crime against nature."

"Me too. You want to know another thing that drives me up the wall? I'll be talking with someone about my books and he'll say, very enviously, 'Well, I suppose you must have a formula.'"

"The writer as alchemist."

"Uh-huh. As if I've got this magic key that makes the process of writing a book a matter of following a recipe. What gets me is when I start thinking my books must follow a pattern so I ought to have a formula, and if I only had the sense to do so the whole process would be a cinch."

"Sure. Here's a formula for running a four-minute mile. Run each of your quarter-mile laps in less than a minute. Now that you know that, are you any closer to breaking the four-minute mark?"

"I'm actually further," I said, "because I'm so much older than I was at the beginning of this conversation."

The Fifth Horseman

All of this became dishearteningly relevant to me in the weeks that followed, when I began to have enormous difficulty with a book which will probably be called *The Burglar Who Painted Like Mondrian*. It is the fifth book in a series of mysteries featuring Bernie Rhodenbarr, a burglar whose life of crime keeps involving him in homicides, which he in turn has to solve. There is, unquestionably, a structural similarity from one book to the next, and you might well think that, having written four of the books, the business of writing the fifth would be about as much of an ordeal as painting by number.

Well, think again. Because I've had the devil's own time making this book work, and the rigors I've gone through may tell us all a little about the process of plotting.

I took my first shot at the fifth Burglar book in the fall of '81, when I wrote a little over a hundred pages of a book concerning the theft of some Early American silver. The book didn't seem to be working and I didn't feel like working on it, and after a couple of months I put it aside and wrote *Eight Million Ways to Die*, which just rolled out of the typewriter. (I never worked harder on anything, as it happens, but the plot never got to be a problem.)

Time passed, and Burglar #5 was overdue. Over the summer I had decided that my flat in Greenpoint needed a painting over the fireplace, and that what I really wanted was a Mondrian, but that what I could afford was something from an old calendar. So I bought a stretched canvas and some paints and brushes, consulted on technique with an artist friend, and painted my own geometrical abstract à la Mondrian.

OK. That gave me a sort of idea for a book. I also had an idea I liked from the aborted effort of the year before; to wit, Bernie and his good buddy Carolyn Kaiser smuggle a corpse in a wheelchair. I came up with another idea, that Bernie would encounter a woman in the course of a burglary and that this would lead to a romantic liaison. I played with all of these ideas, and then I sat down and tried to work up an outline.

No go. I had a whole mess of threads but I couldn't weave them into anything substantial. I figured, though, that I had enough plot components to sit down at the typewriter and see what would happen. I had an opening scene in the bookstore—Bernie runs a secondhand bookshop as a front—and I had the idea of his next paying a call on a man to appraise a library, doing so solely to gain access to an apartment building with a tight security system. Once in, he then burglarizes another apartment in the building.

And I had another idea, too. One of Carolyn's cats would be kidnapped—or catnapped, if you prefer—and the ransom demand would be that Bernie steal a painting. A Mondrian, natch.

I've started writing books with a lot less in hand, and they've worked out fine. So why shouldn't this one?

I got to work, and the pages began to pile up to the left of my typewriter, five, six, eight of them a day, five days a week. The writing went well. The scenes worked, the characters came to life, and other characters I hadn't dreamed of came out of the woodwork and evolved on the page. A book thief who steals only from public libraries, for instance. A newly divorced lawyer training for the New York Marathon. A woman poetry lover. A golden retriever. Other characters from the Bernie Rhodenbarr Repertory Company gave their usual stellar performances—Ray Kirschmann, the best cop money can buy; Denise Raphaelson, Bernie's artist friend; Carolyn; and Bernie himself.

I breathed easier when I passed page 125, which was where the book's first version had ground to a halt a year earlier. I kept on writing, and the words kept on flowing, and the pages mounted up, and all of a sudden I realized that something was wrong.

I had incidents. I had plot elements. I had characters in search of a story. But all manner of things were happening in my book and I didn't have the faintest idea what was going on. Why had a man named Onderdonk inveigled Bernie into appraising his library? What were hairs from a golden retriever doing in the cuffs of a corpse's pants? Who was the young woman Bernie ran into in the Kroll apartment, and how did she fit into what was going on? Who had stolen Carolyn's cat, and how, and why? What connected the Mondrian in Onderdonk's apartment, which someone else had stolen, with the one in the Hewlett Museum, which Bernie was supposed to steal in order to ransom the cat?

If I couldn't answer any of these questions, who could? And if nobody could, how could I keep on writing the book?

For a time I persisted, telling myself to Trust The Process, and feeling all the while like a Christian Scientist with appendicitis. Then, with 175 pages written and a maximum of 75 left in which to Wrap Things Up, I stopped writing and threw up my hands. And my lunch.

"I have to think things through," I told friends. "I'm going to have to start the book over on Page One, and I have to replot the book. The trouble is that the plot has no core to it; it's a whole lot of incidents whirling free in space. I have to find a core for the plot, and then I have to start over."

It sounded good, but how do you think things through? How do you transplant a core into a hollow apple? I didn't know. I knew what I usually did when books ground to a halt. I usually put them in a box and stuck them up on a closet shelf, and there they usually remained. Eventually, years later, I would throw out the box without opening it.

But I couldn't do this. For one thing, I had to deliver a book or resign myself to spending the spring and summer months living in the park and eating grass. For another, I was just not emotionally prepared to abandon Burglar #5 yet again. I had the feeling that, if I didn't find a way to finish the thing, I could forget the Burglar series altogether.

I spent about three weeks thinking, sometimes making notes to myself. I don't know if I accomplished anything during that period. When I'm not actually sitting at the typewriter producing finished copy, I can't honestly tell whether or not I'm working.

Then one night I was having coffee with my friend Laurence Anne Coe. She asked how the book was coming and I told her it wasn't.

"Why don't you talk about the plot with me?" she suggested. "Maybe one of us'll come up with something."

Now I never talk about work in progress. I make that a firm rule, and

I was just about to tell Laurie as much when something stopped me. Perhaps I realized that this particular book wasn't in progress, that it was in limbo, and that it couldn't hurt to talk about it. In any event, some inner voice told me to go ahead, that I had nothing to lose.

So I started talking about all the plot elements I had, and Laurie asked some questions and made some comments, and I said this and she said that, and within an hour's time I knew how to reconstruct the book. I didn't have the whole plot, not by any means, but I now had a central core for the thing which was the book's chief lack until then.

Ms. Coe deserves some credit. She's a producer, and the daughter of a legendary producer, the late Fred Coe, so it's not surprising that she could make a useful contribution to the plotting process. And I deserve some credit, too; I knew when to throw a firm rule out the window and accept help.

I spent another week or two Thinking About The Book, doing a little outlining but still unable to produce a detailed plot summary. Then I started again at the beginning, dropping some characters, changing others, writing some scenes fresh and using others much as I'd written them originally. The book, I am happy to report, is going very well. I'm almost afraid to say so because I've still got 30 or 40 or 50 pages to go and I can't be absolutely certain a wheel won't come off between here and the finish. Writing this kind of mystery is a little like conducting a high school orchestra in that you can't be sure everybody's going to finish at once. But you can say I'm guardedly optimistic.

How do I plot a mystery? I wish I knew.

Secondhand Pros
July 1983

When I was a kid in high school and college, serenely certain that I would one day be a professional writer of fiction, my elders tended to assume that I would reach this goal by first finding some other form of employment that involved some writing. I could start as a journalist, they thought, and write fiction in my free time until I was able to make the pastime self-supporting.

This didn't sound that great to me. I did write for, and ultimately edit, my college newspaper. And I did drop out of school and labor for the better part of a year at a literary agency. But I knew that I didn't want to do journalistic or editorial work for a living, nor did I want to teach. I wanted to write fiction. As luck would have it, I was able to do that right away. If I hadn't been so able, it was my intention to do other things that had nothing to do with writing, those menial jobs that would leave my mind free while supplying me with a well of background material to draw upon in later years. I could see the author's biographical sketch forming in my mind: "After his expulsion from Antioch College, Mr. Block has worked at various occupations, including that of itinerant fruit picker, gandy dancer, navel inspector, and tango instructor. He has wives and children in all of the contiguous 48 states, as well as Costa Rica and Prince Edward Island."

Well, I didn't do any of that, and it's just as well. I'd have made a lousy tango instructor. I know, though, that a great many fiction writers start out in other areas of writing. And I know from my reader mail that many of you out there in *WD*-land have had some success, freelance or otherwise, in nonfiction areas before turning to the liar's trade.

A letter from Nancy Pickard, of Shawnee Mission, Kansas, helped me appreciate the special advantages of you professional writers who have become amateurs at fiction, along with the special problems you face. But let Ms. Pickard describe her own background:

"Here's a brief bio: Journalism degree; two years editorial at local newspaper; three years writing training programs for a lot of money at a national corporation; seven years on my own as a fulltime freelancer, writing everything from audiovisual scripts to radio spots to direct mail, not making a lot of money but having a wonderful time. While I wasn't looking, however, something totally unexpected was creeping up behind me—a desire to write fiction and poetry, God help me. Geez, was I surprised when I realized I was *bored* doing commercial stuff, and that *all* I ever wanted to do for the rest of my life was write fiction and poetry. One day a couple of years ago I asked my husband how he would feel if I didn't earn any money for a long time; he gulped, smiled bravely, and said as enthusiastically as one can when one has lost one's voice, 'Go for it!' I've been going for it ever since, with two unpublished mystery novels, one delightful agent, two published mystery stories, half a dozen published poems, and a ream of rejections to show for it."

One thing that strikes me is Ms. Pickard's realization that writing fiction is a whole new ball game. She took it for granted that she might not earn money for a long time, in spite of the fact that her typewriter had supported her for a dozen years. In contrast, I get innumerable letters from men and women who've never written anything more ambitious than a laundry list who nevertheless expect to publish and get paid for it from the very beginning. I'm not sure why it is, but people who would laugh at the idea of hanging a first painting in the Louvre or singing a first song at Carnegie Hall are infuriated at the thought that their first novels might not be publishable. Ms. Pickard's attitude seems remarkably sane, and very realistic.

Here are some of her observations on the special situation of the pro-turned-amateur:

"It is a great advantage to have made a living at writing. For one thing, we already have a great deal of the self-discipline that fiction writing demands. For another, we have a professional attitude toward criticism that amateurs don't. Not their fault. It's just that we're used to presenting work to clients who may or may not love it, and if we're any good at all, we have that attitude that criticism might actually be helpful to us . . . we might even learn something!"

I agree, and I think there are other assets a writing pro brings to fiction. One is the confidence that one has a professional level of competence with the language. Another, for those who have worked as freelancers, is the ability to live on the edge of financial insecurity without going crazy.

"However," Ms. Pickard continues, "it's hard for us to go from some success and recognition to none. And none. When the form rejections pour in, there are weak moments when we want to yell back, 'You can't do this to me! I'm a real writer! I'm good, dammit!' It takes a period of readjustment for us to realize that we may have been good at selling funeral home services in 60-second TV spots, but we're no better than any other beginner when it comes to fiction."

The voice of Outraged Ego crying out "Don't they know who I am?" is a powerful one. On the other hand, the professional writer is used to rejection, knowing that it's an inescapable part of the process which leads eventually to acceptance. This knowledge may tend to slip away when one rejection follows another, but it's always there.

Fiction writing, Ms. Pickard adds, requires self-discipline of a special sort. "With no client to please and no deadline to meet, we have to become our own client and impose our own deadline. Not always easy for all of us."

Self-image is another problem. "We no longer know how to identify ourselves at cocktail parties," Ms. Pickard reports. "'Freelance writer' doesn't quite do it for us anymore, but 'writer' seems presumptuous and 'novelist' requires a qualifying adjective, like 'would-be' or 'unpublished.' It hurts our professional pride to see that knowing look in other people's eyes, the look that lumps us in with all those other 13 million beginning writers."

My goodness, are there really 13 million of you? No wonder I get so much mail. Personally, I think it's a mistake to tell people at a cocktail party that you're a writer, no matter what level of success you've achieved at it. The ensuing conversation is almost invariably one I'd be happier not having. For a while I told people I was an accountant, which led most people to talk about what *they* did, or how the Dodgers were doing. Then I hit someone who wanted me to prepare his tax return. Mumbling something vague about data processing or systems analysis might be best. Or skipping cocktail parties altogether.

"Most important," Ms. Pickard concludes, "we have to face the fact that we must learn whole new areas of the craft of writing. Having been a professional writer does not make any of us a professional *fiction* writer. We have a lot to learn, and that requires humility, study, humility, hard work and humility."

Indeed it does. Fiction writing starts off by requiring the towering arrogance that enables one to sit down at the typewriter in the belief that someone somewhere will actually be eager to read the productions of our own private imaginations. But that arrogance must be buffered by the humility that leads us to learn our craft and strive to make our work comprehensible and inviting and accessible to the reader. Prior success in an allied area of writing bolsters the arrogance—we have, after all, been paid for our words in the past. The extraordinary difficulties of turning to fiction will, in the course of time, bolster our humility.

And the difficulties are there, and they are extraordinary. I don't know that it is more difficult to write fiction than nonfiction. It's certainly easier for *me* to write fiction, as I prove to myself whenever I commit myself to a nonfiction project. Writing about writing is something else again; it's off the top of my head, it comes out of my own experience, and it feels more than anything else like writing a monthly letter to 13 million friends. But on the occasions when I've done an interview or a piece involving some research, I've felt very much like a beginner. I've come to the conclusion that I'm not very good at nonfiction, that I'd make a lousy journalist, and that it's a good thing I don't have to do it for a living.

Sometimes I think there are constitutional differences between fiction and nonfiction writers. My friend Bill Reel writes a twice-a-week column for the New York *Daily News*, a task I find awe-inspiring. He is similarly awed by the idea of writing fiction. He told me one time that, were he compelled to write a fictional scene set in a restaurant, he'd have to go out, find a restaurant, make a page of notes, and fit that very restaurant into the scene. I, on the other hand, would invent a restaurant to fit the scene's requirement; it might be based on a real restaurant, it might be a composite of several, or it might be a complete fabrication.

This said, I think the fact remains that it's harder to make a living writing fiction. The market is smaller and there are more people trying to write for it. There are people who make a fortune writing fiction, and there are even people who make a modest living, but there are not a great many people who do either. It is a small field, and it has lately been getting smaller as publishers cut back on their lists, squeezing the midlist book out of existence, and as magazines eliminate fiction altogether.

And I'll tell you something. None of that matters. For those of us who were born to write fiction, anything else is a compromise. That's no guarantee that we have the requisite talent, nor is prowess in an allied field, but unless we try, unless we give it all we have, we'll never know if we could do it.

Good luck to all of us.

While this column was being set in type, Nancy Pickard made her first book sale—a mystery to Avon. She writes: "Two years isn't really a very long time to wait for the Break, but still I feel like living proof of the Persistence-Means-Almost-More-Than-Talent School of Writing. Mostly what I feel, however, is wonderful."

Amen, I say. And congratulations.

• 17 •

So Don't Do That!
November 1983

The other day I got a phone call from Mary Ann Allison, who, with her husband Eric, writes under the name of E.M.A. Allison. (E.M.A. stands for Eric & Mary Ann, see? I'm not sure of the wisdom of that kind of joint pen name, but no one asked me, least of all the Allisons, and why should they? Anyway, this column isn't about pen names, joint or otherwise. It's about portions and outlines and complete manuscripts. It's also, as I type these lines, about a week overdue in Cincinnati, so let me by all means Get On With It.)

The Allisons published their first novel in early '83, and a fine first book it was, a murder mystery set in a 14th-century English monastery with a monk as detective. *Through the Valley of Death* is its title, Doubleday is its publisher, and it's an impressive debut. One looks forward to future appearances of Brother Barnabas, and to further fiction from his creators. (That's plural, and with a small *c*. Brother Barnabas's Creator turns out truth, not fiction, and while it may be stranger . . . but I digress.)

Ahem. The E.M.A. Allison team, Mary Ann told me, was having a rough siege of second-novel trouble, not to mention third-, fourth-, fifth-, sixth-, seventh- and eighth-novel trouble. More precisely, they had produced proposals for seven novels since *Through the Valley of Death*, and each had been duly circulated by their agent, and none had sold.

This in itself did not strike me as cause for abject despair. Indeed, I was more struck by the number of proposals Eric and Mary Ann had managed to turn out in a short period of time than by the fact that they'd all been thus far rejected. A great many manuscripts get rejected a great many times before they sell.

But it was the nature of the rejections more than the quantity that bothered the Allisons. Their plots were uniformly criticized as dull, unconvincing and commonplace. "I think we're doing something wrong," Mary Ann told me. "I think we're having trouble plotting, and we wondered if you knew where we could go for help. Is there some sort of workshop you could recommend that focuses on plotting?"

I certainly couldn't think of one, nor could I imagine how the Allisons could profit from a class or workshop. They didn't have trouble generating ideas or getting work done, and their first novel was a well-plotted and professional piece of writing.

"These proposals," I said. "What form have they taken?"

"Three or four chapters and an outline."

"Ah," I said. "Stop writing portions and outlines. Write whole books."

Do you remember the Dr. Kronkheit vaudeville routine? (I think Smith and Dale were the ones who used it for years, and I think Neil Simon borrowed it for *The Sunshine Boys*, and if I'm wrong on either of those points I'm confident 11 readers will write in to set me straight.)

> *Patient (holding his arms up over his head): Doctor, it hurts when I do this.*
> *Dr. Kronkheit: Don't do that!*

Exactly. Doctor, when I write portions and outlines they tell me my plots are no good. So don't do that! Don't write portions and outlines! Write whole books!

Over the years, I've sold books almost every way there is, with the sole exception of door-to-door. I've written complete manuscripts, I've submitted portions with detailed outlines, I've peddled portions with sketchy outlines, I've sent in outlines, detailed or otherwise, without portions to accompany them, and I've occasionally secured a contract on the basis of an idea presented at lunch or over the phone. Each of these methods has its advantages. Each has its drawbacks.

The advantage of offering any sort of partial manuscript, whether it's 80 pages and a ten-page outline or three brisk sentences murmured over the chocolate mousse, is obvious. When it works, you've secured a commitment from the publisher in advance. You'll get some money to live on while you're writing the rest of the thing. (It won't be enough to live on, but I'll tell you something, it never is. And the balance of the advance, yours when you turn in the completed manuscript, won't be enough to live on, either. Let me ask you something. Have you thought at all about computer programming? I mean really *thought* about it?)

That's one advantage of outlines, though. You've got a publisher's commitment. Your book still may be rejected after it's completed—these things happen—but you've got a contract, you've got a little money, and you've got the confidence a contract can give you. In addition, you've got the publisher's input, which can affect the final manuscript for better or for worse.

What, then, are the disadvantages?

There are a few. One is that you can't really show what you can do in an outline. Any number of novels which work magnificently might be quite unconvincing in outline form. I just read *The Clan of the Cave Bear*, Jean M. Auel's astonishing bestseller about life among the Neanderthals, and I don't know that I'd have been eager to sign up that book if I'd read it first in outline form. It works superbly, but it took enormous skill in writing and characterization to make it work, and how can you tell from an outline if an author will have those skills or be able to bring them to bear?

Back in the '60s, I wrote seven books about an adventurer named Evan Tanner. After the first one or two, I sold the books on the basis of a two-page outline, which frequently finessed plot problems with lines like, "In his usual adroit fashion, Tanner finds a way to get from North to South Vietnam," or, "Tanner wraps things up in his usual fashion, but I won't spoil the reader's fun by giving away the ending." I got away with this sort of thing because Knox Burger, then editor at Fawcett, knew the book I ultimately delivered would cut the mustard. I'd done enough books about the character to inspire confidence that I could do the same thing again.

(*Time Marches On Dept.*: Knox is now my agent, not my editor, and the Tanner books will shortly return to print, now published by Jove. I hope you're as happy as I am about this, but I don't see how you could be.)

Plots Have to Grow

Another disadvantage of showing an outline to an editor is that it may not represent as good a plot as your final book will contain. A plot is an organic entity, and it has to have a chance to grow. Even in the case of books which I've outlined rather extensively in advance, my final plot always contains elements that did not show up in my outline, and that were not in my mind when I constructed that outline. In my novels, one thing leads to another. The process of bringing a minor character to life suggests plot developments I could not have thought of before that character existed in the fictional flesh.

In *Writing the Novel: From Plot to Print*, I wrote at some length on the subject of outlining, and one point I stressed is that there ought never to be a question of who's master, the writer or the outline. An outline is no more than a tool, to be amended or scrapped altogether when it ceases to be useful.

But a proposal submitted to a publisher can hardly contain a footnote to that effect. *Editor, take note: The final product will be more convincing and imaginative than this treatment indicates, with a lot of clever developments I haven't yet thought of.* I sometimes think every outline should include this bit of advice, as it's almost always the case, but unless an editor knows your work and knows it well, why should he take your word for it?

Do editors prefer portions and outlines? Or would they rather see the complete manuscript?

I haven't rushed out to take a survey, so I don't know how editors break down. (Oh, sure you do, Larry. Most of them break down from overwork, booze, personal problems, or a combination of all three. Next question.)

Ahem. I know that editors are generally willing to look at partial manuscripts, but what does this amount to? Often they mean little more than that they'll respond to such proposals with either an outright rejection or conditional approval; i.e., if you want to go ahead and finish the manuscript on spec, they'll be glad to look at it again. Now that's encouraging, and new writers need encouragement whatever form it takes, but what does it really amount to? It costs the editor nothing and commits him to nothing, and all he's promised to do is look at the complete manuscript, and he'd do that anyway if you submitted it that way in the first place.

Meanwhile, he may turn down in outline a novel he might have approved had you shown him the whole thing at once. Because editors, by and large, are considerate chaps, and they'd rather not encourage you to write something they fear they'll ultimately reject, so why not reject it in outline form? Why not get it over with?

The editors I know would rather see a complete manuscript. The agents I know would rather show a complete manuscript. You can make a better deal when you've got the whole property in hand. An editor may not *read* everything you send him—he's sane enough to stop reading when he knows he's not interested—but there's an advantage in giving him the choice.

Does this mean it's a mistake to submit portions? No, not necessarily. The outline can be an art form in its own right, and some writers are more convincing in their proposals than in their finished work. (That may lead to problems of another sort further down the line, but meanwhile it gets them a lot of contracts.) If your outlines are effective, if editors respond strongly and positively to them, there are certain distinct advantages in doing business that way. But if they inspire the reactions Eric and Mary Ann have been drawing, the implication is clear, and writing the whole book works to everyone's advantage—both the buyer and the seller know exactly what they're dealing with.

There is, too, an additional problem with selling outlines or partials or even more nebulous proposals. It's a problem of incentive.

I can still recall the first time I sold a book on the basis of an idea. I went to my agent's office, signed my name with a flourish, and walked out on the horns of a dilemma.

I had just earned $750 by writing two words, *Lawrence* and *Block*. Three hundred and seventy-five dollars a word struck me as more than reasonable, and I was pleased with myself. But now I was faced with the prospect of writing an additional 60,000 words for an additional $750, and it didn't seem like an economically sensible thing to do. I did it, but I wasn't happy about it.

• 18 •

Reflection Slips
December 1983

A pair of writers in Kenosha, Wisconsin, are unhappy with the response they've been getting from publishers. They've submitted a query letter and outline to 30 publishers and have garnered replies along the lines of, "Interesting, but not suitable for our list," and "Not right for us at the present time."

"If we're submitting to publishers who state in *Writer's Market* that they need this type of material," they ask, "how can they say 'Not right for our present needs'? If they think the outline is 'interesting,' why do they reject it without asking to see the manuscript?"

This letter reached me just a day or two after I mailed in last month's column, and it gave me an opportunity to pass on the advice I'd just developed in that column—i.e., if you're not getting encouraging results with a proposal, try submitting the complete manuscript. If your query letters are not getting any action, let your manuscript speak for itself. (If it in turn gets rejected 20 or 30 times without drawing any strong positive response, you might want to entertain the possibility that there's something wrong with it.)

This said, the letter from Kenosha raises an interesting question. What is one to make of the language of a publisher's rejection? What does "Not right for us at present" mean? Why don't publishers say what they mean, anyway?

I would submit that publishers say exactly what they mean once you know how to translate their remarks. When a publisher says your manuscript is not suitable at the present, that it's not quite right for his list, that it doesn't suit his current needs, it means one thing and one thing only.

It means he doesn't want to publish it.

And that, when you come right down to it, is all he has to say and all you have to know. That he does not express himself more candidly testifies to his consideration for your feelings. Surely editors must yearn to put the matter more forcefully now and then. "This is garbage!" "I wouldn't line my parakeet's cage with these pages!" "Giving you a typewriter is like letting a child play with a hand grenade!"

Editors rarely behave so brutally, although it happens now and then. There have, over the years, been some legendary rejections. A literary agent of my acquaintance once instructed a hopeful novelist as follows: "I suggest you take the following steps with regard to your manuscript. 1) Go out in the back yard and dig a hole several feet deep. 2) Place your manuscript at the bottom of the hole. 3) Fill in the hole and firm the soil in place. 4) Do not plant anything intended for human consumption in that portion of the garden for at least seven years."

Another publisher returned a book-length manuscript with this notation: "I regret that I must return the enclosed shipment of paper as unsatisfactory. Someone has spoiled it by typing gibberish on every single sheet."

This sort of thing is nasty, and it hardly ever happens. When it does, there are sometimes extenuating circumstances. In the case of the literary agent, for example, the manuscript in question was a piece of racist invective, nauseating in the extreme; the agent's first impulse was to seek out the author and strangle him.

Still, publishers are human (no matter what you may have heard) and everyone has a bad day now and then. Just recently a seasoned professional writer received a proposal back with his own business card attached, the card amended by the addition of a word after his name. The word, some seven letters long, was a part of the human anatomy which, its physiological importance notwithstanding, is rarely uttered as a term of approbation and esteem.

The writer didn't take kindly to being called a forearm. (What word were you thinking of? Why, shame on you!) After an exchange of heated letters and an abject apology from someone at the publishing house, he decided to regard the word in question as the signature of the person who returned his manuscript.

Another reason why publishers are generally gentle in their rejections is that they recognize that their own judgment is not infallible. The best-seller list down through the years has carried innumerable examples of books which were rejected time and time again before some publisher took them on and made them successful. No one wants to go down in history as the man who said no to *Gone with the Wind*, but everyone in the trade realizes that these things happen. How much safer to say that *GWTW* "does not fit the requirements of our list at the present moment" than to go out on a limb and suggest that Ms. Mitchell ought to pound her typewriter into a plowshare and use her manuscript to mulch her dahlias.

When I was first trying to write and get published, the poems and short stories I mailed out came back like boomerangs, each with a printed rejection slip clipped to it. These slips did not utterly destroy me; I don't think I really expected to sell anything at that point, and the slips constituted some tangible evidence that I was at least taking a shot at it.

And I can still recall my delight when I got my first rejection slip with a personal note appended. I can even remember what it said: "Please enclose return postage with any future submissions."

How much I did yearn for the occasional *Sorry* or *Nice—try us again*. I probably read more encouragement into those words and phrases than was warranted, but that was their purpose. They were meant to be encouraging. The editor was saying, in effect, that there was something in my submission that appealed to him. He didn't like it enough to buy it, but he responded to something, and his response moved him to take pen in hand. He wanted to encourage me to keep on writing, and to keep on submitting what I wrote to his magazine.

When we get notes like this, it's only human to want to know just what the editor meant. What was it he liked about my script? What didn't he like? What was he trying to encourage? There's no point guessing, or trying to find out. Maybe your manuscript just crossed his desk on a good day. A day earlier or later and he might have called you a forearm (or worse) instead of encouraging you.

It's interesting, I think, that personal rejections are most often given to those who least require the attendant encouragement. Publishers wouldn't dream of dismissing the work of an established pro, or a manuscript from a reputable agent, with a printed form. Such material may be rejected every bit as swiftly, but the process always involves a note designed to take the sting out of the rejection and provide a reason for the decision.

But the more of a career you've built in the field, the less likely you are to give a damn why Joe Forearm at Permanent Press doesn't want to publish your work. Editorial reactions may be useful in volume; if half a dozen editors pass on a novel of mine, and five out of six of them cite an alleged weakness in the storyline or a lack of sympathy for the lead character, I may want to reevaluate the manuscript in that light before showing it further. More often than not, however, six different editors will find six different reasons to reject a manuscript, and they'll all add up to the message of the form rejection slip—it doesn't fit our present needs, it's not suited to our list at the moment, we like it but not enough to publish it.

Rejection is a blow, and it's kind of editors to soften it insofar as they can. And encouragement is, well, encouraging. But the only real encouragement is a letter with a check enclosed, and those encouraging rejections can become more discouraging than form slips.

In my early years, for example, I kept getting a response that ran something like this: "This author writes well, and while the present manuscript is not quite right for us, we'd very much appreciate a look at his next book." Now there was a reason I was garnering this kind of rejection. I had a natural facility with prose and dialogue, but less skill at putting a book together. Publishers liked the way I wrote but not what I wrote. Hence their desire to see my next book. "What about *this* book?" I wanted to scream. "I just spent months writing *this* book and you're asking to see the *next* one."

But what kind of rejection would have pleased me? None, because any rejection is a rejection, and who wants it? Years and years ago a friend submitted a humorous piece to *Playboy* through an agent, and *Playboy*'s rejection stated, unequivocally enough, "This isn't funny."

My friend was elated. "That's the only way to reject humor," he declared. "No point being mealy-mouthed about it. The only reason to send a humor piece back is because you think it's not funny, so why not say so? Of course they happen to be wrong. It's *very* funny."

Right or wrong, *Playboy*'s opinion proved to be well-nigh universal. But the memory lingers because my friend was the only writer I know of who was ever delighted by a rejection.

How can you best respond to rejection? The ideal way, of course, is to shrug it off and resubmit the manuscript somewhere else as soon as possible. If the rejections you're getting are running to type, perhaps you can learn something from them which will help you revise the present work or avoid similar problems in the future. But when the reasons for rejection are many and varied, and when they amount to no more than another way of saying "Not quite right for us," I wouldn't try too hard to find meaning in them. Recall instead Aesop's story about the father and son and their donkey. When the son rode and the father walked, bystanders criticized the boy for his selfishness. When the father rode, he was criticized. When they both rode, they were denounced as inhumane to the beast. I forget how the story ended, but I think they wound up carrying the donkey.

You risk carrying the donkey yourself when you make too much of the language of a rejection letter. And you can always elect to revise the rejection instead. "We would have gladly purchased your poems but felt they were way over the heads of our cloddish readers," I typed neatly at the bottom of a form rejection I received, duly posting it upon my bulletin board. My friends were certainly impressed.

For that matter, you can always reject the rejection. Some years ago I sent off a portion and outline to a publisher with whom I'd worked in the past. I received no reply for months on end, and quite forgot the whole thing until I received an incoherent note from some new assistant he'd hired, explaining how I could revise the whole thing in a bizarre fashion. I was not inclined to do what he'd suggested, nor, given further developments in my career, did I much want to work for that house anyway.

I was at that time working for a national magazine, so I rolled a sheet of their letterhead into my typewriter. "Thanks very much for your interesting letter," I wrote, "but I must regretfully inform you that it does not meet the current needs of the *Whitman Numismatic Journal*. I hope you'll have better luck with it elsewhere, and want to thank you for thinking of the *Journal*." And I mailed his letter back to him.

I never heard further from him. Do you suppose I should have suggested he try us again?

Call Him Ishmael
January 1984

What do you call your characters? I'm not asking what names you devise for them, or how you come up with these names. I've discussed that question at least twice, and one of those discussions appears in *Telling Lies for Fun and Profit*, should that subject be of more immediate interest to you than the present one. The question for today is not what you will name your characters but how you will refer to them.

Privately, of course, you may refer to them as you choose, and you may indeed choose to be shockingly disrespectful. Agatha Christie, I am told, referred to her faithful series detective Hercule Poirot as "that insufferable Belgian twit." And yet the woman wrote about him all her life. Ah, well. We all know married couples like that, don't we? They abuse each other endlessly, in public and in private, and yet they do stay married.

Ahem. A couple of days ago I was on the phone with my friend, Philip Friedman, author of *Rage* and *Termination Order* and other commendable books. "I want to call a writers' conference," he declared. "Here's what I want to confer about. I'm writing this book and I keep having trouble deciding whether to be on a first-name basis with my characters. It seems like the sort of thing there ought to be a hard and fast rule about, but as far as I know there isn't."

"If there is," I said, "I don't know it either."

"I didn't think there was. Of course," he reflected, a note of envy creeping into his voice, "you never have this problem, do you? You write all your books in the first person, so you can just let Bernie Rhodenbarr or

Matt Scudder refer to the other characters anyway they want. I suppose that's one way to pass the buck, isn't it?"

Now I certainly don't write *all* my books in the first person, though I'll have to admit it's been a few years since I wrote a third-person novel. Still, I have a feeling I'll be at work on a big third-person multiple-viewpoint novel before too long, and when that happens I'll have to confront the question Philip raised. How will I refer to my characters? Shall I call a chap, say, "Philip" or "Phil" or "Friedman" or "Mr. Friedman"?

This can be an occasional problem in real life. When I was at college, there were professors I addressed by their first names and others I addressed by their surnames. And there was a third category toward whom I hadn't quite made up my mind, and I dealt with the dilemma by remaining poised upon its horns—i.e., I called them nothing at all, taking care to tuck neither first nor last name into such sentences as I spoke to them. Eventually the college asked me to leave, although I doubt my behavior in this area was the chief reason for their request.

Back to Fiction

But let's get back to the world of fiction. After all, it's supposed to be more readily comprehensible than real life. That's why we're so much more comfortable in it.

Some observations:

1. Female characters are most commonly referred to by their first names, unless they are Older Women, in which case they are generally called "Miss Sigafoos" or "Mrs. Sigafoos" or, most recently, "Ms. Sigafoos." The use of any of these titles, especially in the case of a younger woman, is a distancing device; it puts the character at a remove from the reader and impedes rather than assisting reader identification.

Female characters of any age are virtually never referred to by unaccompanied surnames. You could refer to a man as Sigafoos, but you'd have to call his female equivalent Linda Sigafoos, or Miss/Mrs./Ms. Sigafoos, or just plain Linda. Calling her just plain Sigafoos will leave the reader assuming she's undergone a sex-change operation while his attention was elsewhere.

(This is emphatically not true in dialogue or interior monologue, which *has* no rules. You can have one character call another anything you please. Whether he's a first-person narrator or a mere spear carrier, he can refer to Linda as "Sigafoos" all he wants.)

Now you may grouse that all of this is impossibly sexist, and I won't presume to argue with you, but so what? I'm afraid there's no help for it, and both male and female writers have to live with it. You may further decry this distinction as hopelessly and pointlessly inconsistent, and I'll agree with you. I won't even quote Emerson's dictum about a foolish consistency's being the hobgoblin of small minds. I'll just suggest that there's little you can do about it.

The point of fiction, after all, is to create an experience for the reader, not to advance the sexual revolution by throwing up verbal barricades. I am perfectly willing to believe the time will come when women as well as men will be called by their last names in stories and novels, but when that happens it will show that a change in societal attitudes has already taken place; it will not lead the way.

2. The sympathetic lead character is most likely to be called by his first name, and other male characters are likely to be so called to the extent that the writer wants us to sympathize and identify with them.

Does this seem curious? (For that matter, does it even seem comprehensible? As I reread the sentence, it seems to have the clarity of an abstract in freshman sociology. My apologies.)

Again we butt up against the jagged wall of inconsistency. Shouldn't all the male characters in a given work be called either by their first names or their surnames? Why discriminate in this fashion?

Well, you don't have to. You can certainly call your lead by his last name; perhaps you feel you'd diminish his dignity if you did otherwise. And you may call unsympathetic characters by their first names. You may, in short, do pretty much as you please. I just the other day read a novel by

David Wiltse, *The Wedding Guest*, and Mr. Wiltse (David? Dave? Wiltse? Never mind.) called his lead Peter, which was to be expected. But he also called one of the bad guys Sam, and called various good and bad guys by first or last names, and if there was any consistent pattern to his choice it eluded me.

3. Children are generally referred to by their first names. You might do otherwise in order to create an arch effect, calling some moppet "young Master Grimes" or "the Chalmers girl" or whatever. But, unless you want to call attention to the auctorial voice, you'll stay with the child's first name.

4. Consistency, hobgoblin or no, is very much to be sought with respect to each individual character. In other words, if you refer to your lead character as James in Chapters One and Two, don't start calling him Cavendish in Chapter Three and Jimmy in Chapter Five. You would likely have called him James Cavendish upon first introducing him to us, but then you'd make a choice of first or last name, and would be well advised to stick to that choice thereafter.

This is irrespective of the fact the other *characters* in the book may refer to him in any number of different ways, as long as it's not confusing and makes dramatic sense. We're talking now about the need for consistency in the voice not of the characters but of the author.

Not every author, let it be said, has been consistent in this regard. The first Ellery Queen novels (third-person novels featuring a fictional detective named Ellery Queen, and published under the byline Ellery Queen) referred to the hero-detective alternately as "Ellery" and as "Mr. Queen." The books were a collaborative venture, the work of cousins Frederic Dannay and Manfred B. Lee, and the lead tended to be either Ellery or Mr. Queen depending who had drafted a particular chapter. An editor might have straightened out this sort of thing; in this instance, an editor did not.

5. Certain characters ought to be called in a certain way simply in the interest of clarity. If you have several characters sharing a last name, for

example, you can't go calling them all Crowinshield. You might call your lead *Crowinshield* and his father *Mr. Crowinshield* or *the elder Crowinshield*. Or you might call all the younger ones by first names and their elders by first *and* last names. You may have to experiment to find out what approach makes for a clear narrative.

6. The sort of fiction you're writing may dictate how you are to refer to your characters. This is more apt to be the case the more specifically the genre's requirements have been defined. If you're writing a romance and hoping to peddle it to a publisher who operates within very firm guidelines, you must fit the form. The guidelines may not stipulate this sort of thing, but your own market analysis will show you what is and isn't done.

You'd think it wouldn't be important, that an editor could always doctor your manuscript to conform to editorial norms. But the editor might not notice that you'd called a hero inappropriately by his last name or a father figure by his first name. He or she might merely note that your book didn't have the right tone to it, and would send it back without troubling to figure out what was wrong.

7. Genre requirements notwithstanding, the most important consideration is your own comfort. When all is said and done, doing what comes naturally is the best policy. I suspect that most writers who get on a first-name basis with their heroes do so not out of a calculated desire to enlist the reader's sympathies but because they *feel* on a first-name basis with the character.

If you know your characters well enough to write about them, you'll probably know what you want to call them. Referring to them in a particular fashion will either feel right or it won't.

And it's essential, ultimately, to do it your way. Once again I find myself drifting inexorably into what Arnold calls "the to-thine-own-self-be-true bit." (Arnold, as some of you may recall, is one of several fictional students who makes an occasional appearance in this column. I don't happen to know his last name.)

Well, I can't help it. Polonius was right. If a piece of fiction is true to its author, it canst not then be false to any man. (Or woman.) The rules, such as they are, are well worth knowing, but in the end no rules are carved in tablets of stone. I suspect Mr. Wiltse called one of his villains Sam because he jolly well thought of him as Sam. That being the case, I suspect he made the right choice.

For your part, Dear Reader, I'd suggest you pay attention to the choices other writers make, and decide what does or doesn't seem to serve their purpose. And then perhaps you'll be a whit better prepared for the great task of being true to thine own self.

• 20 •

Eye Strain

March 1984

A few days ago I listened while my friend Donald E. Westlake traced the development of the American private eye novel at some length and in considerable detail. He concluded unequivocally that the private eye is dead, that a literary form born early in the century has outlived its context, that the fellow with the trenchcoat and the pint of rye is stuck in the '30s and '40s like a fly in amber.

What made this contention remarkable was *its* context—Don chose to present his thesis at Bouchercon. Named for the late Anthony Boucher, mystery fiction's most esteemed critic and a highly regarded writer thereof as well, Bouchercon is an annual enclave of fiercely devoted writers and readers of mystery and suspense. Don thus delivered his talk in the midst of men and women who read and write the very sort of books he seemed to be writing off, and his remarks, you may be sure, were remarked upon.

A couple of hours later I was twice honored; the Private Eye Writers of America presented their Shamus Award to my novel *Eight Million Ways to Die*, and I was installed for a term as the organization's president. In the wake of Don's speech, I felt as though I'd been entrusted with the helm of the *Titanic*.

And since then I've mused a mite. Has the American private eye indeed followed the Great Auk and the Woolly Mammoth into extinction? Is the tough guy in the slouch hat no more than a dead rat in the wall of crime fiction? Mother of Mercy, is this the end of Sam Spade?

More to the point, insofar as all of us as writers are concerned, does any form or class or subgenre of fiction become truly moribund? How can one see this coming, and what can one do about it?

Let me make a distinction first between artistic and commercial lifelessness. Don was not contending that a reading public for private eye stories does not exist, but that an artistically successful book can no longer be written in this mode, its commercial possibilities aside.

Commercial torpor is something rather different. Every sort of fiction, whether category escape reading or mainstream fiction, is subject to trends in the marketplace. Whole categories—mystery, science fiction, gothic, horror—will be hot one day and cold the next. One year almost anyone who can turn out a spy story can find an eager publisher; a year later only a few established leaders in the field can find a warm welcome.

There is a manner in which this sort of thing comes about. (About in which this sort of thing comes? Never mind.) Two or three writers produce novels with a similar theme or of a similar type. The books, because of their own intrinsic merit and because of fortuitous timing, strike a major chord with the reading public. Readers have such a good time with them that they want more. Publishers rush to fill this demand. And writers, inspired by what they've read—and by its success—suddenly come up with ideas in a similar vein.

As the wave nears its crest, more writers—including many with no particular interest in or aptitude for this type of fiction—rush to get in on the act. And some of the writers who once had real enthusiasm for the genre lose it in their third or fifth or twentieth attempt. Readers are turned off—because their appetite has been sated, and because the bulk of new work available is weary and uninspired.

This happens almost inevitably with any category that becomes the rage. That it has not yet happened with romance fiction is curious, but it is still too early to conclude that the romance category will remain immune. Even in such broad areas as mystery and science fiction, this ebb and flow has long operated. While a loyal base of fans in each category has never failed to exist, there have nevertheless been years when publishers sought mystery and SF titles and other years when it was exceedingly difficult to get such books published.

Hardboiled and Overcooked

Don's argument has little to do with the marketplace and its trends. He argues that it is no longer possible to write a *good* novel about a hardboiled private detective, whether or not a receptive audience exists. The detective himself has become more caricature than character. While Dashiell Hammett created private eyes out of his own experience with the Pinkertons, and while Joe Gores decades later developed his Daniel Kearney Associates stories out of his work as a private investigator, contemporary private eye chroniclers draw inspiration not from their own lives but from what others have long since written. While a 1980s private eye may get his clothes from Charivari and his attitudes toward women from *Ms.* magazine, his basic self and his role in life are holdovers from a half century ago.

I wonder. If I wanted to support this thesis, I could cite the several parodies and pastiches written of late. I could also point to the propensity of several writers to make period pieces of their private eye novels, setting them in that black-and-white era when trench-coated knighthood was in flower. Stuart Kaminsky and Andrew Bergman with their '40's Hollywood sets, Harold Adams with his Depression-era South Dakota town, and Max Allen Collins, whose forthcoming *True Detective* is planted firmly and faithfully in early-'30s Chicago, might well reinforce the idea that private eye fiction is more at home in an earlier era. Bill Pronzini's Nameless detective, while undeniably contemporary, is a devoted collector of pulp detective magazines, his avocation constituting a not-too-obscure emotional tie to an earlier time.

Thinking about all of this, I find myself looking for parallels in other areas of fiction. The novel of espionage comes quickly to mind. Eric Ambler very nearly held a patent on the form 40 years or so ago. His tense dramas of innocent but resourceful amateurs trapped in some bizarre

Balkan intrigue were very much the creature of their times. After the Second World War, Ambler's context was gone. The colorful Balkan patchwork quilt had faded in to the monochrome Iron Curtain, and espionage was very much a game for cold-blooded professionals.

And was the spy novel dead for all that? Hardly. It still afforded plenty of room for the fanciful derring-do of Ian Fleming, the moral conundrums of Graham Greene, the convoluted plots of Robert Ludlum, the deadpan brilliance of Len Deighton, the thoughtful despair of John LeCarré, and—but that's enough to cover the point at hand, isn't it? Innumerable writers found inspiration in the basic notion of espionage as a literary context. As the international situation changed, and as our own perceptions of nationalism and patriotism and individual moral responsibility have gone through their various metamorphoses, so too have the books changed. I cannot imagine myself reading a James Bond novel written today (although some are being written, and avidly read). I myself am not much interested right now in reading *any* spy novel, much less in writing one.

But this could change. Someone could write a piece of espionage fiction tomorrow that I might find irresistible. And I might find myself drawn to write such a book myself.

I know some men and women who will read *any* hardboiled private eye novel. This is not to say that they are indiscriminating; they can tell a good book from a bad one, but they are so much in love with the archetypical private eye as American folk hero that they'll willingly read even the inferior examples of the genre. I know other readers who read only selected private eye novels, and still others who read only the relatively rare specimen which is said to transcend its category.

For my own part, I don't much want to read warmed-over Hammett and Chandler, however much I may enjoy the original versions. I don't want to read—or to write, for Heaven's sake—books ostensibly set in present time but inextricably planted in the '30s.

But I don't think that has to be the fate of the private eye novel. It's my conviction that any type of book can be artistically vital if it springs from the heart and soul of the person who writes it. A book that reflects something genuine within its author will indeed transcend the limitations of its form. Real books written by real people *about* real people—real notwithstanding their origin in their creators' imaginations—will always work.

I don't ever want to read another book about Arabs and Israelis. I'll tell you, I'd rather sit on cold stone fences in the Klondike then read a book about Arabs and Israelis. But if the right novelist wrote such a book out of that source within himself from which true fiction springs, I would read it. And I would be glad I did.

I don't read books about rabbits—but I loved *Watership Down*. I'm not interested in Neanderthals, but I found *Clan of the Cave Bear* impossible to put down. I don't like historical novels, but *The Year of the French* was the best thing I read that year. No subject could have interested me less than Gary Gilmore, and no book attracted me less than *The Executioner's Song*, yet I read every word of every page with rapt interest and grudging admiration.

Nor do I find compelling and lively private eye novels all that thin on the ground. I wondered, as I thought about Don Westlake's talk, if he'd read anything much by Arthur Lyons, or Max Byrd, or Stephen Greenleaf, or any of several talented American writers who find they can best express their own inner selves through this particular vehicle.

Perhaps he has, and didn't care for what he read. That's legitimate, certainly. Taste is subjective, and beyond dispute. But the taste of an author, I would argue, is as individual and as indisputable as the taste of a reader, and any character, any genre, any type of fiction is the right choice insofar as it resonates and rings true for the person who writes it.

Overcoming the Ultimate Writer's Block
April 1984

WHO WILL BELIEVE YOU'RE A WRITER IF YOU DON'T? "BUT I DO BELIEVE IN MYSELF," YOU SAY. YET, SUBCONSCIOUS NEGATIVE THOUGHTS CAN SABOTAGE YOU.

What's the biggest factor in determining writing success? Any of you have any suggestions? Yes, Arnold?

I know it's not talent, sir.

What makes you so certain?

Because you wrote a piece called "It Takes More Than Talent," sir, so I figure that knocks talent out of the race.

Good thinking, Arnold. That's not to denigrate the importance of talent, by the way. A feel for language, an intuitive understanding of how to arrange words in their best order, a sense of what is and is not dramatically effective—all of the elements that make up what we call talent are enormously important. But a great many writers with a generous supply of genuine talent never get anyplace in this business, while other writers who haven't been so abundantly supplied with talent become astonishingly successful. So talent helps, but its presence is no guarantee and its absence no certain bar.

Yes, Rachel?

I'd like to nominate perseverance, sir.

Perseverance, Rachel?

Yes, sir. Perseverance. Sticking to a purpose or an aim. Never giving up what one has set out to do. Persistence, tenacity, diligence, pertinacity.

I see.

Writing story after story after story, book after book after book. Shrugging off rejections and getting the manuscript back into the mail the day it's returned. Keeping at it, sir. Never backing off never saying die. Don't give up the ship, boys. I have not yet begun to fight. Darn the torpedoes, full speed ahead. I only regret—

Darn the torpedoes?

Well, this is a family magazine, sir, and I thought—

Uh, yes, Rachel. Thank you. And I agree that perseverance is essential to a writer. In a field as competitive as ours, with the odds so high against us, we need the tenacity of a barnacle. But perseverance in and of itself is not enough. There are writers who persevere all their lives, who turn out mountains of copy and move those mountains back and forth through the mails, and who get little for their troubles outside of a wall papered with rejection slips.

Yes, Edna?

You wrote a column recently on courage, sir.

That's true, Edna. I did indeed. I write a column every month, Edna, and sooner or later I suppose I'll make my dentist happy and write one on the importance of daily flossing. I suppose it's important to a writer, though perhaps less so than courage and perseverance and talent and imagination and, oh, any number of other auctorial assets.

But if I were going to single out one essential asset, one chief determinant of a writer's success or failure, I'd point to the writer's own ability to believe.

To believe, sir?

To believe.

In what, sir? In Divine Providence? In the Great Pumpkin? In the Tooth Fairy?

Only for those who make a habit of daily flossing. No, what I'm getting at is the writer's capacity to believe in his ability and in the validity and value of his work. It is my conviction that the writer who believes in himself and his work can succeed, while the writer who does not can only fail. There are, to be sure, degrees of belief and disbelief, even as there are degrees of success and failure. And the deeper and stronger one's belief in self, the more absolute is one's success.

Proving the Pudding

This sounds highly theoretical, impossible to prove, and lighter than air. For the proof of the pudding, we can turn to an area as basic and sweaty and down to earth as the allegedly wide world of sports. Athletes, who we are so quick to presume work almost entirely with their bodies, tell us time and time again that it's all in the mind, that mental attitude and mental preparation makes the difference between the thrill of victory and the agony of defeat.

Boxers glower at each other at the weigh-in. Outfielders refuse to change their socks during a winning streak. Cornerbacks get hypnotized. Tennis players take est. Athletes of every sort do everything they can think of to psyche themselves up and their opponents out.

And what they believe, the beliefs they hold within their minds, determine their capacity to perform.

It's easy enough to prove this. For years on end, every runner believed the four-minute mile was an insurmountable barrier, that human muscle and bone could never best it.

Then one man, Roger Bannister, broke the unbreakable barrier.

And then, in almost no time at all, *every* top miler was breaking the four-minute mile. Once runners ceased to believe in the inviolability of this barrier, it ceased to *be* a barrier. They now believed they could break four minutes, and the next thing you knew they were doing so.

Let's look at another sport. Let's look at weight lifting. Picking up and pressing increasingly heavy iron objects would certainly appear to be a purely physical challenge with purely physical limitations. A given set of muscles can do so much and no more. A good mind-set might allow an athlete to have a better day than he usually has, but how much can the athlete's belief system have to do with the pounds he can lift?

The lifters themselves will tell you it has *everything* to do with it. More than diet. More than anabolic steroids. Maybe even more than training.

There's a difference, of course, between telling yourself you believe something and actually believing it. I can tell myself I can grab a car by its rear bumper and lift it into the air, and I can give myself all the little pep talks in the world, and I won't get anything more for my troubles than a pulled muscle and some shortness of breath. But every once in a while somebody does lift up a car by its bumper, somebody who never previously lifted anything much heavier than a briefcase, and he does it because the car happens to have backed onto his child.

When we are faced with the task of explaining such phenomena, we can usually come up with something. We can talk scientifically about adrenaline. We can say that a Higher Power added His strength to the father's. Or we can say that the man believed in every atom of his being that he could lift that car, that his need and desire to do so were so great that he did not have any room in his mind for the belief that he could fail.

Back to the Books

What does all this have to do with writing?

It's a fair question, in that you don't buy this magazine and read articles like this with the hope of running a four-minute mile or changing a tire without a bumper jack. What can our personal beliefs about ourselves and our work do to help us write better fiction and achieve more success with it?

I submit that it plays precisely the same role for us that it does for the runner and the weight lifter. The more completely I believe in myself, the more I am able to employ the talent I possess. My belief in my ability and in the worth of my work will enable me to work to the limit of my capacity. I'll generate the best possible ideas and make the best decisions throughout.

Does this sound suspiciously like *The Little Engine That Could*? Perhaps it does, but there's more to it than that. If all you did was sit down for 15 minutes before your daily stint at the typewriter and tell yourself, over and over, that you're a terrific writer and you're about to do excellent work, I suspect that, in and of itself, would greatly improve the quality of your work and the success you'd have with it. But it wouldn't do much to erase the negative beliefs that stand in your way.

Don't you think you have negative beliefs? Of course you do. Everybody does, and trying to deny them by sheer force of will doesn't accomplish a whole lot. Here are just a few of them; maybe you'll recognize some of them as old friends of yours:

I don't have enough talent. I don't have the self-discipline. I don't finish what I start. People won't be interested in what I have to say. I don't know anything about people. I'm not good enough. Editors don't like my stories.

Are any of these familiar? And what others can you add to the list?

These negative beliefs, whether or not you are consciously aware of them, are powerful instruments of self-sabotage. If you believe that editors do not like your stories, you will act in such a way as to support this belief. You will write stories that editors won't like. You will submit your stories to editors who won't like them. One way or another, you will struggle to confirm that negative belief.

Years ago I knew through correspondence a successful businessman who insisted that all he wanted on earth was to have a story of his accepted for publication by a national magazine. He was convinced that editors would not buy his stories, and he went to great lengths to make this belief prove itself. He had plenty of talent. His narrative skills were more than adequate and his imagination was up to par. But he sabotaged himself incessantly.

False Confessions

He decided he would write confession stories because at the time the confession market was the most accessible one for a neophyte writer. He wrote reams of confession stories, and he got the tone right, and in story after story he violated every editorial taboo in the field. I remember reading his stories with astonishment—how could anyone as knowledgeable as he was submit stories as patently unacceptable as these? I thought at the time that the guy was crazy. I see now that he was unconsciously committed to proving the truth of his belief—i.e., that editors would never buy stories from him. And indeed they wouldn't, and they never did.

I know some writers who are not, by any objective standard, very proficient. Yet they keep turning up on the bestseller list, to the considerable puzzlement of other writers who simply cannot understand their success. "Old Sigafoos can't write his name in the dirt with a stick," one writer will assure another. "What's the matter with the reading public? Are they all crazy?"

They may be, but that's neither here nor there. What Mr. (or Ms.) Sigafoos has going for himself (or herself) is a strong positive belief in his (or her) ability to write successful fiction. The strength of this conviction is palpably present in the finished product, and it carries more weight with most readers than deft prose, unsplit infinitives, or a good ear for dialogue. All of these technical aspects are important, but they seem to be less important overall than what the writer believes about himself and his work. (Or herself and her work. Or itself and its work. Or—*arrrghhhh!*)

Similarly, I know some writers whose work delights me. I enjoy reading them, and so do many of my friends, but they don't go over big with the reading public. Not, I don't think, because they go over anybody's head, but because their excellences are ones of technique and style, while their lack is a lack of conviction, of inner belief.

Belief in oneself is rarely a constant. I believe more strongly in my abilities as a writer at some times than at other times, and more or less in respect to a particular work. And I can see now that the books of mine which have failed to a greater or lesser extent have owed much of their non-success to a failure of belief.

Let me give you an example. I've alluded occasionally in my columns to a World War II thriller I wrote which manifestly Did Not Work. I had come up with what I recognized as a sound commercial idea, but it was not really *my* kind of idea, and I had enormous difficulty writing the book. I wound up bringing in a collaborator to revise the work, and he helped it a good deal, but ultimately the book didn't distinguish itself artistically or commercially.

Now I could say that I was wrong for the book and it for me from the beginning, and I could let it go at that. But as I look back on the experience of writing the book, I can recall vividly how I was beset by doubts almost every day I worked on it. I kept telling myself that what I was writing was garbage, that it lacked any conviction, that the characters were flat and uninteresting, that the plot lacked tension.

Maybe I'm mistaken, I would also tell myself. *Maybe I can't see the picture because I'm standing inside of the frame, and maybe if I just keep on keeping on, why, it'll all work out fine. Maybe this is better than I think it is, and anyway I've got a contract to fulfill and I better get to it.*

So I got to it, and I doggedly turned out my five pages a day, day in and day out, and tried not to dwell on how rotten they seemed to me. But in my unconscious mind I held onto the thought that I couldn't write this kind of book and that it was no good, and is it any wonder that this thought manifested itself on the five daily pages I was turning out? I believed I was writing badly, I believed I could only write badly, and what do you think I did?

I wrote badly.

Get in a swimming pool sometime, if you're a swimmer, and swim a lap in the ordinary fashion. Then swim a second lap, and on every stroke shout out: "I can't swim! I can't swim!"

You'll be lucky if you don't sink like a stone. And the only thing that'll keep you on top of the water is the fact that you know what you're shouting is a lie. Even so, even with that knowledge, what you're shouting is going to make swimming harder for you.

Now imagine how you'd do if you believed, consciously and unconsciously, that you couldn't swim. How far do you think you'd get?

That's about how far I got with the World War II book. Of course my character walked through it like an empty suit of clothes. Of course the dialogue was stilted and the interaction of characters unconvincing. With every stroke, I was telling myself and the world that I couldn't swim.

Yet, I could write other books and do fine with them, both artistically and commercially. Some of those other books were as far from my usual type of writing as the WWII book was. If the truth be known, I've written so many different kinds of books over the years that I'm not sure I *have* a type of writing. But I believed in my ability to write them, just like that poor beleaguered little engine that could, and so I did.

Changing Your Mind

What good does it do us to know all this? How can you make your beliefs conform to your desires, so that your fiction is as successful as it can possibly be?

It's simple, really.

All you have to do is change your mind.

Is that hard to grasp? Does it seem astonishing to entertain the notion that we can change our minds, and in so doing alter our ability to write well? It may not be hard to acknowledge that a mental attitude affects our writing ability for better or for worse. Writing, after all, is more demonstrably a mental activity than running or weight lifting, so why shouldn't it be at least as subject to mental influences as those endeavors? But even so, isn't what we believe about ourselves and our abilities a given? Is it possible to change those beliefs?

It is, if the beliefs are false. All we have to do is replace them with truths.

Let's get down to cases. I'm going to say part of a sentence, and then you take a breath and finish the sentence for yourself. "*What keeps me from writing successfully is—"* Now take a breath and finish the sentence. Arnold?

I have nothing to say to people.

Terrific. Rachel?

I'm not good enough.

Wonderful. Gwen?

Society and the publishing world is biased against women writers.

Great. Jason?

I lack self-discipline.

Marvelous. Gordon? Lucia? Everybody, shout 'em out!

I don't have time to write.

I'm too young.

I'm too old.

I lack life experience.

I can never finish anything.

Rejection would destroy me.

Nobody wants to listen to me.

I have boring ideas.

My ideas aren't commercial.

That's just wonderful, class. And now's a time for all of you in our home audience to participate. Close your eyes (after you've finished reading this paragraph) and say *What keeps me from writing successfully is* and take a breath and say the first words that come into your head. Write them down and do it again. Keep going until you have four or five wonderfully negative ideas about yourself as a writer.

Worst Things First

The chances are that all of these negative beliefs are inhibiting you. But pick the one that seems to resonate best, that sums up what's keeping you from writing well and succeeding with what you write. That's the one to work on first.

If you've read this far, you can probably understand how this belief of yours is standing in the way of your success. By holding this belief, you create a corresponding reality. If you believe you can't finish what you start, you confirm that belief by *not* finishing what you start, and then you can tell yourself you were right to think so in the first place. If you believe your ideas aren't commercial, your mind helps out by obligingly refusing to come up with any commercial ideas. If you believe you lack life experience, your mind fails to turn the experience you possess into the raw material for fiction. If you believe people don't want to listen to you, you'll say (and write) things they won't want to hear (or read).

Fine—the negative beliefs you hold are damaging, even paralyzing. But how can you possibly change them?

You took the first step in that direction when you said them aloud and wrote them down. Negative beliefs are most devastating when we don't know we have them, when we cut them off at the source through the mechanism of denial. Now all you have to do is take that negative belief and turn it into a positive one.

Does that sound like a combination of mental jujitsu and wishful thinking? Perhaps it does, but please remember that these negative beliefs have one remarkable thing in common.

They're all lies.

They're lies and you *know* they're lies. Rejection would destroy you? Oh, the hell it would. Nobody ever died of a rejection slip, and nobody ever succeeded without accumulating plenty of them along the way. Rejection wouldn't destroy you, but thinking so has been crippling you for years.

You don't have time to write? Nonsense. Anyone who has time to read an article like this one has plenty of time to write. And you know you do, because you've read enough books (including my own *Writing the Novel: From Plot to Print*, and if you haven't read it what are you waiting for?) that explain clearly enough how a page or two a day adds up to a novel in remarkably little time. Anyone can become a writer on an investment of an hour a day, and anyone can find that time by getting up one hour earlier, and you already *know* that; everybody knows it.

So now it's time to turn your negative belief, the lie you've been telling yourself, into a positive one. Turn that idea inside out, and play with the wording until you've created a positive affirmation of your own ability to write successfully. All right, let's hear it.

> *I have something important to say.*
> *I'm a terrific writer.*
> *My identity as a woman strengthens me as a writer.*
> *I am self-disciplined and energetic.*
> *I have all the time I need to be a writer.*
> *My life furnishes me abundantly with the material for fiction.*
> *Rejection won't hurt me.*

That's good, Aileen, but maybe you can make that more forceful and affirmative.

> *Rejection enhances my self-esteem.*

That's wonderful. Let's hear some more.

> *I always finish what I start.*
> *My ideas are vibrant and inventive.*
> *Editors love what I write.*
> *Everyone is interested in what I write.*

Get the idea? You there at home, take your own negative belief and turn it into a positive affirmation. Write it down. Write it down again. Say it out loud. Say it out loud *again*. Louder! Again, and *louder!*

This affirmation is powerful all by itself. Just saying it over and over will have a strong positive effect upon your writing performance. (You may not believe it can change anything. That's OK. Do it anyway, and you'll believe it when it works.)

How can you use the affirmation? By saying it over and over to yourself, obviously. You can say it aloud or silently, as you prefer and as circumstances permit. Some people like to make tapes and play them over and over. You can make a loop tape that will repeat indefinitely, and you can play it as you drift off to sleep. People who've tried this report that it's especially effective, because the brain seems to be most receptive to this sort of suggestion when you're right on the verge of sleep.

I find affirmations most effective when I write them, because the process of writing them down permits me to use a response column to release my own resistance to the affirmation. (The "That's an Affirmative, Sir!" sidebar shows just how a response column works.)

You see, while we've already determined that the negative things you've been telling yourself are lies, some of these affirmations look at first like pretty shaky truths. If every manuscript you send out comes caroming back by return mail, how easy is it going to be for you to write *Editors love what I write*? You write it down, and a little voice in your head mutters a word frequently found on the floor of dairy barns.

That's what the response column is for. You take a sheet of paper, and you draw a line a little to the right of the center of the page. And at the left you write *Editors love what I write*, and in the right hand column you write your response. And you keep doing this 15 or 20 times.

Your affirmation is the truth. Your response—and it will vary each time, as you'll see—is the negativity you're releasing and getting rid of. Your responses will continue changing over the days and weeks, and eventually you won't get any negative responses. When this happens, you'll know the truth of the affirmation is beginning to penetrate into your unconscious mind. At this point you continue using the affirmation but drop the response column. And you take another negative idea, turn it into a positive, and start working with it.

It's a good idea to write the affirmation in first, second, and third persons, as in the example in the sidebar. You can type or handwrite the affirmations. Sondra Ray, a pioneer in the use of affirmations and originator of the Loving Relationships Training, types affirmations because she can do them much faster that way. I type everything I write *but* affirmations; writing them by hand seems to connect me more intimately to the process. Try it both ways and see what works for you.

And the process will work, believe me. Does it mean anyone who works with affirmations can be a successful professional writer? Not necessarily. Talent helps, and motivation helps, too. But I will say that anyone who works effectively with affirmations will be less at the mercy of implanted negative thoughts, and will consequently write better and more successfully. The first step in getting your own way is getting out of your own way, and affirmations are as good a means toward that end as I know.

So keep at it, boys and girls. And before you know it, Rachel, you'll have your picture on the cover of *Time*.

I'll believe it when I see it, sir.

Absolutely, Rachel. And vice versa.

THAT'S AN AFFIRMATIVE, SIR!

Let's say your most inhibiting negative thought is Rejection will destroy me. Consequently, fear of rejection has kept you from submitting material, perhaps even from writing it. When you do submit something and it's rejected, your own belief makes the experience a devastating one.

So you create for yourself the positive affirmation *Rejection enhances my self-esteem*. Now what kind of nonsense is that? Nobody gets a heightened sense of self-esteem out of rejection. This isn't an affirmation, it's a load of used oats.

But what the hell, you decide to work with it anyway, using a response column. Maybe your first entry looks something like this:

AFFIRMATION	RESPONSE
Rejection enhances my self-esteem	*What nonsense!*

But you keep on with it and see what happens:

Rejection enhances my self-esteem	*No it doesn't. It crushes me.*
Rejection enhances my self-esteem	*How could that be true?*
Rejection enhances my self-esteem	*It tells me I'm no good.*
Rejection enhances my self-esteem	*It makes me feel awful.*

After five or six entries in the first person, you change to the second person, like so:

Larry, rejection enhances your self-esteem	*It hurts, hurts, hurts!*
Larry, rejection enhances your self-esteem	*How could it?*
Larry, rejection enhances your self-esteem	*It could kill me.*
Larry, rejection enhances your self-esteem	*Well, no. I've lived through it before.*
Larry, rejection enhances your self-esteem	*By making me see I can survive it.*
Larry, rejection enhances your self-esteem	*Acceptance would enhance it a lot.*

Now you reword the affirmation in the third person:

Rejection enhances Larry's self-esteem	*Then Larry must be nuts.*
Rejection enhances Larry's self-esteem	*At least he's taking chances.*
Rejection enhances Larry's self-esteem	*I don't think this process is working.*
	It's still a load of used oats.
Rejection enhances Larry's self-esteem	*Maybe it's possible.*
Rejection enhances Larry's self-esteem	*Maybe.*

Gradually the negative responses lose their force as the affirmation becomes implanted. Before you know it, the outrageous proposition that rejection enhances your self-esteem has become true. At that point you stop being paralyzed by fear of rejection, write more freely, submit more freely, and have a better chance of acceptance. Furthermore, those rejections you do garner wind up enhancing your self-esteem!

Don't be alarmed if you find yourself resisting the process. Just do it anyway. When I started using affirmations, I hated the whole thing. So the first affirmation I created for myself was *I enjoy writing affirmations*, and it took a surprisingly short time to become genuinely true.

• 22 •

Self-Analysis
April 1984

My first piece for *WD*, and a sort of prototype for this monthly column, was entitled "Where Do You Get Your Ideas?" It was written in a motel room in North Carolina in October of 1975, published just about 15 months later, and how was I to know where it would lead me?

One of innumerable places to which it has led me was Catonsville, Maryland, where I taught last June at the Maryland Writers' Conference as the guest of Michael Scott Cain, himself a fine writer, a teacher of writing, and a *WD* contributor. One of my classes centered on fictional ideas and their origins, and I encouraged my students to suggest some of the sources for such ideas.

One man raised his hand. "I think all fictional ideas come from the self," he said.

"Well, uh, yes," I said, "but I was thinking in more specific terms." And I went on to talk about some books and stories of my own, and to illustrate how they had been sparked by a bit of factual information, by an offshoot of someone else's experience, by some particle of overheard conversation, or by some reworked real-life incident. A few students shared similar examples from their own work. And damned if that first guy didn't stick his hand in the air again.

"I think this just proves my point," he said.

What point, I wondered, was that?

"About ideas coming from the self," he said, relentlessly. "Either it's *your* experience or it's something *you* read or something *you* overheard or something *you* learned about. The self is always involved."

"Well, yeah," I said, a little impatiently. "But when you've said that, what have you said? Obviously the writer has some connection to the idea or he wouldn't be making it into a story, but, well, so what? How does it help us to know that?"

I suppose he gave up at this point, and I emerged from the discussion feeling vaguely frustrated. It was clear to me that the fellow had been saying something that was meaningful to him, and it had seemed only tautological to me, the literary equivalent of proving mathematically that A equals A.

Ah well. Months passed, and one day I had a blinding flash of the obvious. There are indeed certain ways in which writers produce ideas—and in this connection you might want to read "Where Do You Get Your Ideas?" in my book *Telling Lies for Fun and Profit*. But there is something that makes an idea right for one writer and wrong for another, and that is the extent to which the idea does or does not vibrate in harmony with something deep within the writer's inner self.

I'm not talking now about the sort of thing that happens when, say, a writer of historical romances gets a great idea for a science fiction story while having no interest in or talent for the writing of science fiction. I've discussed that problem before—indeed, I've made myself a victim of it, trying now and then to write books because I've come up with strong commercial ideas and not pausing to realize that they were not ideas for my kind of book.

I'm talking here about something a little subtler, a little more personal than that.

So let's get down to cases. I've often referred in these columns to a series character of mine named Evan Michael Tanner, an eccentric chap who appeared in seven novels of international adventure which I wrote in the middle and late '60s. Tanner, in case you never made his acquaintance, is rather a quirky fellow. A shard of North Korean shrapnel pierced his skull and destroyed his sleep center, and he's been wide awake ever since. He's spent the 24 hours of the day ghosting term papers and doctoral theses for students, learning every language spoken on the planet, and joining such disparate lunatic fringe organizations as the League for the Restoration of Cilician Armenia, the Latvian Army-in-Exile, the Internal Macedonian Revolutionary Order, and the Flat Earth Society. In his initial appearance in print, *The Thief Who Couldn't Sleep*, Tanner sets out in pursuit of the lost gold hoard of Balekesir and winds up unwittingly fomenting a revolution in Macedonia.

I've previously reported that Tanner owes his origin to the dovetailing of several minor bits of data. First I read a long article in *Time* which explored the nature and functions of sleep and mentioned in passing that a handful of human beings did seem to exist without any sleep whatsoever. The writer posited the existence of a sleep center in the brain as a physiological entity.

A while later, I was looking up something in the *Brittanica* and happened on the fact that a Stuart Pretender to the throne of England still existed. The House of Stuart had last reigned in the person of Anne, who died without living issue in 1714, but the Stuart line had continued, and now some minor Germanic princeling was at its head, although he didn't seem much inclined to press his claim.

My first thought was of a plot at this late date to restore the House of Stuart. Then I conceived a character who didn't sleep, who supported himself by ghosting in the groves of Academe, and who had many of the other attributes which eventually constituted Tanner. A year or two later, when an acquaintance told me of his own true-life adventure attempting to recover some long-lost gold coins in Turkey, everything fell into place and I sat down and wrote the book.

The book worked fine. It didn't make me rich or get me on the Carson show, but it turned out to be the start of a series that is even now returning to print this year. And that's how I explained Tanner's genesis in the past, and as much as I knew about it.

Not too long after I came back from Catonsville, I took an intensive seminar which explored, among other things, the deeply held thoughts and beliefs that affect one's life. I was told that everyone has one or more of these primal laws, and that typically one's entire life may amount to an attempt to disprove one's primal law. A common example of this is the child who grows up knowing inside that she is ugly—and who ultimately becomes a model.

Primal laws and the way they adversely affect our writing careers—and what we can do about them—compose a key section of "Write for Your Life," the intensive seminar for writers which I've created and am offering in various locations nationwide. I mention the subject here as a way of showing how my own primal law played a central part in Tanner's evolution.

My primal law is "I don't belong here." I don't fit in here, they won't like me here, they don't want me around. I'm an outsider here, I'm not welcome here. Wherever *here* is, it's not where I belong.

And who was this Tanner character? Why, he was a guy who was welcome and at home everywhere he went. Drop him into any corner of the world and he'll speak the local lingo well enough to pass for a native. He blends with his surroundings in a way that would make a chameleon blush. All he has to do is cross a border and he invariably finds a friend, some ditzy comrade Tanner knows through correspondence. A Croat separatist, a Transylvanian irredentist, a fellow Flat Earther—Tanner has buddies everywhere, and each one sees him as someone different, because Tanner literally becomes the person he thinks they want him to be.

"I don't belong here." That's my primal law. So I created in Tanner an alternative self who belonged everywhere. In order to do this, of course, he fragmented himself to an extraordinary degree. And he sacrificed the ability to sleep, as if spending time in an unconscious state would amount to a loss of control. If he slept, if he let go for a moment, these buddies of his might find out who he really was. And then they would know he didn't *really* belong.

I want to let go of this before what began as an illustrative example turns into a public display of self-psychoanalysis. Suffice it to say that Tanner owes rather more of his essential nature to his author's own inner conflicts and anxieties than I would ever have suspected.

And that, I am quite certain, is why the books work, why the character remained vital and alive for me throughout seven novels. Tanner was sparked, to be sure, by one item in *Time* and another in the *Encyclopaedia Brittanica*. He was highlighted by other bits of data collected here and there, and his personality was formed of parts of me and parts of a couple of friends of mine. And his first adventure was based on something that actually happened.

But my mind chose to make fiction of Tanner because he emerged, quite without my conscious awareness, from the very depths of myself. I didn't even know I held this fundamental belief that I didn't fit in, so I could hardly consciously create a character to move in counterpoint to that primal belief. But, consciously or not, that is precisely what I did.

I can only guess that all of the characters who work optimally in my fiction represent similar efforts to resolve inner contradictions. It's often said that all viewpoint characters are projections of the self. They are, as it were, the people I would be if I were them. And I can certainly see aspects of my personality and circumstances echoed in such of my characters as Bernie Rhodenbarr and Matthew Scudder. As dissimilar as they may be, each has fairly obvious points of origin in his author.

But this is something else, and something more deeply hidden from me, certainly. It speaks rather profoundly, I think, about the extraordinary resourcefulness of the mind—of its ability to use the writing of fiction to exorcise inner demons, and too of its capacity to make from the resolution of inner turmoil a useful, profitable, entertaining entity.

Where do ideas come from? Indeed, from the self. Those bits of odd data that coalesced for me into the character of Tanner did so because they combined to strike a chord that resonated with something deep inside. In order to make something out of them, I had first to add to them something of myself, something I didn't even know was there.

A mysterious business, this business of fictioneering. I've been at it, man and boy, for a cool quarter of a century. And I'm still just beginning to find out what it is I've been doing all these years.

• 23 •

Nonstop Writing
May 1984

Could do a column on automatic writing. Just keeping the pen moving pen or pencil keep it going might be a good column not that I partic want to write a column right now I'm two weeks early Automatic writing—tell 'em about Write for Your Life describe ways of using the process—first thing in the morning when blocked etc. I don't know if I really got enough for a column or if there's any point to it. I'd actually rather be doing something else no I wouldn't This is self-indulgent scribbling away like this even if I can use it as illustrative material still what real value does it have? I think that should be enough to give 'em the general idea.

The italicized nonsense in the preceding paragraph is the verbatim transcript of a piece of nonstop writing I did just before I began drafting the rest of this column. It's reproduced here not merely because I delight in getting paid for what a less resourceful writer might use to line the bottom of his parakeet's cage, but also to illustrate a process I've occasionally called automatic writing, but which is also variously known as speedwriting and fast writing.

None of these terms, I might point out, is altogether successful. Automatic writing has long been used to describe a technique of spiritualism in the same ballpark as the Ouija board. Speedwriting is a form of shorthand ("f u cn rd ths, u cn gt a gd jb"). And fast writing is what you do when you're up against a deadline.

The process I'm talking about is something rather different. It consists simply enough of writing without pause, writing without stopping to think of the right word or even the right thought. Perhaps we might call it Nonstop Writing, because that's precisely what it is. You start writing and you don't stop.

One of the early processes in my Write for Your Life seminar consists of everyone's doing five or ten minutes of nonstop writing. When I explain the process, I tell my trainees that there is no way you can fail to do it perfectly as long as you keep writing. If the pen is moving, you're doing it right.

I presented Write for Your Life in New York this past November. Two days later I began work on a new novel, *Like a Lamb to Slaughter*. On the first morning, I sat down at my new desk in my new office, in front of a reconditioned—and new to me—typewriter. I pushed the machine gently aside, opened a spiral-bound notebook, and began writing as follows:

> *Here we go again. Here we go gathering wool in May. Who is this guy Charlie what's he about anyway? What's Charlie do for a living? Not what he wanted to do. He wanted to be an artist. He wanted to be a carpenter Jesus was a carpenter Nice middle-class guys don't do that so he does something else but has a shop full of tools downstairs. No, doesn't fit Charlie. His best friend it might fit. This is stupid I don't feel like writing anything anyway I should have stayed in bed I'm tired What about Charlie anyway . . .*

I went on in this vein for a full ten minutes, closed the notebook, did my usual 20-minute prework meditation, then returned to the typewriter and wrote the book's first eight pages with unaccustomed ease. In the three weeks since then I've followed the procedure every day and I'll tell you something, I think I must have learned a valuable lesson at my own seminar. Because the stretch of nonstop writing I use to start each day seems to center my thoughts on the book, to get my creative juices flowing, and to make it easier for me to start getting words on paper.

It stands to reason. Athletes use warm-up exercises to get their muscles loosened up, and this warm-up period seems to work in much the same fashion, limbering my writing muscles and getting me ready to start writing at full tilt.

What, you may ask, is the point of doing this exercise at a fast pace? Why must the pen keep moving without a pause? Why does one have to scribble away so furiously that one doesn't even have time to think?

The answer, I suspect, lies within the last question. It is precisely because one doesn't have time to think that nonstop writing works. The little editor in the mind, the naysayer who can find fault with anything I write, never gets a word in edgewise. The point, for once, is not to get it right but to get it written, and so there's no need to censor what goes on the page, no need to worry about logic or syntax or word choice or prose rhythm, no need to do anything but continue making marks on the paper.

Once I've done this for five or ten minutes, a blank sheet of bond paper becomes rather less intimidating. I can afford to let the editor function then, I shape each sentence before committing it to the page, I make changes and additions and deletions as I go along, and it's a good thing; my nonstop scribbling is not something anyone would care to read.

(Jack Kerouac, I might note, wrote whole novels in what he called his "spontaneous bop prosody," a near thing to nonstop writing. The process did very likely unblock his creative energies, but the books seem to me to lose in craft what they gain in energy.)

While my mental editor wields his blue pencil, his voice is softer and less intrusive after my session of nonstop scribbling. It's just easier to get past the fear of writing and into the act of writing.

Stops and Stopgaps

Nonstop writing has other applications. Here are a few that come to mind:

1. *Wake-Up Writing*. A friend told me about this technique a few years ago, and it was old stuff then, so I'm certainly not claiming to have invented it. The process goes as follows: the minute you wake up in the morning you take up a pad and pen or pencil and scribble without pause until you've filled a page with your jottings. What you write need not be tied to your current writing project; indeed, you don't have to be a

writer, or to be interested in writing, to start your day in this fashion. You may write about a dream or start free-associating about some childhood memory. One time I woke up with a vague idea for a column and wound up a few minutes later with a surprisingly detailed outline for a column which turned out to be a cinch to write. But that was an isolated example, and not really the point of the exercise.

What *is* the point of the exercise? To clear the mind, I suspect, and to do it through writing. The process helps generally to unblock creativity, and I would think it ideal for a writer to be holding a pen or pencil while unblocking his or her creativity. I don't know what other value wake-up writing might have, but I would certainly recommend experimenting with it.

2. *Night-Night Writing.* A lot of people, writers and nonwriters alike, write a journal entry every night before going to bed. Some journals are a record of the day's events, some an emotional history of their authors, and some a vehicle for literary self-expression. For those who find formal journal-keeping tedious, a nightly stint of nonstop writing might prove a less structured alternative. I would guess that it would perform essentially the same functions as wake-up writing, but would conclude the day rather than kick it off.

3. *Stopgap Writing.* My usual routine when at work on a novel calls for me to do a certain number of pages a day Monday through Friday, with the weekends off. This past Saturday I decided to do a page of nonstop writing as a way of keeping my hand in and staying in contact with the writing process.

I think I'll try to continue this activity and see if I like it enough to make a habit of it. It strikes me as a way to stay connected not only to writing but also to the specific book I'm working on, while allowing me the rest and diversion I require of the weekend. It takes so little time and energy that it doesn't impinge on my leisure.

Similarly, I can see value in performing this exercise on enforced days off—when I have to interrupt my schedule for research or business appointments, for example. And it might be very useful during the extended periods of time off I enjoy between books. I like to treat myself to long vacations, but it might do me good to stay in touch with my identity as a writer through daily nonstop writing.

4. *Writing Through Blocks*. I don't know that nonstop writing will cure writer's block; I somehow doubt that the cure is that simple. But I think some of us might find it a useful and manageable way to write *while* blocked. Even if "real" writing gets done, a blocked writer could dash off a daily page of gibberish, crumple it up and throw it away, and sustain himself with the knowledge that he did write *something*. If you give yourself permission to declare yourself a success as long as you do your ten minutes of nonstop writing, you'll lessen the negative effects of a blocked period on your self-esteem. (If you give yourself permission to declare yourself a success whether you write *anything* or not, you're even better off. But that requires a level of self-love not all blocked writers can readily attain.)

5. *Getting Organized*. Before getting started on a prose project, a book or a story or an article, nonstop writing can serve a useful organizational function. When I'm starting out or when I hit plot problems, I frequently talk to myself on paper, just rattling on about what I'm writing in the hope that something useful will come to light. The trouble is that I'm frequently inhibited by the very elements that make the process essential—anxiety, confusion, uncertainty, doubt and fear. If I make myself write without a pause, these factors have less of a chance to get in the way.

Don't Stop Now

How do you *do* nonstop writing? In simplest terms, you start anywhere and you don't stop until you're finished. You can allow yourself run-on sentences, you can abandon a line of thought in mid-word and switch to something completely different, you can leave slips of the pen uncorrected—it doesn't matter. No one's ever going to read this garbage.

You probably won't even bother reading it yourself. It's not designed to be read, it's designed to be written.

I use a pen and a ruled spiral-bound notebook. You can use whatever works for you. I don't use a typewriter because the machine gets in the way. I'm more connected to the process by hand and less concerned with typos and such. A typewriter is faster, to be sure, but who cares? The idea is to go at full speed, whatever that is. But you're not getting paid by the word, or by the words-per-minute.

I write about whatever comes to mind—or, more accurately, what comes to hand, since this frequently constitutes a bypass operation on the mind. Sometimes I write about not wanting to write, or about having nothing to write about. It doesn't matter.

As long as the pen keeps moving, I know I'm doing it right.

• 24 •

Gone Shopping
June 1984

I just gave myself permission to stop writing.

Actually it was yesterday—yesterday as I write this, which is a couple months before you get to read it. I often have the feeling as I work on this column that I'm not so much writing to you as I am speaking the words right at you. It's occasionally disconcerting to realize that the poor words have to hang in the air for a few months before you get to hear them. I wore a parka to work this morning, with the hood up and the collar buttoned. It's an old parka, it should have been replaced last year, and now, as you read all this, my faithful old parka will have been carted off by the sanitmen.

Unless there's a garbage strike. There could be a strike between now and then, there could be a lunar eclipse, there could be a coup d'état in the Middle East and a revolution in Africa. Maybe they'll have cured the common cold by the time you read these lines, maybe they'll have squared the circle and boxed the compass and colonized the moons of Jupiter. Maybe—

Enough. After close to a year of banging my head against assorted walls, yesterday morning I walked over to my agent's office and told him I was getting nowhere on a book that was several months overdue at my publisher's office. I further stated that I did not know when I could deliver the book, that I was not at the moment sure I could ever deliver it, and that I didn't intend to write the book, or any other book, or even to think about writing a book, for at least six months. Possibly longer. Maybe ever.

My agent understood. Isn't that wonderful? I think it is. He understood, and he sympathized, and he told me not to worry about it. I have never been quicker to take any piece of advice from anyone. I instantly stopped worrying and I haven't worried since. Giving up on the book filled me with the sense of relief and accomplishment I can ordinarily attain only by *finishing* a book.

I don't expect to spend the next six months (or longer, or forever) in a monastery, or in a coma, or watching raindrops roll down a window. I'll be doing my column, and occasional articles and short stories. I'll be doing some teaching—I've just arranged to undertake the Mystery Writers of America writing workshop, and I'll be putting a lot of energy into my new Write for Your Life seminars. I've got some appearances booked at writers' conferences in the coming season, and I'd like to add a few bookings to my schedule. I'll have plenty to do.

But I won't be writing a book, and I won't be thinking about writing a book, and I hope and pray I won't be beating myself up for *not* writing a book.

So there.

How, you may wonder, does all of this come to be in my column, which is after all not a personal journey but a presumably instructive monthly musing on the topic of writing fiction? Where does this Block fellow get off writing about not writing? Who cares if his parka's falling apart? Who cares if his *life's* falling apart?

Let me assure you that, while the former may be, the latter is emphatically not. And let me suggest that, if this is a column about not writing, then that is an activity to which most of us devote a great deal of time. With the possible exception of Isaac Asimov, I can't think of anyone who doesn't spend more time not writing than writing.

So I'd like to tell you a little about the writing and non-writing I've been doing over the past year.

Not Gone Well

I've had stretches before when things have Not Gone Well. I'm not mad about the term writer's *block*, if only because the word has enough work cut out for itself as the surname of a major American novelist. But this is a rose which, by any name, smells less than sweet to most of us. I've had times when my life was so disorganized that I couldn't seem to get anything done, and I've had times when I took a wrong turn somewhere in the course of a book and couldn't make it work. I've had times when the words just wouldn't come, when my mind turned out to be every bit as blank as the fresh page in the typewriter. And I've written about some of these times, and how they felt, and what I did to get out of them.

But this has been different.

Let me explain just what it's been like. Sometime in January of '83 I finished my last book, *The Burglar Who Painted Like Mondrian*. (No, hang on a minute. Let's not call it my last book. Let's call it my most recent book.) I then took a couple of months off, as is my wont, and then commenced thinking about the next book. My publisher had already commenced so thinking, and had taken to asking me what the new book's title would be, and what it was about. My publisher does this sort of thing.

He thought, and I agreed, that the next book should be about Matthew Scudder, a series character of mine. I supplied a title, *Like a Lamb to Slaughter*, which I felt would fit any book I might chance to write about Scudder. Not like a glove, not to a T, but 'twill do, 'twill do. My publisher promptly engaged an artist to prepare a cover, and I went into a huddle with myself to figure out what would happen in this book I was doomed to write.

What happened, after a couple months with no plot ideas whatsoever, was the blinding realization that I didn't *want* to write a book about Scudder. The character had had a major catharsis in his previous appearance in *Eight Million Ways to Die*. I felt complete with him, I wanted to give him a rest.

So in May I went into seclusion in Cape May, New Jersey, to figure out what book to write instead.

I stayed there for a week and couldn't come up with anything useful. I came back, and some more time passed, and I decided that the publisher wanted a Scudder book and the public wanted a Scudder book and what difference did it make what I wanted? Meanwhile, my publisher was pressing me for a blurb about the book for his catalog, and I had somehow agreed to deliver a manuscript by October.

I got an idea, at least for a strong opening sequence. I sat down, and in the space of a couple of days I wrote 40 pages and change. And I stopped because it just didn't feel right. It felt wooden and lifeless and inert and I put it in a drawer and left it there.

A month or so later, I started it over. I didn't go back to what I'd written, I threw all that out, and I started in at the beginning and got into it. The writing went well, and this time it wasn't lifeless. I was writing good scenes and I could tell I was making them work. I clipped along at a rate of six, eight, ten pages a day, and I got 120 pages done in three weeks or so, and then one day I struggled to get out a page or two, and then the next day I didn't do anything, and the day after that I wanted to quit.

Just like that. It seemed to me that there was no plot developing, that I had a third of a book written and some things happening but I didn't know where I was going, I had no feeling for what I was writing, and I couldn't bear to write any more. I put the book aside thinking that I would get back to it in a few days, in a week, in a couple of weeks, and as time passed I knew I didn't want to get back to it at all. I hated it, I didn't want to look at it let alone resume writing it, and I decided it was a mistake to have started it in the first place, that I never should have let myself be pressured into writing another book about Scudder, that it was all hopeless and the hell with it.

I went to my publisher and told him I couldn't write another book about Scudder for the time being. He took this news reasonably well and allowed as to how he could understand why this might be the case. But he already had *Lamb* in his spring catalog and wanted to let his salespeople continue to take orders for it. Could I write a book about Bernie Rhodenbarr, my other series character, and his sales force could just explain that the spring book had turned out to be a Rhodenbarr book instead of a Scudder? I said I could probably do that. Could the Bernie Rhodenbarr book be called *Like a Lamb to Slaughter*? I told him it could not, and he shrugged with acceptance.

Promises, Promises

I went home and remembered an idea I'd had a year or two back for a non-series suspense novel. I'd cooled on it for a time, but now it excited me again, and, wonder of wonders, it would fit the *Lamb* title and jacket to perfection. I called my publisher, told him this, and promised the book in February.

Then he began pestering me for new blurb material for his ads announcing the spring list. I refused to be specific.

In mid November I sat down to write the book. I was hot to do it, and I did eight pages the first day and the pages rolled without a hitch. At the end of three weeks I had 140 pages written. During the weekend I had enormous anxiety about the book, and Monday morning I decided I didn't like it, and that I dreaded going to the office and looking at it. I didn't go to the office. I took a week off, and I took another week off, and I realized I wasn't going to do any more work on the book. I was going to abandon it. I *wanted* to abandon it.

I tried to think of something else to write. Because I had to deliver the book in February, and I hadn't said anything very specific about the book, all I had to do was deliver *a* book, and if I really pushed in January and February, well, I could come in with it, perhaps a little bit late, but—

Then I got an idea for another book about Scudder.

Like a Writer to Slaughter

Is this beginning to sound crazy? It sounds crazy to me, but it's what happened. I got an idea for a book about Scudder and it just plain felt right to me. On January 3rd I went to my office, sat down and wrote ten pages of *Like a Lamb to Slaughter*, about Scudder. It felt fine. I wrote ten pages a day, five days a week, and when I hit a hundred pages it was like hitting a wall. I took a day off. I took another day off. But I went back the third day, and I hung in there, even when it didn't go well, and—

And somewhere around page 130—does the exact number matter? I could look it up—somewhere around there, I was done. I felt I'd been marking time, sending Scudder on meaningless errands. I was lost. The book was dead. I couldn't write anymore.

In the days that followed, I decided that I was perfectly willing to believe that any of the three substantial chunks of novel I've written this year are probably OK. Objectively, I think they're well written and acceptable. But they're books I'm clearly incapable of finishing. There's no point in my trying to complete one of them, and there's even less point in picking myself up and dusting myself off and trying to write a fourth book. If at first you don't succeed, try, try again. If you still don't succeed, quit.

I can think of a lot of reasons to explain this condition. My life has changed in innumerable ways (all of them for the better) in the past year. I think I have to have time to integrate those changes before I can write a sustained work of fiction. My writing will very likely change to reflect these inner changes—it always has in the past—and maybe I won't be able to write more about Scudder. If so, fine. I can live with that.

In the meantime, I can only recall the legend I saw recently on an overpriced T-shirt: "When the going gets tough, the tough go shopping."

I quit.

Fear of Writing

August 1984

Good morning, class.

Good morning, sir.

Today I'd like to talk a little bit about fear. But first let's have a show of hands. Raise your hand if you ever experience any fear in connection with your writing. Thank you, thanks very much. You can put your hands down now. Arnold, I believe you were the only one in the class who didn't raise a hand.

I was afraid to, sir.

I see. Well, that's understandable, Arnold. One of the things many of us are afraid to do is admit we're scared. That can leave us sitting at our typewriters and whistling in the dark, and it's tough to get much accomplished that way.

One of the initial exercises at my Write for Your Life seminar is designed to bring fear out into the open. Participants begin by reeling off all their fears, first about the training seminar itself, then about writing in general. When all of these fears are acknowledged and shared, they lose a great deal of their power.

For one thing, it's a comfort to know you're not the only scared person in the crowd. How many of you heaved a little sigh of relief a few minutes ago when you saw everybody else's hand up along with yours?

Except for Arnold's, sir.

Except for Arnold's, Rachel. Indeed.

Perhaps Arnold was afraid to raise his hand because he thought he'd be the only frightened person in the room. As it happens, most people are afraid of writing, and fear is by no means the mark of the amateur or neophyte. In *The Craft of Interviewing*, John Brady quotes Gloria Steinem, who explains that she knows she is a writer because writing for her meets her three tests of métier: when she's doing it she never feels she really ought to be doing something else, it's a source of satisfaction and occasionally of pride, and, finally, it's terrifying.

A year or two ago I wrote a column on courage. I said then that I considered courage at least as important an item for a writer as a sharp pencil or a word processor, and I haven't changed my mind about that. But by courage I certainly didn't mean fearlessness. It doesn't take the least bit of courage to do something that holds no fear for you in the first place. The truly courageous person is the one who feels his or her fear, and faces it, and goes ahead and does the task anyway.

> *A fear I have about this column is I'll never get the damned thing written.*
> *Another fear I have about this column is that I don't have enough to say on the topic.*
> *Another fear I have about this column is it'll be too airy-fairy with no nuts-and-bolts stuff to hung onto.*
> *Another fear I have about this column is I'm repeating myself in it.*
> *Another fear I have about this column is nobody will be interested in it.*
> *Another fear I have about this column is some cynical jerk will write me a nasty letter about it and I'll be depressed for a week.*
> *Another fear I have about this column is even if I get it done I won't be able to think of anything to write next month....*

I could go on. And I'll tell you something, it might help if I did. Before I started listing these fears, I didn't know what most of them were. I knew it was taking me a while to get this column attended to, and I knew I'd made a false start at a column on this same subject a month or two ago, but I didn't know just what it was that was holding me back.

And it helps to know.

Most of us grow up thinking that what we don't know won't hurt us, a sort of ostrich approach to life. I've come to believe that *only* what we don't know has the power to hurt us. We can prevail over anything—so long as we are able to take a straight-on look at it.

Let me give you an example. A lot of years ago, I was writing sexually oriented nonfiction books for a paperback publisher. My agent managed to sell another publisher, a more substantial one, on a book proposal of mine. This second publisher would be paying twice as much money in advance as I had been receiving from the first publisher.

And I just plain couldn't seem to get started on the book. I put it off, I did other things, I sat in front of the typewriter and stared at it. I was scared of it.

Before I got into deadline trouble, I figured it out. I had things scrambled in my mind. Because I was going to be getting twice as much money for the book, I figured I had to give the new publisher something special, something that was twice as good as what I'd been turning out. And I didn't know how I was going to manage that, since I'd been giving the books my best shot all along.

Once I saw what the fear was, I saw too that it was ridiculous. The new publisher was dealing with me because he liked what I'd been doing for the first publisher. He expected something *as* good, not something twice as good. I'd been writing books of that ilk easily and effortlessly all along, and now I relaxed and took a breath and wrote the new book easily and effortlessly, and the new publisher was perfectly delighted with it and it sold well, earning its advance and more, and leading to several more contracts with the new publisher, and for even more money.

Now if I hadn't—yes, Gwen?

Aren't you going to tell us the name of the book, sir? Or the name you wrote it under?

I'm afraid not, Gwen. Now where was I?

Oh, yes. If I hadn't known that I was afraid to write the book, and if I hadn't pinpointed the source of that fear. I wouldn't have been able to relax. I might have failed to deliver the book altogether. I might have tried too hard to produce a masterpiece and wound up failing to supply what the publisher had wanted all along. But, because I was able to face the fear directly and work through it, everything worked out fine.

The process of listing your fears when you're stuck on a project, or about to start something new, or just feeling anxious, can be invaluable. Do it as a written process, as I demonstrated at the beginning of this section. Or do it with a friend who will acknowledge each fear you state with a nod or a quick thank you—you don't want someone who'll try to talk you out of your fears or tell you they're groundless. If you run out of fears right away, make up some more. Any fear you make up will have some validity, and it will be worth your while to write it down or say it out loud.

> *A fear I have about writing is that I've been at it too long and I'm all written out.*
> *Another fear I have about writing is I'll show more of myself than I want to in my work.*
> *Another fear I have about writing is that I'm losing my enthusiasm for writing fiction.*
> *Another fear I have about writing is I'm not good enough to make it really big.*
> *Another fear I have about writing is it's not fun anymore.*
> *Another fear I have about writing is that my internal self has undergone a lot of changes in the past couple years and I won't be able to incorporate these changes in my work.*
> *Another fear I have about writing is—*

Oh, that's enough. A fiction writer with this many fears would seem to deserve the title of The Cowardly Liar. It's useful, though, to root out and list these more general fears about writing. Once you've found out what your fears are, you can devise affirmations to reverse them. (See my article "Overcoming the Ultimate Writer's Block," in the April *WD* for an explanation of how to work with affirmations.) The following affirmations specifically address some of the fears uncovered above: *I am a never-ending source of wonderful ideas, it's safe for me to reveal myself to others, I have what it takes to succeed as a writer, writing is easy and fun for me.*

Fear of Trying

If you're not at all afraid of writing, you may be doing something wrong.

I started off writing soft-core sex novels. I wrote under various names, low ceilings and economic duress, and I went on doing this for a long time.

At the beginning, this was a fine training ground for me. Each book was a challenge of one sort or another. I learned a lot about writing and got paid a living wage while I was at it. I had fun, too, and I satisfied the urge to see my work (if not my name) in print.

In the course of time, I ceased to benefit much from what I was writing. There was no challenge left in the field for me, and I wasn't having any fun with it. It had turned into a job, and not a very good one, and I didn't know how to get free of it. I was utterly without fear of what I was writing. I wanted to write something better and more challenging, but I was profoundly afraid to give up the sure sales and the easy money and try writing something I might not be able to bring off.

I didn't let myself know I was afraid of this. I stifled the fear at the source and told myself instead that I didn't have any good ideas for a better book, or that I would be ready to do something decent in a while.

I'm overstating this—I always made intermittent attempts at writing better books, and I didn't spend eternity writing dirty books, just a year or two longer than might have been best for me. It's easy now to see that it was fear that kept me there, and that the absence of fear about what I was writing was the first sign that it was time to write something else.

Fear of Flopping

A friend of mine was in a class once. The participants were invited to sharpen their leadership skills by taking turns leading the class. My friend wanted to take his turn, but he was afraid, and he let the chance go by.

That night, annoyed with himself, he sat down and made a list of all the things he had wanted to do in his life that he had missed out on because of fear. And he decided then and there that fear would never again stop him from doing something he really wanted to do.

That decision changed his life. He hasn't taken up hang-gliding or burglary, or become addicted to risk-taking for the thrill of it, but he goes ahead and does the things he really wants to do whether he's afraid of them or not. One of his fears is fear of failure, and not everything he does is an unqualified success, but so what?

You have to know what your fears are to face them and overcome them. It's not the dimension of the risk that determines the bravery of the act. The person who jumps out of an airplane or plays a game of Russian roulette may simply be more afraid of appearing a coward than of the direct consequences of the act. It might be an act of courage to give up the secure job that keeps you from writing fulltime. It might be ill-advised, and not what you want to do in the first place. The commendably courageous act varies with the individual and with circumstances.

And that's enough about fear, because I'm afraid we're out of time. If you'll pass your homework to the front of the room, and—yes, Arnold?

I didn't do the assignment, sir. It held no challenge for me.

Then I don't see how I can give you a passing grade, Arnold.

That's what I was afraid of, sir.

• 26 •

Character Studies
September 1984

Chekhov wrote somewhere that the writer should know everything about his characters—their net worth, their shoe size, their medical history, and so on. It doesn't matter that none of this data may be passed along to the reader. The writer knows it, and hence perceives the character more completely, and thus writes out of a fuller sense of the person.

This would seem sound enough. There is a school of thought that contends a drawer in an onstage desk, though it remains unopened throughout the play, ought to be fitted out with the appropriate contents, so the company will perform more realistically for this note of realism. I don't know if this is true, and suspect most actors are far more influenced by other factors than by the contents of unopened drawers, but I get the point.

But how do we become so intimately acquainted with our characters? What can we do to make them real for us, so that we will be more capable of making them real for our readers?

One time-honored method consists of writing about the character in one form or another prior to using him or her in fiction. You might jot down notes about the character, all at once or over a period of time. The notebooks of prominent writers commonly disclose innumerable entries of this sort, ranging from a sentence to a few hundred words. Somerset Maugham's *A Writer's Notebook* is stuffed with such material, and one cannot always tell whether the subject of an entry is a person of Maugham's acquaintance, someone he's heard about, a fabrication, or a combination of fact and invention.

Another technique consists of formally developing sketches of principal characters before starting a first draft, but after an outline has provided you with their bare bones. A page or so about each character, to which you may or may not ever refer again, can deepen the level of intimacy between them and you.

I did something of this sort when I first set out to write a series of books about Matthew Scudder, my ex-cop turned unlicensed private eye. I've reported before that Scudder was originally conceived as a series character, and I had special reason to prepare a detailed sketch of him, as I sold the series to Dell on the basis of the lead character, not the specific plots of the initial three books.

I don't have my notes, but I must have written a couple hundred words about Scudder—how he'd been a tough cop with an elastic code of ethics, how he'd killed a child with a stray bullet while foiling a holdup, how that incident had somehow led him to leave the police department and his wife and children, landing in a 57th Street hotel and settling in for some years of hard drinking. I remember noting that he accepted jobs grudgingly, that he set fees arbitrarily, that he preferred to work for clients he disliked. I had his fondness for churches in there, and his curious habit of tithing. I noted that he didn't know why he tithed, and that he did indeed do a lot of things without knowing why.

Around this time, I recall sitting up one night with a couple of writer friends and telling them what I knew about Scudder. After I'd been babbling for a while, one of them looked at me in awe. "You sound," he said, "as though you're describing a real person."

Well, of course.

Because I knew Scudder so well—and let me stress that I was not literally describing a real person, that he was entirely a fabricated character, although a keen-eyed observer would not have had too much difficulty discerning similarities between his life and my own—because I knew him as well as I did, it was very easy for me to see the world through his eyes and write effectively from his point of view. Because I further had a particular affinity for him, I was able to write five books and three novelettes about him and to let him grow in each book, so that (I think) he improved significantly with age.

In contrast, I knew next to nothing about Bernie Rhodenbarr when I sat down to write *Burglars Can't Be Choosers*. I sat down and started typing, and Bernie took shape on the very first page, breezing past a doorman with a Bloomingdale's shopping bag in his hand. I hadn't even known the book was going to be light and sophisticated until Bernie's patter sent it in that direction.

As a result, Bernie took some time defining himself, although his essential character has probably stayed pretty much the same. He got the bookstore and the lesbian sidekick in the third book, took up jogging at the end of the fourth. And, more fundamentally, he became less hapless and rather more forceful as the series progressed.

In the most recent book, *The Burglar Who Painted Like Mondrian*, there's a scene a few chapters from the end in which Bernie, compelled to sneak for the fourth or fifth time into a high-security building, gives up in despair and ducks into a bar around the corner. He sets out to get drunk and gets picked up by a woman who turns out to live in the building in question—at which point he struggles to get sober enough to go home with her with larcenous (or do I mean burglarous?) intent.

The woman absolutely took shape on the page. I didn't know anything about her in advance—in fact I didn't know that was how Bernie was going to get into the building, not until a chapter or two before it happened. I just took Bernie into the bar and there she was, supplying her own dialogue and doing a good job of it. Chekhov notwithstanding, I didn't know anything about her on a conscious level before I wrote the scene, and afterward all I knew was whatever got on the page. Not her shoe size, nor her medical history, though for Bernie's sake I hope the latter's fairly clean.

Somehow, though, I must have known her. Because she came to life nicely in that scene.

This past spring I began conducting a 12-week workshop in mystery writing under the auspices of Mystery Writers of America. Unlike most classes and workshops, there's no reading aloud of student work, a process I've always found insupportably tedious for all concerned. We read each other's work on our own time and criticize it at leisure. Thus we have to find other processes to keep amused during the two hours of class time.

At this evening's class (yes, I'm writing this in the middle of the night) I initiated the following process: Each student selected a character he or she had written about, was writing about, or planned to write about sometime. Then we took turns. A student would talk about a character for a few minutes, and then we would go around the room, each of us asking a question about the character.

"The only unacceptable response," I explained, "is 'I don't know.' This is fiction. Make up something, and do it without elaborate thought. There are no points deducted for inconsistency. Just let it happen."

It turned out to be a lot of fun. (It was fun for me, and that's my chief criterion when I'm teaching. And when I'm writing, come to think of it. *If it's fun to write, it's fun to read* is a good working principle.) I think much of the fun derived from the fact that it was a process of discovery, for the questioners and for the questionee.

One of my students knows a tremendous amount about her characters before she starts writing. She selected not the lead character from her novel-in-progress—I'd have expected her to know that character in detail, having read a comprehensive character sketch she'd done—but a character from a short story she'd just begun working on. Seven of us asked her three questions each, ranging from specifics about her character's romantic life to the nature of her tennis game, and almost every answer came from data already assembled; the writer had already thought it all out, and had assembled more information than would ever appear in the short story. The drawers of her onstage desk were crammed full.

Another writer used a character he'd sketched hazily in his notebook, the projected lead character for a largely undefined novel. His character took shape in the course of our questioning.

I think the process worked as well as it did because it stretched the creative imaginations of all of us, questioners and questionees alike. I don't know how it will change my students' relationships with their characters—I suppose I'll find out next week. But I suspect it enlarged our understanding of what characterization is all about.

Wanna play?

OK. Pick a character, one you've written about to one extent or another. Now take a pencil and paper and answer these questions about him:

What does he like for breakfast?
What's his astrological sign?
What did his father do?
What's the single most shameful thing he ever did?
What kind of car does he drive?
Is he faithful to his wife?
What does he wear on his day off?
How much money did he earn last year?

Afterward, one of my students asked if there was any way you could work the process on your own. In a sense, you've just done it—but in another sense you haven't; you've had me playing the role of interlocutor.

I told her that you couldn't really do it on your own or you'd just be doing a character sketch in another form. What made the process work was that you had someone else to ask you the questions you wouldn't think of on your own, and thus to stimulate your creative ability. "But the process would work fine one-on-one," I said, "and the person you do it with wouldn't have to be a writer. Anyone could do it with you."

The spontaneous nature of the process probably has something to do with its success. One has to supply an answer quickly, before the censoring mechanism can think the whole subject to death. Come to think of it, a similar sort of time pressure attended the birth of the process; I thought of it on the way to the class, and will be using it in classes and at seminars, I suspect, for years to come.

Then I came home, flushed with enthusiasm, only to remember that I have a column due in a couple of days. And wouldn't you know it? Necessity went and mothered another invention, and here we are.

Neat, isn't it?

The Guts of the Fiction Writer
Basics of Fiction

IT TAKES GUTS TO BE A FICTION WRITER — GUTS TO CONSTRUCT A WEB OF CHARACTERS AND PLOTS AND THEMES FROM DEEP INSIDE OURSELVES FOR ALL THE WORLD TO SEE.

If the writer of fiction has need of a totem animal, I submit that he might do worse than consider the spider. The humble arachnid spins his web out of his own guts, makes of it a work of art and a masterpiece of engineering, rests comfortably within its confines, and uses it to snare his dinner.

Even as you and I.

For where else does fiction originate? It comes from deep within, and we do not merely spew it forth. No, we construct it with art and with craft. And, if we have done our work well, it shelters and feeds us.

I don't know if others have remarked on the spider as metaphor for the writer. I should be surprised if they haven't; the image is a fairly obvious one, and first struck me over 25 years ago, when I was a second-year college student writing poetry that was every bit as sophomoric as I. Just the other day I unearthed an Elizabethan sonnet of mine based on the spider-writer image, and I can't wait to earth it again. The final couplet

> *Letters are digits and a brain a lever,*
> *Intestines thought-reels that give line forever*

strikes me as the sort of thing Alexander Pope might have done if he'd had no talent.

I thought of the spider—if not yet the sonnet—a couple of months ago when *WD*'s editor first proposed a piece on what it takes to write fiction, and suggested its present title. "You could deal with 'guts' in both senses of the word," he suggested. "The inner workings of a fiction writer and the courage and integrity necessary to make a go of it."

All I could think of was that spider.

My first thought was to be a writer. I didn't know what sort of writer I'd be and I don't recall caring much one way or the other. I was 15, an English teacher had found something promising in some composition I'd written, and writing suddenly struck me as something that I could do and something that was worth doing. My immediate desire was to *be* a writer. I didn't know—or much care—what I'd write or what sort of writer I'd be.

More recently I've had occasion to take a long look backward at my early years. I have come to believe that most of us tend to be shaped in large measure by ideas we pick up about ourselves and the universe at birth or not long thereafter. One notion I seem to have acquired early on was that it was not appropriate for me to gain attention by making a fuss or creating a lot of noise.

I've been told that I didn't cry in infancy, that when I did once howl for 20 minutes my parents called the doctor. "All babies cry," the poor man advised them. "Well, I know that," my mother said, "but he never did before."

What a perfect answer writing was for me! I could get attention—indeed, I could seek attention from the entire world. And I could do so in utter silence, and from a great distance. No one would be near me while I did my silent work, and I would be nowhere around when people read what I'd written, and applauded or hissed.

I talked about this at a recent seminar, and most of the people in the room were nodding in recognition and identification. I wouldn't be surprised to learn that many writers—and others in the non-performing arts as well, painters and composers and such—have similar ideas about getting attention, wanting it, even craving it, but deeming it unsafe or unwise or unseemly to be open and loud in the seeking of it.

I suppose all art is a cry for recognition, for acknowledgment, for applause. Even the recluse sheltered by a pen name must be sending the stuff out for a reason. Even the secret writer who keeps his poems and stories in a locked trunk has a reason for writing them down instead of keeping them locked in the confines of his own mind. Everything I write cries out something along the lines of *Look at me! See how good I am! See how clever / thoughtful / informed / sensitive / decent / honest / brave I am! For God's sake look at me!*

The cry of the fiction writer is probably a little different from that of the reporter. *Look how knowledgeable I am*, the journalist calls out. *See how much I know, and how good I am at telling it to you.*

The fictioneer carries a somewhat different message. *This is who I am*, he announces, *but it's not really who I really am. I want to show you the real me. But I'm not sure you'll like the real me, so I'm just telling you a story. It's a nice story, isn't it?*

Most of the fiction writers I know have a lot of ambivalence in the area of letting people know who they are. On the one hand, we want to be known. We have a very real need to show ourselves to others. On the other hand, we don't think it's safe. We've got the bone-deep conviction that, if people know who we really are, they'll hurt or reject us.

This is me, we cry out. *But not really!*

In a sense, my own growth as a writer has been largely a matter of becoming increasingly willing and able to reveal myself in my work. This is not to say that I consciously withheld myself from the reader in my earlier work. It's more that I didn't know how to use my own self in my writing. Even when I used characters whose experiences and circumstances ran parallel to my own, I kept myself somehow out of my own work.

Remember the child's rhyme?

> I put my whole self in
> I take my whole self out
> I give my whole self a shake shake shake
> And turn myself about

Isn't that precisely what fiction writers do all the time? We put our whole self into our work, then take our whole self out, shake the box, and turn ourselves around.

With time, as I continued to write and continued to grow as a writer, I somehow became able to put more of myself into my characters. This is not to say that they are me or that I am them. Indeed, all of my characters are somehow aspects of myself, but with time they have held more of me as I have learned—and dared—to show more of myself.

The first Evan Tanner novel, *The Thief Who Couldn't Sleep*, was a big step forward for me. The book was hardly autobiographical. If Tanner was based on anyone, he was based on a couple of friends of mine. But Tanner's eyes became a pair of windows on the world for me, and I lived in his skin as I had not done in any previous creation.

In the mid-'60s I was for a period of a year or two a compulsive client of Times Square streetwalkers. I did not understand my own behavior, and I don't know that I examined it too closely at the time. But I did use it as the basis for a novel, *After the First Death*, and that constituted an unprecedented show of guts for this particular fictioneer, and in both senses of the word. By letting Alex Penn act out my own compulsions in print, I spun a work out of my own innards and showed uncharacteristic courage in the process.

But not all that much courage, it seems to me now, and not all that much of my inner self, either. I read the book now, and although I like it well enough as a piece of writing, I am struck by how differently I would handle the same material if I had it to do over. I'd let a lot more of my own self into Penn, I'd be rather more honest about the nature of his fears and longings.

This is not to say that I regret the way I wrote *After the First Death*, or that I would welcome the chance to write it again. Just as it has taken me time and practice to learn the techniques of writing, so it has taken time and practice to learn courage and self-revelation.

Sometimes one is able to trace an author's progress within the evolution of a single character. Ross Macdonald's Lew Archer comes immediately to mind. In the first few books, Archer was a sort of kid brother to Raymond Chandler's Philip Marlowe, a wise-cracking cynic whose origins in the work of other writers were not hard to detect.

As Macdonald went on writing, something happened to Archer. The voyages of self-discovery forced upon the author found expression in his creation. More and more of Macdonald got funneled into Lew Archer, and the fictional detective became increasingly his own man and less and less the heir of Spade and Marlowe.

I look for similar metamorphoses in my own series characters and am unable to see them. I wrote seven books about Tanner, and it seems to me that he's not much different in the last one, but then those books were all written in the space of a few years, not over several decades like the Lew Archer books. Still, I went through changes during those years; you'd think Tanner would show some of those changes, and perhaps he does to an eye other than my own.

Bernie Rhodenbarr changed some in the course of the five books thus far written about him. Or perhaps it's more that his life filled out with the addition of a bookstore for him to operate and a best friend to hang out with. Matthew Scudder has undergone great changes in the course of five books, but in his case it seems to me more a matter of the books constituting a single long novel, in the course of which Scudder is affected by what he undergoes. He's changed by the time *Eight Million Ways to Die* is over, not because I'm writing about a different person, but because he's been altered by what he has experienced.

*   *   *

I just read through the last paragraph, then looked over the ones immediately preceding it, and wondered at the way I was discussing fictional characters as if they were real.

And I thought of something a friend of mine, herself a novelist, once said about fiction writers in general.

"Anyone who spends the most meaningful hours of the day in the exclusive company of other people who do not exist, and who are indeed the product of his or her own imagination," she said, "is apt to be a little weird."

Well, I can't argue with that.

A major portion of my writing seminars center on how negative ideas held consciously or unconsciously in the mind work to sabotage one's writing success. I talk about the manner in which these beliefs get in one's way, and how to unearth them and reverse them, primarily by working with written affirmations.

Each seminar participant selects the one negative thought that seems to be the most basic impediment to his or her own success and then creates a positive affirmation to reverse it. We use a couple of processes to help our minds internalize this new positive thought.

At a recent seminar, one woman's complaint was that she had trouble concentrating on her fiction, that the more meaningful a piece of writing was to her, the less likely she was to complete it. In the course of the self-analysis process, it became clear that the negative thought at the bottom of all this was that it was not safe for her to reveal herself to others, that people would not like her if they really knew her.

This woman wrote out several affirmations for herself and shared them with the rest of us. The one she was reluctant to read at first was one which resonated the strongest. It was "To know me is to love me."

I told her I thought that was the one she should work with. "I know it is," she said, a little grudgingly. "I got a chill up the back of my neck when I said it."

That section of the seminar continues with a paired process, in which one person says his new affirmation over and over to his partner, who then says it back to him repeatedly.

When her partner said to her, over and over, "Jan, to know you is to love you." Jan couldn't stop crying.

> It's safe to let people know who I am.
> The less I keep to myself, the more I have to give.
> The more I reveal myself, the safer I am.
> The more I share with others, the more I have for myself.
> To know me is to love me.

These are all powerful affirmations, and all of them address themselves to the negative thought that stood in Jan's way—and that blocks a great many of us fictioneers. One can create infinite variations on this theme, and can use any or all of them to one's profit.

We all have a desire to reveal ourselves in our work, whether we're writing moral fables about kittens and bunny rabbits or shoot-'em-up adventure yarns or romance novels. And we all have some difficulty putting ourselves completely into our work, even those of us who gush autobiographically in the manner of Thomas Wolfe and Earl Thompson.

The more we internalize the notion that it's safe and desirable to reveal ourselves in our work, the more successfully we'll be able to do so.

Am I suggesting that every fiction writer is no more than a frustrated autobiographer? That if Edgar Rice Burroughs had been less neurotic he'd have written his own story instead of Tarzan's?

No, of course not. The fictioneer is concerned with revealing himself and with gaining applause through this revelation, but these are not his sole concerns.

He is also concerned with creation.

"If a poet is anybody," wrote E.E. Cummings in his introduction to *Is 5*, "he is somebody to whom things made matter very little—somebody who is obsessed by Making. Like all obsessions, the Making obsession has disadvantages; for instance, my only interest in making money would be to make it. Fortunately, however, I should prefer to make almost anything else, including locomotives and roses. It is with roses and locomotives (not to mention acrobats Spring electricity Coney Island the 4th of July the eyes of mice and Niagara Falls) that my 'poems' are competing.

"They are also competing with each other, with elephants, and with El Greco."

The fictioneer is obsessed with making up stories. "Once upon a time," he says, and we are off. He may be telling of something that actually happened to him or someone he knows. He may be spinning a plot wholly out of his imagination and setting it in a locale he never visited outside of dreams.

It doesn't matter. It's all very much the same thing. He is fabricating a world out of thin air and inviting you to enter it. "This is all make-believe," he tells you in advance, "but I want you to believe it while you're in it."

And so we do. We enter into a compact with him, putting our skepticism on Hold the moment we hear the words *Once upon a time*. Or *Call me Ishmael*, or *Through the fence, between the curling flower spaces, I could see them hitting*. Or *The day broke gray and dull. The clouds hung heavily, and there was a rawness in the air that suggested snow*. Or *Alice was beginning to get very tired of sitting by her sister on the bank and of having nothing to do*.

We suspend our disbelief. We enter this world of the fictioneer's making even though we are well aware of its unreality.

"My husband thinks he's a chicken," said the woman in the old joke, "but I don't know as I want you to cure him, Doctor. Because we get a good price for the eggs."

"All right," we say. "I believe in Madame Bovary, and Mack Bolan, and Rebecca of Sunnybrook Farm. Why not? I can use the eggs."

Truth is stranger than fiction.

Heard that before, have you? Well, then, look at the converse.

Fiction is more plausible than truth.

Because it has to be. The people who write for the newspapers have it a whole lot easier than those of us who turn out novels and short stories. All they have to do is tell the story. It doesn't have to be believable and it doesn't have to make sense. They're dealing with facts, and they can be smug about it.

"This is what happened," they say, and we can like it or lump it.

Now there was a wire service story a while back about a child named Dewey McCall whose father ran over him with a huge piece of earth-moving equipment, a backhoe or something along those massive lines. The kid wound up squashed under the tread of this thing with nothing but hard-packed earth under him. When the father backed the machinery off of the kid, Dewey was flat as a flounder and, according to an eyewitness, "his little eyes were bulging."

Relax. I am not telling you a horror story. Dewey turned out on examination not to have sustained any serious injury whatsoever. He regained his original shape like a rubber doll trod underfoot, and the only visible evidence of his travails were some treadmarks on his little chest. A few tons of heavy machinery parked on top of him for a few minutes there and he didn't even wind up with a nosebleed.

How'd you like to try to get away with that in fiction?

Oh, you could do it. If you were writing fantasy or science fiction in which you postulated that Dewey was immortal, or under some sort of mystical protection, your readers would readily accept his invulnerability to death by squashing. Heroes from Achilles to Superman have laid claim to our voluntary suspension of disbelief.

You could even get by with it as an inexplicable miracle, if you placed it in the right kind of context. Suppose you're writing the story of a man, and in the first chapter the man's son goes through what Dewey went through, and the father is forever after affected by what has happened. You could get away with that.

But as a general thing, you couldn't just toss off a miracle on this scale and expect the reader to buy it. Miracles and major implausibilities aside, you can't have inconsistent behavior and random chance and coincidence play a major role in fiction without infuriating the reader. We demand a balance in fiction, an inner logic, which we are not always able to detect in life itself.

Years ago I wrote sexually oriented nonfiction under a pen name. What I did, essentially, was fabricate case histories with the aim of informing the reader in a particular area of human sexual behavior—and, to be sure, of appealing to his prurient interests in the process.

It was a pleasure to write this stuff. The stories were supposed to be true, and they thus were not under the constraints imposed upon fiction. The human lives of which I was writing could take abrupt and unlikely turns. They could have all manner of loose ends and could bear no end of inconsistencies. I had in my arsenal the journalist's ultimate weapon of factuality, against which there is no defense. "You have to believe this," I was in effect saying, "because it happens to be the truth, and I don't care if it makes sense and comes out even. Facts are facts."

Oh dear. Interestingly enough, before I was done writing these books they had begun to evolve into a sort of legitimacy. Readers wrote to me, I engaged in correspondence and conducted interviews, and ultimately a majority of my case histories were indeed based on fact. And it was at that point that I began to get occasional criticism from my editors. In one book, I recall, one case history out of a dozen was drawn from a real interview. It was specifically singled out by my publisher as unconvincing, and less realistic than its fellows.

* * *

Sometimes I think it takes guts to write fiction. And other times I think what it really takes is arrogance.

Consider the colossal effrontery of the fictioneer. He sits down at his desk and makes up a story, assuming that the product of his own imagination will keep other people, total strangers to him, interested and enthralled. He invents characters and trusts that these strangers will care mightily what happens to these made-up people.

The flip side of all this arrogance is anxiety and insecurity. Why should anyone waste his time reading my made-up stories? Why should people care what happens to my characters? And where do I get off deciding what happens next? How do I know what my characters think / feel / believe? What entitles me to decide how their fabricated lives will turn out?

It helps if I can learn to operate less on arrogance and more on humility. Most of us find out in the course of time that we've got a lot to be humble about. For all that it seems to demand arrogance in advance, the profession of fiction-writing tends to constitute a humbling experience in the long run.

What has served most to humble me over the years has been the increasing realization that my work has so often succeeded not because of me but in spite of me, that it has been most effective when I've taken my own hands off the wheel and let some other driver steer the car. In my very best books, it has sometimes seemed as though I've had precious little to do with the writing, as though the books have largely written themselves. In all of my writing, the most effective dialogue has been that which my characters supplied themselves; I've sat at the typewriter feeling rather like a courtroom stenographer, jotting down lines that other voices have shouted or whispered deep within my mind. I do my best work when I feel least like its source and most like its channel.

Of course, I impose a certain conscious control upon what I write. I make sure that it's in grammatical form, that there's a structure and a logic to it, that the spider's web is geometrically sound. But the more I let go of trying to figure things out and make them happen, and the more I allow myself to tap into some universal source I don't presume to understand, the better my work turns out.

Mozart said musical composition was the easiest thing in the world. All he had to do, he explained, was take the trouble to write down the music he heard in his head.

I find my thoughts returning to the spider. "The humble arachnid," as I called the creature in the first paragraph.

The word comes from mythology. Ovid tells us that Arachne was a mortal who excelled all other maidens in weaving. Both her finished work and her own grace and skill at the loom brought her admiration. Arrogant as any writer, Arachne challenged the goddess Athena to compete with her. Athena accepted the challenge.

In her tapestry, the goddess wove the stories of those who had dared to compete with the gods and had been punished for their pains. Arachne, undaunted, wove into her web the weaknesses and foibles of the gods themselves. Then, in Jessie M. Tatlock's retelling of the myth:

> *Athena herself could not but wonder at the maiden's skill, but her arrogance aroused her resentment. She struck the delicate web with her shuttle, and it crumbled into bits; then she touched Arachne's forehead. A sense of her impiety rushed over the girl; she could not endure it, and hanged herself with a skein of her own silk. But Athena did not wish that so skillful a worker should die; she cut the skein and, sprinkling upon her the juice of aconite, transformed the maiden into a spider, that through all ages she might continue to spin her matchless webs.*

Do you suppose there's a lesson there? I have a hunch there might be. Just a gut feeling, you could call it.

Length Wise

January 1985

Remember Procrustes?

Oh, sure you do. He was that chap of old with a most remarkable bed. So proud of it was he that any traveler who put up at his abode had to sleep in it. If the sojourner was too short for the bed, Procrustes had him stretched. If he was too tall, Procrustes had him shortened with an ax. Thus the bed fit everyone, because everyone was made to fit the bed. I bring this up because—yes, Rachel?

But that's terrible, sir.

Uh—

People would be killed, sir! Innocent people!

Rachel—

Is something being done about this man? Attention must be paid, sir. Perhaps a protest march would help.

Rachel, it's a myth.

A myth, sir?

A myth. A story. Fiction. Somebody made the whole thing up. And I brought it up today because it struck me that many of us find ourselves treating our stories as Procrustes treated his guests, stretching or shortening them to fit the requirements of the marketplace.

How long should a piece of fiction be? A chapter in a novel, I seem to recall having written, ought to be long enough to reach from the preceding chapter to the next one. Similarly, a short story or novel ought to be long enough to extend from the first word to the last. Lincoln said much the same thing of legs—i.e., that they ought to be long enough to reach the ground.

Is that all there is to it? I think not, especially in view of my experiences writing *When the Sacred Gin Mill Closes*, a detective novel which, publishing schedules being what they are, ought to streak like a comet across the literary sky just about the time this column finds its way into print.

When the Sacred Gin Mill Closes had its origin in early '84. I had promised Robert Randisi, guiding spirit of the Private Eye Writers of America, that I would provide a short story about my hard-drinking ex-cop, Matthew Scudder, for a PWA anthology he was editing. When it came time to write the story, I sat down and did so with no regard whatsoever to length. I knew Bob would publish it irrespective of its length as long as it was a good story.

The story ran somewhere around 8,000 words, which is not a particularly handy length from a marketing standpoint; it's longer than most magazines want short stories to be, and not really long enough to be a novelette. It was, however, a decent length for that particular story. There was plenty of plot and incident to carry the word count, and yet there was room for mood and character development.

My wife Lynne liked the story so much she got me to show it to my agent, and he liked it enough to send it to Alice Turner at *Playboy*, and she liked it enough to buy it and print it prior to its inclusion in *The Eyes Have It*, the PWA anthology. If I'd set out with the intention of writing a story for *Playboy*, I would not have turned out something 8,000 words long. I probably would have come in at about half that length, and I rather expected Alice to cut the story substantially after she bought it. (As it turned out, I don't think she cut more than a hundred words or so.)

What does all this mean? That stories have to find their own length, and consideration of market requirements cuts creativity off at the knees?

Not exactly. Because I'm not done with the story yet.

Around Christmas of '84, I was getting ready to end a year-long sabbatical from fiction writing. (The only fiction I'd written all year was the

Playboy story, which I'd called "By the Dawn's Early Light.") I'd had it in mind to write a book about my burglar character, Bernie Rhodenbarr, but an idea for such a book wouldn't come into focus. I knew I wasn't going to write a sixth book about Matthew Scudder; I'd tried several times and gotten nowhere, and I wasn't going to make that mistake again.

Well, you never know, do you? As the new year approached, I found myself thinking more and more of Scudder and wanting to write a book about him. And it struck me that I already had a plot to work with. I could expand "By the Dawn's Early Light" to novel length. All I had to do was turn each word into ten words and I'd have a proper 80,000-word novel.

It's not terribly difficult to puff up or trim down a story. Around the time that I was starting work on my book, I had the job of writing an introduction to *The Case of the Dancing Sandwiches*, by the late Fredric Brown. Brown had originally written the story as a novella, which was published as a mini-paperback; some years later he set about doubling its length and changing the locale from New York to Phoenix, with the aim of book publication; he died with the expanded version uncompleted, and both versions were now being made available to collectors. Putting two words where one was merely requires that you run your scenes a little longer, that you describe settings in greater detail, that you take time and space to tell the reader a little more about your characters. If you don't do this very well, the result will be choppy and overblown; if you're good at it, no one will suspect the work had ever been shorter.

The task I was facing was rather different. While the basic plot of the short story, in which Scudder is hired by a saloon acquaintance to compile evidence against the men who burglarized his house and murdered his wife, might be sufficient to carry a novel, I felt it wasn't strong enough by itself. I decided to let Scudder work on three different cases at once, giving the story three plot lines that worked together while remaining distinct from one another.

Scenes sketched in a sentence or two in the short story became fully developed in the novel. Characters were more fully limned, settings more elaborately detailed. Scudder himself had time for more rumination.

In the story, I had simply announced that "all of this happened a long time ago." In the novel, I specifically set the action in the summer of '75 and worked to re-create that time. The bar scene was background to the story; in the novel, it became almost a character itself, tying the several threads of the story together.

When I started out, I wondered if I would be able to turn 8,000 words into 250 pages. *When the Sacred Gin Mill Closes* wound up running not 250 but 350 pages in manuscript, and I don't think there's a sentence in there that's present merely to pad things out. I think it's the best book I've written.

Why am I telling you all this?

Perhaps to suggest the difficulty in stating how long a particular story ought to be, "By the Dawn's Early Light" was the right length when it was written, and it was still the right length when it had been expanded into a full-length novel. I'm sure that a condensed version of the short story could also have been the right length. If, when I sat down to write the original story, I'd known that Randisi didn't want to look at anything over 4,000 words, I'm sure I would have come in at that length, and I suspect the story would have worked.

A while back I got a letter from a reader bemoaning the fact that she couldn't sell a story she had written. It was a generally unmarketable length—18,000 words, something like that—and she insisted in her letter to me that it could not have been longer or shorter than that. Well, I doubt it. I think there are any number of ideal lengths for the development of a fictional idea, and it is up to us to choose the length that suits us. This choice may be predicated wholly on aesthetic considerations, in which case we may wind up writing an 18,000-worder now and then. It may be primarily commercial—we know that one-page short-shorts for *American Grommet* run a thousand words, and our story is thus going to be no shorter than nine hundred, no longer than eleven hundred.

Most of the time our choice takes both elements into consideration. When I was writing the fifth Scudder book, *Eight Million Ways to Die*, I was a little concerned that the book was running so long. It wound up 450 pages in manuscript, and that's about twice the length of the typical first-person private eye novel. I felt it needed the extra length to best develop the book's several themes, so I went ahead in the hope readers would agree with me. Still, I was sustained by the knowledge that 450 pages was not an *impossible* length for such a book. If I'd felt that the book needed 700 pages, my awareness of commercial realities probably would have led me to overrule that feeling.

Cold Cuts

How do you know how to make something come out a certain length? Suppose you have a certain story to tell, and you want to tell it in a certain number of words. How, by other than Procrustean means, do you get it to come out right?

You learn, and you learn by doing. After you've written a certain number of 4,000-word stories, you get the sense of what a 4,000-word story is. Same thing with longer fiction.

When you drive a particular route, after the first time or two you don't have to use a road map. And, later on, you find that you no longer have to pay conscious attention to landmarks. There comes a time when you assure people that you could drive it in your sleep.

You learn, too, by reading. When you immerse yourself in the kind of fiction you want to write, when you read all the fiction of that sort you can find, good and bad alike, you learn on a subconscious level what works and doesn't work in that kind of story. Story length is just one of the aspects your subconscious learns to keep track of.

Understand, too, that your stories don't have to come out the right length the first time you write them. Quite a few writers almost invariably write long, cutting substantially when they revise. Robert Ludlum's books typically are half again as long in their first draft as in their final version; Sidney Sheldon deliberately writes long, feeling that he produces a richer book by putting everything in and cutting back later.

Other writers do just the opposite. Richard S. Prather starts with an outline, expands that to a detailed chapter outline, expands that to a 30,000-word draft, and finally doubles the book's length in the rewrite. Others do a similar job of turning a spare first draft into a full final draft. The first draft is just plot and incident, which they can handle best by not worrying about other considerations while writing it; the second time around, they can allow themselves to fill in description and characterization and mood.

For my own part, nonfiction is more a Procrustean bed for me than fiction is. My occasional book reviews for *The Washington Post* are supposed to be 750 words long, although I don't suppose the government would fall if they were a little longer or shorter than that. However, they always seem to come in at the appointed length without much conscious attention on my part.

My *WD* columns are supposed to run around 1,750 words, and I've been doing them for so long that it's no strain for me to come in at the right length, I could drive this road in my sleep. And, should I find myself one month with more or less to say, I'm fortunately blessed with an editor who is a far better host than Procrustes. Accommodating chap that he is, I can always count on him, knowing that he would never

Spilling the Beans
February 1985

Once upon a time, many long years ago, when John F. Kennedy was in the White House and I was in the seventh grade, a friend of mine showed me the first chapter of what he hoped would become a novel. In that chapter, a chap named Parker was walking across the George Washington Bridge from New Jersey to New York. A fellow stopped his car and offered him a lift. Parker told him to go to hell and went on walking.

Hostile fellow, Parker.

I asked my friend why Parker was so testy. While I was at it, I asked him why Parker was walking across the bridge, and what he would do when, like the legendary chicken, he Got To The Other Side.

"I don't know," my friend said. "I figure I'll write the book in order to find out."

He went on to find out a great deal about Parker. My friend, whose name was Donald E. Westlake (and still is, come to think of it), went on in the course of time to write 20 books about Parker, all of them published under the name Richard Stark and all of them returning to print now. I sometimes think Don had a great advantage in knowing so little about his lead character when he set out to write that first book. Many of us know altogether too much.

Sir, you've told us a writer can't know too much about his characters.

I have?

You've quoted Chekhov to that effect.

Hmmm. So I have, Rachel.

You said, sir, or maybe it was Chekhov—

People often confuse the two of us.

—that a writer should know everything about his characters, including those things he doesn't plan on disclosing to the reader.

Ah. Thank you, Rachel. There, I think, is the heart of the matter. Many of us may not *know* too much about our characters, but we tell the reader altogether too much. Don, blissfully ignorant of Parker's nature and origins, couldn't overburden the reader with data. He had an intuitive sense of who Parker was, enough to render him as a living character, but he didn't have a lot of hard facts on hand.

Many of us have more elaborate dossiers compiled on our lead characters by the time we start writing about them. Often we'll dish out this material like over-generous chefs, drowning entrées in a sea of sauce. No sooner has the hero shuffled onstage than the reader is told virtually everything the author knows about him.

This is rarely necessary. You don't have to read a biography of Beethoven before you listen to the Fifth Symphony. Indeed, you'll be more likely to read the man's life with interest *after* having become familiar with his music.

Similarly, you don't have to know a great deal about a character before seeing him involved in a dramatic situation. After you've watched him in action, then you'll be more receptive to being made acquainted with some of the facts of his life.

It seems to me that writers who use first-person narration are most apt to tell us too much too soon. One of the dangers of the first-person mode, and one of the reasons writing teachers traditionally inveigh against its use, is the difficulty the new writer often has in getting his lead character to keep his trap shut. With the best will in the world, no end of writers allow their presumably charming narrators to turn into garrulous ear-bending bores.

Have you ever known anyone who seemed to operate on the premise that every thought had to be voiced, that unspoken ideas might otherwise build up and explode the cranium? I haven't known many such folk (and

I'd like to keep it that way) but I keep running into them in fiction. Writers who are, if anything, rather guarded in their own conversation turn around and create characters who gush all over the place. It's almost as if they believe they're not playing fair with the reader if they let a character think or do anything and keep it to himself.

This does seem to be a fault of the new writer, and one which is readily outgrown in most cases. We soon learn a sort of narrative economy. Perhaps we notice what editors cut out of our work. Perhaps—and this may be especially true with first-person writing—it's in large part a matter of getting it out of our system; after a certain amount of excessive self-expression through the medium of an autobiographical lead character, we begin to tire of the sound of our own voices.

Refried Beans

Even the writer who has outgrown the gusher stage may run into the problem of telling us too much when working with a series character. There's a real dilemma here. The writer must consider two kinds of readers—those who have read earlier volumes in the series and are consequently familiar with the character's past, and those who are encountering the character for the first time. (There's an intermediate class as well, consisting of readers who have read earlier books but need to have their memories gently refreshed.)

This can be tricky. By the time you've written half a dozen books about a character, you've learned a lot about him and lived through a lot with him. So have those faithful readers who've been with you from the beginning. Obviously you can't dish up all of this for the first-time reader, but how and where do you draw the line?

In my own novels about ex-cop Matthew Scudder, the one scrap of background data with which I've always felt the need to acquaint the reader is the particular traumatic incident which triggered Scudder's decision to resign from the police force, walk out on his wife and children, and take up residence in a cheap hotel. Here's how I presented this material in *Time to Murder and Create:*

> *I looked at my coffee and thought about it. A summer night, the heat almost visible in the air, the air conditioning working overtime in the Spectacle, a bar in Washington Heights where a cop got his drinks on the house. I was off duty, except you never really are, and two kids picked that night to hold up the place. They shot the bartender dead on their way out. I chased them into the street, killed one of them, splintered the other one's thigh bone.*
>
> *But one shot was off and took a ricochet that bounced it right into the eye of a seven-year-old girl named Estrellita Rivera. Right in the eye, and through soft tissue and on into the brain.*

One version or another of the Estrellita Rivera bit appears in each of the Scudder novels. In the two most recent books, *A Stab in the Dark* and *Eight Million Ways to Die*, I held the data back, feeding it in a little at a time. *WD*'s Bill Brohaugh noticed this and suggested the theme for this month's column, thinking that my reasons for changing the form of the Estrellita Rivera revelation might make interesting reading.

Indeed they might, if I had a clearer idea of what they were. Perhaps I was simply tired of writing variations of that paragraph. Perhaps Scudder's own progressive journey was making him more guarded and less quick to pick the scabs of his memory. Perhaps I saved the revelation for a later spot in the story because I wanted a particular sort of impact in a particular scene—I think that's very likely what I had in mind in *Stab*.

I don't suppose it matters. Every series writer has to wrestle with his own equivalent of the Estrellita Rivera bit. Ed McBain, who couldn't possibly recap the histories of all his 87th Precinct cops in each book about them, does seem incapable of withholding the explanation of Meyer Meyer's curious name and its purported relationship to his alopecia. And Don Westlake, who started out knowing no more about Parker than his last name and his surly disposition, wound up learning so much about him that each of the first several books spent an increasing amount of time and space acquainting new readers with prior developments, telling why Parker has a new face, why the mob is after him, how he got the mob off his back, and so on. Finally Parker had too much of a history and his creator stopped trying to get it all written down for each new reader. And a good thing, too.

Beans and Berns

Just as you don't need to tell your reader everything you know about your character, or everything he knows about himself, neither do you have to describe and explain everything he sees or does.

In a book where everything is seen through the eyes of a single character, it may seem as though the reader has to be told everything. This would seem to be the case particularly in first-person narratives, where anything pertinent that is not mentioned may seem as if it has been unfairly withheld from the reader. How can I be playing fair if Scudder sees something and doesn't see fit to mention it to the reader at the time?

In my experience, a certain amount of withholding can be perfectly legitimate. I may have Scudder pick up on a clue, for example, and explain what he has found without explaining the mental connections he makes. Or I may have him mention that he goes into an apartment and sifts through a box of papers for 20 minutes, without mentioning until later on what he learned in the process.

In *The Topless Tulip Caper*, my narrator, Chip Harrison, states quite simply that he enters an apartment at a particular time, and in the next sentence announces that he left the apartment at a particular time. A scene later, when he reports to his boss, Leo Haig, we learn what he found in the apartment.

And, in several of my books about burglar Bernie Rhodenbarr, he scurries around in the penultimate chapters, slipping in and out of offices and residences, falsifying evidence and otherwise greasing the wheels of justice. The reader rarely knows just what Bernie's up to and just where he's doing it, but there's enough information to set up the payoff scene later on.

My stories about Martin Ehrengraf, the criminal criminal lawyer, are not in the first person but illustrate the same point. Ehrengraf fakes evidence, frames the innocent, and commits murder to establish his clients' innocence, yet the reader is never told precisely what Ehrengraf has done and never sees Ehrengraf actually doing anything. This is essential, in that the character would be altogether too grim if you ever saw him do what he does.

And I think that covers things, class. If anything, I may have fallen into the trap I warned you against and told you altogether too much. If there are no questions, I think we'll—yes, Arnold?

Did Mr. Westlake ever find out Parker's first name, sir?

He did indeed, although he has not yet chosen to share this information with his readers.

Do you happen to know it, sir?

Uh-huh. But I'm not going to tell you.

Opus 100

May 1985

This may be my hundredth piece for *Writer's Digest*.

Then again, it may not. It's hard to know. I started writing this column eight years and a couple of months ago, but it appeared every other month for the first year, alternating with a column on cartooning. At the same time, I've intermittently published a feature article or interview in addition to my column, and I've had articles in *Writer's Yearbook* and other annual volumes. Ninety-two or ninety-three columns, let us say, plus seven or eight assorted pieces—well, it's certainly *close* to a hundred.

Close enough, I should think, to serve as the excuse for a column's worth of musing and stocktaking. Some thoughts, if you will, on what it has been like to murmur in your ear once a month, what it has meant to me and what I may have learned in the process.

This past September I was in Cincinnati to present the Write for Your Life seminar. I visited the *WD* offices, of course, and one morning I was interviewed by Jean Fredette for *Fiction Writer's Market*. As a prelude to our session, she mentioned the approximate number of columns I'd done for the magazine, plus my two books on writing. "You realize," she said, "that you've probably written more words about the writing of fiction than anyone else alive."

What an astonishing thought! Could she possibly be right? Let's see, the column probably averages 1,750 words. *Telling Lies for Fun and Profit* (Arbor House) doesn't really increase the total, being a collection of the first four years of columns, but *Writing the Novel: From Plot to Print* (WD

Books) must add another 75,000 words, and—well, any way you look at it, it's been something like a quarter of a million words.

Now, I knew the last eight years had been reasonably productive ones for me. I'd published something like nine novels and two books of short stories. But had I also written a cool quarter of a million words *about* writing?

It would seem that I have. Perhaps someone else somewhere has written more, and if so, more power to him. Or her. The distinction, if that's what it is, is certainly not one I sought.

I swear I never thought it would come to this.

In August of '76, I drove into Cincinnati on my way from Los Angeles to New York. I had already sold an article to *WD*, although it was not to appear in the magazine for a couple of months, and I'd routed myself east through Cincinnati to have lunch with John Brady, then editor of *WD*. I had it in mind to convince him that the magazine could use a regular column on the writing of fiction, and that I was just the person to write it.

At the time I'd had many books published, most of them mystery and suspense novels. I had never taught writing, and the only other writing I'd done *about* writing was a piece on dialogue I'd sold almost 20 years previously to a long-defunct periodical called *Author and Journalist*.

Since then, while my primary career as a writer of fiction has grown in a gratifying fashion, I have found myself with a whole second career as a writer about writing. I took a holiday from book writing in 1984, thinking it would be a restful sort of sabbatical, and wound up working harder than I'd ever worked in my life, creating and presenting a seminar for writers and building it into a whole business. I've traveled all over the country toward this end, to the great profit of the airlines if no one else. I've produced an affirmations tape and gone into the mail-order business to distribute it effectively. I had not the faintest idea that all of this would come to pass when I sat down to lunch with John Brady.

* * *

What effect has all this concern with writing had upon me? Most noticeably, I suppose, it has made me ever so much more conscious—while reading and while writing—of the whole *process* of writing. I've mentioned elsewhere how much writing transforms one as a reader, leading us to read everything that passes before us on two levels, as an innocent reader and as a more knowledgeable writer. We become more aware of another writer's technique, which at once makes us more critical of poor work and more admiring of good work. Even when we are most caught up in a narrative flow, a part of our mind remains detached, observing, taking notes; at the very moment that we are being moved to tears, that portion of the mind notes just *how* we are being moved to tears.

Writing about writing magnifies this process enormously. I read, now, as a reader, as a writer, and as a teacher of writing, and everything I read thus becomes grist for a mill that grinds exceedingly small indeed. A two-line description of a minor character will suddenly give me an idea for a column. I probably get a dozen ideas for a column every month, a dozen at least of what *seem* to be ideas. The idea that's still there when it comes time to sit down and write the column is the one that winds up getting developed, but in the meantime I will have done a great deal of thinking about various aspects of writing.

When I was first writing these columns, I would twice a year get urgent appeals from Cincinnati for a list of my proposed topics for the next six months. At first I furnished such lists, but somewhere along the way I managed to convince Brady that he was asking the impossible. Trying to think of six ideas at once, I would realize that I could not think of a single idea, that I had run hopelessly and permanently dry, that the only solution was to cease doing the column at once.

Somehow, miraculously, I come up with an idea every 30 days. While I don't exactly take it for granted, I've stopped worrying every month that I'll never think of another topic. Something that I read always manages to trigger something. Some thought I have, some remark I overhear, provides me with the raw material for another 1,750-word look at the curious business of fictioneering. I'm glad the columns aren't longer than they are. I don't know that I could regularly come up with ideas worth developing at, say, 3,000 words. But an idea doesn't have to be all that big to cover the space set aside for my column, and, month after month, I seem to find them.

I suspect a great value of this column to me, if to no one else, is that it has allowed me to go through things in print. A lot has happened in my life in the past eight years, and, while I haven't written here about too much of that, I have written at length about the particular problems I've had with the fiction I was writing at the time. I've started books and abandoned them, run into walls and kicked the walls down, gone from depression to elation and back again, and often what I've been going through at the typewriter has been what I've mused on the next month in *WD*.

I've found, too, that the columns I've written about my own problems have often been better received than those which would seem to be of more practical value. I've occasionally felt more than a little self-indulgent, mouthing off in print about my own irritations and aggravations and then getting paid for it. I've felt that I should be turning in a higher proportion of nuts-and-bolts columns, filled with good, practical suggestions regarding the technique of writing.

Yet the response from readers—and *WD*'s readers have to be the world's most responsive—has suggested that, time and time again, those very columns with the least in the way of practical information have had the most real value for the people who've read them. The more this has been proved to me, the more I've been able to realize that successful writing has very little to do with the facts one has managed to amass, that one can most effectively *teach* writing not by imparting data or by showing what is right and wrong in a particular piece of work, but by inspiring a reader to do what he or she is already fully capable of doing.

In the course of all this, my writing in these pages has linked me to all of you out there. I have had letters from hundreds upon hundreds of you over the years. I've met many of you this past year at seminars. But I've felt very genuinely connected to all of you, even if our sole contact has been through this column.

Writing is lonely, and as writers we create most of the loneliness ourselves. We write in order to make contact with the rest of the world and count ourselves failures if we aren't published and our only contact is with our work. And yet we tend to hold ourselves back, to hide in our work, to refrain from sharing the most important parts of ourselves.

Writers need each other. I've come to believe that the greatest value of writers' conferences, far outweighing the professional contacts one might make or the manuscript analysis one might receive or the imperishable truths a lecturer might impart, is the opportunity to spend a few days in the company of people who are going through the same thing. At Write for Your Life, participants are commonly struck by the impact of sharing on a deeper level than they're accustomed with other writers; that sharing of self is very much a part of the process of opening people up to their own creative potential.

I share a great deal of myself in my fiction and more in my personal relationships. But I know that there are aspects of myself that I can share most effectively once a month in this magazine, and for that opportunity I am deeply grateful.

This column is about fiction. I discovered early on, however, that my readers were as apt to be persons with no great interest in writing fiction. Some months, to be sure, I don't focus specifically on fiction, but even when I do, I'm apt to hear from nonfiction writers who found what I had to say applicable to their area of concern. A column on characterization, for example, will draw a response from someone doing personality profiles for a trade journal. A piece on dialogue will strike a chord with an interviewer.

And why not? I haven't written poetry in a quarter of a century, but I frequently find Jud Jerome's column provocative—and his concerns not that far removed from my own. I cannot write about fiction without writing first about writing—and neither, I suspect, can anyone else.

Similarly, I can't write about writing without writing about writers. And increasingly I've come to see that all writers have a great deal in common, irrespective of what it is they write.

I've learned a great deal writing this column. About writing—which is to say that I've learned something about myself and about all of us. When I look ahead, on an occasion such as this, I find the prospect of writing, say, *another* hundred pieces more than a little daunting. For heaven's sake, I haven't got that much to say.

But I *have* got that much to learn.

· 31 ·

No Message
March 1986

The other day I was watching a televised interview with a filmmaker who had recently produced a documentary on sculptor Duane Hanson. Hanson, as you may know, has devoted his career to sculpting astonishingly real representations of real people in real-life situations; his "Museum Guard," posed attentively along a gallery wall, is frequently asked directions by exhibit-goers. The sculptor goes to great length to obtain this effect, making casts of his models, affixing real hair to the sculptures' skin surfaces, etc., and the interviewer asked the filmmaker why Hanson took such pains.

"He's trying to show the pain and struggle of working people in contemporary society," the filmmaker said.

"What nonsense," I said.

Moments later, Hanson was on the screen, and the interviewer was asking him essentially the same question. Hanson said something about using realism as a way of presenting his view of the human condition.

"You know," I said to my long-suffering wife, "I wonder if the present Congress might be induced to pass a bill enjoining plastic and graphic artists from using words to explain what they're doing. I mean, that was almost as bad as the paragraphs artists write for the front of their exhibition catalogs. 'In my most recent paintings, I find myself stressing the linear antipathy of massive forms of light in contradistinction to cattogrammatic and syncogrammatic antipodes of stasis.' There oughta be a law, and perhaps the time is right for it."

"Some civil libertarians might object in the name of the First Amendment. Freedom of speech and all that."

"That's nit-picking," I said. "Besides, we're dealing with a crisis here. How much more can the public take?"

Lynne gave me a look. "The thing is," she said, "artists are generally operating intuitively when they take one or another direction in their work. Then, when they're asked to explain themselves, they're called upon to supply an answer that they don't know themselves. That's why those statements come out like gobbledygook, or seem to have nothing to do with the artist's work, or wind up sounding impossibly pretentious."

"Precisely the point of my proposed law. Let the work of art speak for itself."

"But the public wants those statements."

"That," I said, "is impossible to believe. Nobody even looks at them except us compulsive readers who read cereal boxes and mattress tags."

"Not true," she said. "People read them, even if they can't make head or tail out of them. They want to be assured that the artist knows what he's doing."

The Medium is the Message

Later on, I found myself thinking back over that conversation, and it set a few trains of thought rumbling deliberately down the track. It struck me that I don't have any special distaste for the aesthetic pronouncements of painters and sculptors; any artists, it seemed to me, made a mistake when they set about trying to tell you what they were getting at in their work. It's at least as objectionable when writers do it, using a group of words in an attempt to explain or justify another group of words.

"Why did you write this book? What were you trying to say in it? What's its message?"

It seems to me that the answer to that question *is* the work itself, not an essay or a paragraph about the work. When I write a book, I'm not trying to say anything. I'm trying to create a book, to tell a story, to make something. If there's a message in anything I write, the book is not a vehicle in which to transport that message. The book itself is the message.

When I was in Cincinnati last summer, I got to talking about a related topic with *WD*'s managing editor, Thomas Clark. Tom had just finished reading a few thousand entries in the magazine's annual writing contest, a chore I had myself performed some years ago. He mentioned a phenomenon with which editors are likely to be familiar—i.e., that many of the least successful stories were often very obviously centered on something the author cared very deeply about. Perhaps they had been written to neutralize an early trauma, or to come to terms with a recent loss. Perhaps the author had been inspired by the desire to convey a recent insight to the world at large. Whatever its underlying motivation, story after story showed enormous emotional involvement on the part of the author, while inspiring in the reader nothing but a certain amount of boredom and distaste.

At the same time, the very best fiction—in the *WD* contest or on library shelves—also consists of deeply felt experiences and profound conviction transformed into the stuff of fiction. To echo Yeats, the worst are full of passionate intensity—but so are the best.

Later, thinking about our observations in the light of various stories I'd read over the years, a couple of points struck me.

First of all, it seemed to me that certain fictional use of real experience cannot be realistically judged by ordinary aesthetic standards. When we use portions of our lives and of our inner selves in an attempt to come to terms with ourselves, when we cauterize the raw edge of the past by writing about it, it is far off the point to ask how well it succeeds as fiction. I have read any number of stories that must have been exceedingly painful for their authors to write, and the writing of which must have been an enormously valuable act of human courage. Who cares, ultimately, whether the scenes came to life for the reader, whether the characters emerged as wholly realized human beings? Isn't that beside the point? When writing functions in this fashion as self-directed psychotherapy, we err if we demand that people be entertained and enlightened by the process.

In this context, I'm reminded of a letter I received from a woman who wanted to write the story of her child's early death. She planned to write a book-length manuscript for the sake of doing so, but with no intention of publishing it, and she wanted some technical advice. I suggested that she avoid worrying about technique, that she concentrate only on writing honestly and directly, since publication was not her goal and its requirements not her concern.

There is, it seems to me, nothing at all wrong with writing for ourselves. We always write for ourselves, and if it profits us to write certain pieces exclusively for our own benefit, to produce fiction manuscripts that function more as journal entries, who is to say we've done wrong?

Message Center

That said, we can now ask ourselves why some deeply felt fiction succeeds as fiction while some does not. One could brush the question aside easily enough by saying that some of us write better than others, that some of us use experience to our profit while others struggle with it. I suppose this is true, but I think there may be more to it than that.

It seems to me that the best fiction (or painting, or dancing, or anything) carries a message, and that the message is one of which the artist is largely unaware. If I have the desire to write a novel, let us say, and if I know in advance what I want to say in that novel, why on earth should I bother to write it?

Suppose I am struck by the realization that God is Love. That's certainly a worthy message, although I wouldn't want to claim to be the first person to come up with it. Now if I sit in the corner and mull things over until I come up with an idea that will tell the whole world that God is Love, I am very likely to write a perfectly lousy book. I'd be a whole lot better booking a half-hour of cable TV time on Sunday morning, or leasing a billboard.

Does this mean God is Love is a rotten message for a work of fiction? Certainly not, and you could probably summon up the titles of a few novels that carried that particular message. If they're good novels, the writers probably wrote the books to *discover* the message themselves.

Because a work of art is a work of discovery. It is not a polemic, and even those successful works of art deliberately designed to carry messages generally succeed in spite of their authors' intent; the writer winds up doing more than he set out to do, carrying a deeper message beside the one he originally had consciously in mind.

When I wrote *Eight Million Ways to Die*, I had a notion of what it was going to be about. I knew that book had a couple of principal concerns—the lead character's need to come to terms with his alcoholism, the nature of contemporary life in New York City, the capricious and highly arbitrary selection system of the Grim Reaper. Writing the book, I found out what it was I had to say on these subjects. I found out, after the book was finished, that the book had other themes, perhaps as important, of which I was not consciously aware while writing it.

Message Received

I am sure this is true of virtually everything I have written. Sometimes, rereading a novel years after having written it, I'll be struck by a way in which I unconsciously echoed something in my own life. I've written no end of notes to myself in my fiction, and I'm sure I've deciphered only a small percentage of them.

I don't suppose Duane Hanson knows why it is his role in life to produce extraordinary sculptures of ordinary people. I don't suppose Mondrian knew why he was drawn to paint grids and fit them out with squares of primary colors, although he developed an elaborate aesthetic justification for his style of painting. Nor do I suppose those of us who write fiction know why we choose the plots we do, or people them with the characters we do.

We are not philosophers, though our philosophy will be implicit in what we write. We are not preachers, though occasionally our work may have more impact than a sermon. We are only storytellers. If we tell our stories honestly and courageously, we can safely trust that they will carry the right messages.

• 32 •

Hands Off!
June 1986

About a year ago as you read this, I was having lunch with a fellow employed in the book production department of a Major Publisher. He had been recommended to me as one of many production people who undertake similar duties on a freelance basis for self-publishers and other lunatics. I had decided that I was interested in self-publishing a book about my Write for Your Life seminar and we were lunching together to explore the possibility of his handling everything for me.

I listened as he told me what services I would require, how he would handle them, and what costs I could expect to suffer. "You'll need this," he said, "and you'll need that, and you'll need—"

I nodded, quite caught up in the thing.

"And you'll need a copy editor," he said.

I made my way out of the fog. "A copy editor?" I said.

"To go over the manuscript before it goes to typesetting."

"That's what they do, all right," I said. "How much does a copy editor get?"

"Oh, it depends," he said. "A couple hundred dollars."

A warm glow spread through me. I was the publisher. If I didn't want to have a copy editor, I didn't have to have one. And I'd be saving a few hundred bucks in the bargain. There have been times, over the years, when I would probably have paid that much to be spared the services of a copy editor.

Besides, copy editing would take time—a minimum of a week to get it into the copy editor's hands and back, and another few days to get it to me so that I could go over the copy-edited manuscript. Every day I could save in the self-publishing process was all to the good. One of my chief reasons for self-publishing in the first place was so that I could have the books in six months instead of fifteen, and the last thing I wanted to do was squander a couple of weeks on a process I would prefer to do without anyway.

"We won't need a copy editor," I assured him.

I don't suppose the relationship between writer and copy editor has to be an adversarial one, but that seems to be the way it generally turns out. The copy editor's job is to correct grammatical and stylistic errors and inconsistencies in the author's manuscript before it is set into type. Since it is commonly the author's personal conviction that such errors do not exist in the first place, the two rarely get off on the right foot.

The copy editor puts in long hours with the aim of improving the author's work and rendering it clearer and more accessible to the reader. The writer receives the manuscript back with sentences rewritten, repunctuated, and otherwise distorted from their original form. Where he purposely used a construction that might have displeased his seventh-grade English teacher, the copy editor has helpfully straightened things out.

Some writers, let it be said, don't care a whole lot. They aren't terribly interested in small points of style, have little confidence in their ability to decide where the commas belong, and are grateful that someone will take the whole mess out of their hands and create a semblance of order. Experts on some subject or other who produce a nonfiction book in their area of expertise frequently fall into this category. They are not real writers in the first place, they put style a poor second to substance, they require heavy editing, and they rarely object to it.

Among fictioneers, a different attitude prevails. Most novelists of my acquaintance have a horror story or two about copy editors. Some of them are instructive. Some of them are outrageous.

Donna Meyer writes Regency romances as Megan Daniel. A recent manuscript of hers got heavy editing by what must have been a singularly pigheaded copy editor. Donna had her characters say such things as "He was like to fall down any minute" and "I scarce had time to think about it," this being common usage in ordinary speech in the Regency period. The copy editor systematically changed *like* to *likely* and *scarce* to *scarcely* every time either word was used in this fashion. Donna had to go over the entire manuscript, taking out what the copy editor had inserted.

Now you would think that, after the eighth or tenth correction, the copy editor might have at least entertained the possibility that Donna had written it her way for a reason, and that her choice might even be legitimate. This does not seem to have occurred to the copy editor. Some of the thoughts that occurred to Donna, on the other hand, are not suitable for publication.

In *Mystery Scene*, Warren Murphy reports one of the most awe-inspiring instances of creative copy editing I have ever come across. (A thoroughgoing copy editor might change that last sentence to ". . .across which I have ever come." Never mind.)

"Not long ago," Warren recounts. "I wrote a scene in which I said something like 'The two Japanese sat in the corner talking.' Some copy editor changed this sentence to 'The two Orientals sat in the corner conversing in the soft vowels of the Land of the Midnight Sun.'"

Warren pointed out, reasonably enough, I would say, that Japanese do not talk in soft vowels, that the Land of the Midnight Sun is about as far as you can get from Japan without leaving the globe, and that he reserves the right to select his own collaborators.

This sort of creative copy editing doesn't happen often, and thank God for that. More than 20 years ago I had some experience with a paperback house that believed in a similar sort of collaboration with its authors. While the copy editors there were less imaginative than Warren's copy editor, they made up for it in diligence.

I wrote several books for this particular house, all of them soft-core sex novels which I published under a pseudonym. Somewhere along the line, I happened to flip through one of the published books and encountered a sentence I didn't recall writing; the construction seemed unlike me. I got my carbon down from the shelf, flipped through it to the page in question, and discovered the sentence had been rewritten. I checked some more sentences and discovered that virtually all of them had been reworked to one degree or another. If I had written a compound sentence, someone had split it into two simple sentences. If I'd written two short sentences, someone had hooked them up into a compound sentence. I read several pages, gagged, threw the book against the wall, and made it a point never to open copies of my books from that publisher. Years later I found out that this particular house subjected every book they published to this sort of treatment. They employed several people whose job it was to edit every manuscript in this fashion. They evidently thought it was necessary, for reasons I cannot begin to guess; there was no rhyme or reason, and certainly no rhythm, to their editing, and I doubt they ever improved a book in this manner. It must have cost them a fortune, too.

The kind of copy editing to which most of us are subjected is of a much gentler sort, but it is nonetheless irritating. What I find most irritating is the copy editor's propensity to repunctuate my manuscripts.

Punctuation gives the copy editor a marvelous opportunity to make his or her presence known, and this is important for reasons beyond ego. The copy editor, after all, has to *do* something to the manuscript in order to justify having been paid to work on it. In recent years, more and more publishing houses have phased out their own copy editing departments and now employ freelancers. If a freelance copy editor doesn't make a lot of changes, the publisher might suspect the manuscript has been given short shrift. But, if the copy editor takes out commas where the author has put them in, and inserts them where the author has left them out, such a suspicion need never arise.

And what sort of change could be easier and safer? Punctuation, after all, is an arbitrary business. And the writer is happy enough if you leave the spelling of his name unchanged. He's certainly not going to get upset about a couple of commas.

Some of us, to be sure, don't. But I do. After 25 years in the business, I know where I want a comma and where I don't. I use punctuation for effect, not in obedience to some rule book or style sheet. I want a sentence to fall upon a reader's inner ear in a particular way, and that's why I punctuate a sentence as I do. My approach is intuitive rather than logical, and I'm satisfied that I punctuate correctly.

And so, I might add, do other writers, some of whom punctuate very differently than I do. Donald Westlake uses more commas than I do. Brian Garfield uses far fewer. Were I assigned the chore of copy editing their books, I would not dream of adding commas to Brian's sentences or yanking them out of Don's. It's abundantly clear to me that they both know what they're doing. (Once, incidentally, the two of them collaborated on a novel. How they fought over commas!)

Another task of the copy editor is to correct the writer's grammar. I am perfectly capable of ill-using my mother tongue, and am willing to have such mistakes called to my attention. But my characters are even more likely to make mistakes, and it maddens me when someone sees fit to correct grammar in dialogue. The way my characters abuse the language is one of the ways in which I establish them for the reader. I don't want their acts cleaned up for them.

Most of my novels are written in the first person, and this creates a gray area as far as grammar is concerned. While I do not allow a narrator as much leeway as I give a character in dialogue, still I do not require that he speak like an Oxford don.

Red Flags and Yellow Flags

Does the copy editor have to be the enemy?

No, of course not. Many times over the years I have been spared embarrassment by a copy editor who caught a mistake that escaped my attention. I have found, though, that it is important to let the copy editor know in advance that you don't want your manuscript tampered with in a cavalier fashion. On several occasions I have included with the manuscript a note something like this:

> "To the Copy Editor: The author of this manuscript is a fanatic and a pain in the neck. Do not repunctuate arbitrarily, do not correct grammar or syntax in dialogue, and flag all proposed changes throughout the manuscript."

To flag changes, the copy editor attaches little squares of yellow paper to the pages where changes are proposed, instead of going ahead and making them on the manuscript. The author can then go through and locate these changes and enter them or not, as he or she prefers. This makes it easier to spot proposed changes, and it makes the whole process more cumbersome for the copy editor, and discourages gratuitous meddling.

In my self-publishing venture, I found it at once liberating and unsettling to operate without a copy editor. In a sense, I was walking a high wire without a net; any mistake that got past me would turn up in print. I'm sure there are such mistakes. I'll have to live with them.

If I can't stand it, just look for me in the Land of the Midnight Sun, sitting in the corner, moving my soft vowels.

· 33 ·

First Blood
July 1986

Have you ever had anything published? Have you been paid for anything you've written?

Those are our lines of demarcation, aren't they? We use them to divide the world of writers. Every few days during seminar season I'll get a call from someone who's considering taking my Write for Your Life seminar. "I may be too much of a beginner to belong in the room," I'll be told. "I've never had anything published." What a painful confession! Or, as a variation on the theme, "I've been writing for years, but I've never actually made any money at it."

I always assure my callers that levels of success and experience are immaterial at Write for Your Life, that writers of all sorts participate as equals and gain equally from the experience. Whether they believe me or not, I'm sure they bring into the seminar room the same feeling of inadequacy, of being of dubious legitimacy in the great siblinghood of writers. They have not been published. They have not been paid for it. They are not real writers in their own eyes, let alone anyone else's.

Think back and remember. How important it seemed. How terribly important it seemed!

I was 15 when my first writing was published, and I remember it as clearly as if it happened 32 years ago. The Maurice Evans–Judith Anderson production of *Macbeth* had recently been shown on network television, even as my eleventh-grade English class had lately studied the play. Inspired by this, I wrote a letter to the editor of the *Buffalo Evening News* in which I acted the part of a yahoo who was alarmed and outraged by all of this unseemly violence on the television screen, and understandably concerned about its possible effect on our youth. "Let's all get together," I urged my fellow readers, "and clean up television." I signed the thing "Allor Bryck," which had the same letters as "Larry Block," but not in their usual order.

And the editors printed it. Didn't cut it, didn't change a comma. There I was, in print, where everybody (my parents, my friends, my English teacher) could read every word.

It is, to be sure, the lot of the subtlest satirist to be misunderstood. Several citizens, champions of culture, wrote in to support the Bard, I can only hope that Shakespeare's shade was comforted by their allegiance; for my part, I was purely delighted to see that there were actually folks out there dumb enough to take the piece seriously.

But there were headier thrills still in store. Steve Allen, then hosting *The Tonight Show*, occasionally read crackpot letters to the editor to his audience, and one night he chose Allor Bryck's bid for immortality.

Poor Steve. I think that was the beginning of the end for him.

The first money that ever came to me as a direct result of something I'd written was when I wrote home from scout camp asking for five bucks and my dad sent it by return mail. But that doesn't count.

The first money I got for something I wrote was the dollar Mel Hurwitz paid me for a love poem, which he in turn presented to his girlfriend. I don't know what he may have received in exchange. I doubt that he tried to pass it off as his own work—the chap could have levitated more easily than he could have written a poem—but then why should he? When he gave a girl flowers, he didn't pretend that he'd grown them.

The first money I got from a publisher was the two dollars *Ranch Romances* paid me for a filler. I don't remember the item. It was something I'd clipped and sent in. It was the fall of '56, and I was back at college after having spent the summer working as a mail boy at Pines Publications, publishers then of Pocket Library paperbacks, and a slew of magazines, *Ranch Romances* among them. I had met, among others, a woman named Helen Tono, and it was she who accepted my contribution and sent me the two bucks.

Well, you know what they say. It's who you know, right?

In February of the following year, I spent a weekend in New York, staying with some friends who had a loft on the Bowery. (Four of them split the $60-a-month rent. That space would bring $3,500 a month now. I'll tell you, if you want to get rich, forget this writing dodge. Get into real estate.)

One night, a friend and I spent an hour or so in the Salvation Army's Bowery mission, watching the bums endure a service as the price of a bowl of soup. At the time it seemed like a lot to make a man go through, though in retrospect I don't suppose the prayers did the fellows any harm. At any rate, we walked out of there giggling.

Back home, I wrote about the experience. I already owned a copy of *Writer's Market*, and in it I discovered that the Salvation Army had a magazine called *The War Cry*, which paid a cent a word for material. So I wrote how my fiancée and I had gone slumming one cold winter night, and how we had found our way into the Sally looking for laughs. "We came to scoff," I wrote, "and we remained to pray."

They bought it. Seven dollars and fifty cents, a cent a word, and they paid by return mail.

And they printed the story. I had a hell of a time finding it. *The War Cry*, after all, is not that widely disseminated on newsstands. But I did eventually get hold of a copy, and I wonder what happened to it. I can't imagine I would have thrown it out, but I certainly haven't seen it in years.

"We came to scoff and we remained to pray."

I trust God will forgive me for that one. As Heine said, it's His profession. Even as committing this particular sin was part of mine.

* * *

Just a few months after *The War Cry* broke the ice for me, *Manhunt* took a short story I'd written the previous summer and rewritten twice since then. The story was 2,000 words long and I was paid a hundred dollars for it. It appeared under my own name in what was one of the top markets in the crime fiction field.

During the following year I sold with some regularity to other crime fiction magazines. I hit *Manhunt* another couple of times, but most of my sales were to markets that paid a cent or a cent and a half per word. I placed some articles at $75 a shot with some low-level male adventure mags. ("Lemmings Ate My Knees," "I Made Love to a Bear in the Fight Against Communism—and Lived!" That sort of thing.) With the technical assistance of a paramedic friend, I wrote a piece for *True Medic Stories*. ("My name is Brad Havilland. I'm 42 years old and I'm the best bowel surgeon in the state.")

During that year I made a couple of attempts at writing novels, but I didn't really know what I was doing and they died in embryo. Then, in the summer of '58, I wrote a lesbian novel that sold to Fawcett. The market for soft-core sex novels opened up and I began writing regularly for it.

I was a professional writer.

When exactly did I become a professional writer?

I don't know. I'm not sure where you draw the line, or if there's a line to be drawn. I am sure, though, that all of those early efforts were part of the gestation and birthing process for the professional writer I was in the process of becoming. I was learning to see myself and to be seen by others as a person who wrote for publication, a person who made money through his literary efforts.

Is this the road one must follow?

Certainly not. I know no end of writers who can recount similar stories, writers who have found themselves writing the damnedest things in order to break into print and turn a dollar. I also know any number of writers who did nothing of the sort, but who developed their craft by keeping their focus on their writing itself. When they had matured to the point where their work was ready for print, then and only then did they direct their attention at marketing it. At the time, they might have looked askance at me as a hack, even as I might have dismissed them as dilettantes. Now that we're all of us less insecure, and hence more tolerant, we can see ourselves as having followed different but equally legitimate paths to a similar goal.

For those of us who take the path I took, publication and pay are enormously important. It does something for us to see our words in print. It does something, too, to be paid cash for them.

It validates us. It tells us that we're good enough to be published and paid for it. Whatever our greatest doubts about ourselves, it is one small voice assuring us that they're not true, that we're adequate.

Sometimes, too, we get fooled. Because publication and payment are so important, we come to believe that they're the only things that *are* important.

"The man who has made a financial success of writing is in the worst danger of all," John O'Hara wrote in the introduction to *And Other Stories*, "and it is hardly a secret that I am one of those who has made money. But I believe, and I suppose I have always believed, that the writer who loafs after he has made a financial success is confessing that the money was all he was after in the first place. That was never my idea. Much as I like owning a Rolls-Royce, for instance, I could do without it. What I could not do without is a typewriter, a supply of yellow second sheets, and the time to put them to good use."

Early publication and early payment are important. And, ultimately, recognition and financial success may be important. But they are rarely why we started writing in the first place, and they are rarely why we continue to write, and continue to take delight in it.

Would I go on writing now in the absence of the rewards of print and profit? I don't know for certain that I would, but neither can I say unhesitatingly that I would not. I'm not sure that I would have any say in the matter.

For writing, like virtue, is very much its own reward. This is not to say that there are not other secondary rewards, and we can comfortably enjoy them just as O'Hara enjoyed his Rolls. I certainly do. I get the same thrill holding a copy of my latest book that I got seeing my scrambled name in print beneath that first letter to the editor. And I still get a considerable feeling of satisfaction opening envelopes and taking checks out of them.

It's a pretty good deal, isn't it? No wonder everybody wants to be a writer.

• 34 •

Buckling Down
December 1986

Good morning, boys and girls.

Good morning, sir.

As I write these lines, I'm seated at the dining table in a rented beachfront condo about two and a half miles south of my own house. I moved in here 18 days ago and have been living here all by myself ever since, and—what is it, Rachel?

I'm very sorry, sir.

You are?

And if there's anything any of us can do, sir, you need only ask. If you'd like us to speak to Mrs. Block, we'd be happy to, and I'm sure the two of you can Work Things Out, and—

That's very considerate of you, Rachel. As a matter of fact, however, everything is fine between Lynne and me. My temporary relocation is symptomatic not of marital discord but of a determination to Get Things Done. I moved in here, not to sulk or mope, but to buckle down.

A couple of months ago Natalee Rosenstein, my editor at Berkley, sent over a screenplay for me to read. Berkley had just acquired novelization rights to the film, she explained, and she and publisher Roger Cooper thought I would be just the person to transform the screenplay into a novel. This struck me as highly unlikely, but I read the screenplay (*Black Widow*, by Ronald Bass) and found it to be an excellent piece of work, and a storyline I could see myself exploring in fiction.

I told my agent I would like to undertake the project, providing the terms were attractive. He hammered out a deal with Berkley that was more than generous. I spoke to Natalee, and she told me that Berkley would need the complete manuscript by September so that the book's publication could be timed to coincide with the release of the film sometime in the late spring of '87. At the time, I was in the middle of seminar season, with the last seminar set for June 28th. I couldn't start work on the book before then. In addition, I had already committed myself to participating in the Antioch College Writers' Conference the fourth week in July. And I had hoped to begin work during the summer on a collaborative nonfiction project I'll be doing with an undercover narcotics agent.

One thing was clear enough. *Black Widow*, if it were to be done, would have to be done quickly. In *Writing the Novel: From Plot to Print*, I talk about the virtues and rewards of steady daily production. If you write a page a day, I point out, you will complete a good-sized novel in a year. A page is not a burdensome amount of writing for most of us, and a book a year is considered prolific by most of the world, so it's doing it day in and day out that makes the difference.

Well, that's nice. But if I wrote this thing at the stately pace of a page a day, I'd still be knocking out pages around the time that the movie reached the theaters. Slow and steady would not win this particular race. I would have to write this book fast, and the faster the better.

I knew what that meant. It meant isolation. It meant going off somewhere by myself and locking the door. Locking myself inside and locking the rest of the world out.

And getting the work done.

Fleeing the Wolf

Isolation has on several occasions been my response to writing problems. In the late '60s, for example, I moved to a small farm in western New Jersey not far from the Delaware River. It was a lovely spot, and I was instantly happy there, and for six months I did not write a single usable word.

Finally, with a book due under contract and the wolf at the door, I took a train to New York, checked into the Hotel Royalton, and wrote the book I'd been stuck on in a scant week. On another occasion, unable to find the way to approach a particular novel, I went to Philadelphia and holed up in a hotel there, with satisfactory results.

Some years later, while living alone in New York, I had to do revisions on a recently completed novel and couldn't seem to get anywhere with them. I checked into the Lambertville House, a hotel some three miles from the farm where I'd been unable to work for six months, and I revised the book in a week's time.

Why does isolation work?

First of all, it immediately distances one from ordinary day-to-day life. The distractions that crop up on one's home turf are not around. With *Black Widow*, it was particularly important that I escape such distractions, because there were going to be a lot of them.

With seminar season just ended, there would be a lot of unanswered correspondence around the house, a lot of loose ends to be tied off. The mail would bring letters and book orders every day. The phone would ring.

I should point out that I am blessed with a wife who not only keeps other people away from me while I'm writing but can even be counted on to leave me alone herself during such times. I have, too, a comfortable and well-equipped home office; it does contain a phone, but one that can be readily unplugged. Couldn't I have sufficient privacy—isolation, if you will—without leaving the house? Couldn't I retreat to my office immediately upon awakening and remain there undisturbed all day?

Not the same thing. The house would still be full of other things with a claim on my attention. Distractions didn't have to force their way into my office in order to throw me off stride. If I knew they were right outside my door, I'd be tempted to open the door and go out after them.

I've mentioned before the importance of prioritizing writing. Most of us seem to get more work accomplished if we make writing the first thing we do each day, not only because we hit the desk with our minds fresh and uncluttered but also because we are assigning a priority to our writing by doing it first.

Isolation prioritizes writing wonderfully. Locked away in my comfy condo, I could paraphrase Vince Lombardi: Writing was not just the first thing, it was the only thing. I'd brought nothing with me that was unrelated to the job at hand. I was there for one reason only, to write a particular book. I did not have to list chores in order of importance, because I had only one chore.

The fact that I had to pay a month's rent on the condo helped keep me focused on the priority of the writing, too. After all, I had shelled out money to be here. I had saddled myself with a substantial business expense, considering it a worthwhile investment. If I didn't get the work done, I was wasting my money.

OK, these are all solid arguments for renting some private work space. But why move in? If the place was only a five-minute drive from the house, why not make the drive first thing in the morning, work all day, then return home for a dinner and a decent night's sleep?

Well, I suppose I could have done that, but then I wouldn't be isolating myself with the book. I'd be working days in a rented office, and each night I'd return to a house in which there were a lot of things going on in addition to the book I was writing. So it would not have been the same at all.

If I am to get good work done at the pace I had set for myself, I cannot be involved with my work only during those hours I spend at the typewriter. The writing goes on whether or not I'm at my desk. Indeed, I remain involved in the process while I sleep. It goes on for 24 hours a day.

As a result, I'm not terrific company when I'm deeply involved in a book. I may feel like company, I may seek out company, but I tend to have trouble tracking conversations. I may ask you a question and not be able to listen to your reply. I tend to be short-tempered and impatient, and may cut out abruptly and go off by myself again.

Another reason for making isolation as complete as possible is that it forces the mind to turn inward. With no one for company, no one to talk to, the mind talks to itself. Attention that might be dissipated elsewhere is directed instead upon the book. This is why I find isolation valuable not merely when I want to write something rapidly, but also when I want to break through on something that I've had trouble coming to grips with. (Something to grips with which I've had trouble coming? Hmmmm.)

While working on *Black Widow*, I called Lynne once or twice a day. But I didn't give her the number at the condo, nor did I give that number to my agent or anyone else. In fact, when the phone rang once with a wrong number, I turned off the bell altogether. I did not want interruptions. And I did not make any outgoing calls until I had at the very least completed most of what I was going to write that day, and usually waited until the day's work was finished altogether.

What kind of hours did I put in?

That's difficult to answer, because I didn't think much in terms of hours and didn't keep track of them. I got out of bed whenever I happened to wake up, made a cup of tea, proofread the previous day's work, and got started. (Another advantage of isolation is that it eliminates the need for clocks and schedules; I could stay up late, sleep late, take naps, and let the work take whatever pace it wanted.) I had it in mind to do a certain number of pages every day, and I didn't call it a day until I had completed my quota. Sometimes this took six or seven hours and sometimes it took longer. During the day I would interrupt myself innumerable times to lay out a hand of solitaire, and would take occasional longer breaks to fill in a crossword puzzle. When I was done for the day I would watch baseball on television. (Sometimes I'm able to read other people's fiction while I'm working like this. On this particular occasion I couldn't focus on it.)

How did it go?

Black Widow ran 343 pages, and I started it on July 1 and finished it on July 15.

The Romance of Writing

I should point out that this particular project lent itself to this sort of treatment. It had been clear to me right away that I ought to be able to write the book rapidly, if only because I didn't have to spend a whole lot of time figuring out what was going to happen next. The screenwriter had already worked that out for me.

(As a matter of fact, there were a lot of things I had to work out in terms of plot and structure, and the work was a good deal more demanding than you might suppose. I'll have some thoughts on the difference between books and screenplays, and the business of adaptations in either direction, in a future column.)

I made some advance preparations, too. I read the screenplay through half a dozen times and thought out my approach. I bought the books I would need in order to write scenes set in Houston, Seattle and Maui. I did some library research on a rare disease that figured as a plot element in the script. I so arranged things that I was ready to hit the ground running, and I brought what I needed so I wouldn't have to interrupt the work once it was under way.

There are books I would not care to write in this fashion, books I like to live with and within for a more extended period of time. Sometimes, writing at a more leisurely pace, one discovers the book within oneself as one goes along.

In the main, however, it has been my experience that most of my best work consists of books written in a rather short overall span of time. I don't always need to isolate myself in order to write quickly; *Write for Your Life* was written in two weeks last summer, in the very house I chose to leave in order to write *Black Widow*. In that instance, however, I knew just what I wanted to say and how I wanted to say it, and I probably could have written the book on a card table in the middle of Times Square if I could have found a way to keep the junkies from stealing my typewriter.

Isolation is a useful sometime tool for some writers. It would drive some people crazy, but I seem to thrive on it. And—yes, Rachel?

And it's romantic, isn't it, sir?

Wildly romantic, Rachel. The lonely writer, fighting it out in splendid isolation, sequestered with his muse. But you want to know what's really romantic, Rachel? After the book's done and on its way to your agent, and your wife makes her very first visit to the condo, and you spend an illicit night together.

Now *that's* romantic.

• 35 •

Are You Sure Alfred Knopf Started This Way?
1987 Yearbook

A WRITER BECOMES PUBLISHER IN THIS ACCOUNT OF ADVENTURES IN SELF-PUBLISHING. PLUS: INFORMATION AND INSTRUCTION FOR OTHERS CONSIDERING PUBLISHING A BOOK BY THEMSELVES.

It was a Monday, the 20th of January, and the country was celebrating Martin Luther King's birthday, but on Estero Boulevard it was just another day on which my books were not arriving from the manufacturer. When the Ryder van began backing into our driveway, a little after noon, though, I decided it was altogether fitting and proper that the day be observed as a national holiday.

"The books are here!" I cried. And rushed out to greet the driver.

There were 107 cartons of the little darlings. My daughter Jyl was visiting, and she joined me and Lynne to form a sort of box brigade, shuttling the cartons from the back of the truck up a flight of stairs and into what a previous owner had thought was the house's fourth bedroom, but which was clearly intended to be a stockroom and shipping room.

Twenty-five years ago I was writing soft-core sex novels under a pen name. I had a publisher who wanted to give me more work than I could handle, and a friend introduced me to a fellow he thought might be able to subcontract some of the books from me. The friend's friend was delighted with the opportunity. He had a wife and infant daughter, and had been forced to shelve his dream of writing; he was then making ends meet by unloading trucks in a warehouse.

Now, a quarter of a century later, I was unloading trucks in a driveway.

"I dunno," I said to Lynne. "Are you sure Alfred Knopf started this way?"

For many self-publishers, the alternative is no publication at all. Writers turn to self-publishing when they've been unable to interest commercial publishers in their work.

My own circumstances were somewhat different. By the time I was thinking of writing *Write for Your Life*, I had published more than 30 books with commercial firms. Two were instructional books for writers, *Writing the Novel: From Plot to Print* (Writer's Digest Books) and *Telling Lies for Fun and Profit* (Arbor House). Both books had sold well and remained in print, and with both publishers I enjoyed an excellent personal and professional relationship. I had every reason to anticipate that a book version of my seminar for writers would be welcomed by either of the two.

It seemed to me, though, that self-publishing would serve me better. I had several reasons to think this.

First of all, I had cause to believe that I could merchandise the book very effectively myself. The book struck me as an ideal mail-order item. Whether or not I published it myself, I would want to sell it at my seminars and through the mails.

I knew how to do this, and I knew that I enjoyed this sort of thing, because I was already in the mail-order business, having already sold more than 2,000 copies of my cassette *Affirmations for Writers*. Even before that, I'd bought up remainder stocks of a couple of my out-of-print novels and peddled them through the mails. The mail-order business is more efficient when you can offer more items to your customer, and the book I wanted to write was wholly compatible with the products I was already selling.

If I let someone else publish *Write for Your Life*, I couldn't sell it effectively by mail. I could at best buy copies from my publisher at a 50% discount, and you need a larger margin than that to come out ahead in mail order. (Ideally, your total cost on your product, including your mailing expenses, should be no more than a third of your price, and it's best if you can keep it down to a fourth. Otherwise you don't have a sufficient cushion to promote your product effectively.)

I would probably lose store sales by self-publishing my book, but I decided store sales were secondary. Besides, if the book did well, I figured it would be easy enough somewhere down the line to get a commercial book distributor to take it on. First things first; my primary market was reachable through mail order, and self-publishing looked to be the best way to go after that market.

But that was just one reason. Time was a strong second reason. I hadn't written the book yet, but I already knew one thing. I wanted copies in a hurry.

The sooner I had books, the sooner I could start selling them. More to the point, the sooner I sold them, the sooner they could start selling the seminar. One of my chief motives in writing the book lay in the fact that I had trouble explaining to people what the seminar was and wasn't. I wanted to write the book so that it would put people in a position to decide whether or not the seminar was something they could use.

I also wanted to make the book available to graduates, so that they could take the seminar home with them. And I wanted to make the material accessible to the overwhelming majority of writers who would never have the chance to take the seminar. All of these factors made me want books as soon as possible. I certainly didn't want to wait a year or more, and I had to expect at least that much waiting time with a commercial publisher.

I wanted books in time for the seminar season in the spring of '86. I wasn't going to be able to start *writing* the book until August of '85. A glance at the calendar provided a powerful argument indeed for self-publishing.

Finally, and perhaps most important, I wanted to do it because I wanted to do it.

Most of the writers I've known have had fantasies of self-publishing. Here was a chance to fulfill that fantasy, and with a book that seemed to lend itself to that treatment. I had learned a lot and had a lot of fun making my affirmations tape. And I'd enjoyed selling it, too.

One of the processes in the seminar consists of coming up with actions one can take to add to one's bank of experiences. A way I could add to my own bank of experiences was by publishing my own book, and I couldn't wait to get started.

As a first step, I read *The Complete Guide to Self-Publishing*, by Tom and Marilyn Ross (WD Books). Then I very nearly decided to say to hell with the whole thing.

The book is excellent, let me say, and I recommend it wholeheartedly, and without reservation. It tells you exactly how to contend with the entire business of publishing your own work, from writing and product development through the whole process of book production, and on to advertising and promotion and distribution. It's all there, and it's presented clearly and concisely.

And it almost scared me off.

It was the material on getting the book produced that intimidated me. The authors explained just how to deal with typesetters and printers, how to get bids from various firms, how to make decisions about paper and page size and type. The more I read, the more I felt incapable of handling all of that. It sounded impossibly complex.

A week or so after I read the book, I was having lunch with a friend named Richard, a sales rep for a major trade publisher. I talked about my desire to publish *Write for Your Life* myself and my concern about my ability to handle the production adequately.

"It seems to me," I said, "that there ought to be people who handle that whole process for you."

"There are," he said. "I know a lot of guys who work in the production departments of publishing houses. They do all of this every day for their employers, and they handle book production for self-publishers on a freelance spare-time basis."

"Could you recommend one?"

"I could recommend several," he said, and did.

I called only one of them. It was, after all, the third week in July already, and we were moving from New York to Florida on the 25th of the month. So a couple of days after my lunch with Richard, I sat down to lunch with a fellow I'll call Lou. I told him what I wanted to do, and he said he'd be delighted to help me do it.

"The book's not written yet," I said. "I'll be able to start work on it around the first of the month, as soon as we're settled in our new home. I know what I want to say in it and I don't think it should take more than a month, two months at the outside, so I can have the manuscript to you by the end of September."

In that case, he said, I could probably have books in February. I allowed as to how it would be nice to have them earlier than that.

"You could," he said, "but you'd pay a price for it. Publishers have gotten books out in three days, but the costs escalate when you rush things."

I decided I could live with a February delivery, although January would be better and December better still. I asked what role I would have to play in the production process.

"You give me the manuscript," Lou said, "and I'll give you the finished books. Along the way, you can participate to whatever extent you want. Some clients don't want to hear from me until the books are ready to ship. Others want to consult about typefaces and paper and everything else."

I said I would like to be kept in the picture. Then we talked about Lou's compensation. There were, he said, two ways freelance book production people worked. Some of them billed the client for a straight 10% of total production expenses. Others quoted a figure to the client, paid the printing and typesetting and binding costs themselves, and pocketed the difference.

"I prefer to work the first way," he said. "Otherwise I'd have an incentive to get the book produced as cheaply as possible."

That made sense to me.

How many copies would I want to print? The per-copy cost would be lower the more copies I printed, but the overall cost would rise. I said I was thinking in terms of 5,000 copies, and Lou told me that was a good number. He suggested that his estimate include two sets of figures—for a 5,000-copy first printing, and for a 3,000-copy first run to be followed if necessary by a 2,000-copy reprint.

By the end of the lunch hour, we had agreed that he would get estimates of presswork, binding and printing costs, and send me a letter enumerating the probable schedule of the whole process and an estimate of the costs. I left the restaurant confident that I had found the right person, and that it would not be necessary to interview anybody else. If I had had more time available, I probably would have met with two or three of the other people Richard had recommended, but I don't see how I could have made a better choice.

We moved on schedule, and had been in Florida for several days, waiting for our furniture, when Lou's letter reached me. He had secured several estimates, and had prepared a detailed breakdown of fixed and variable costs. According to his figures, a first printing of 3,000 copies would cost me $2.55 per book. Upping the run to 5,000 copies would bring the per-copy cost down to $1.83.

He also included a rough schedule, which looked something like this:

9/30: Ms to me

10/11: Designer's text layouts (tissues) in for approval (2 weeks)

10/18: Designer's text layouts OK'd and ms sent to compositor (1 week); cover concept discussed and assigned to artist for tight comp (3 weeks)

11/1: Sample pages in from compositor for approval (2 weeks)

11/8: Sample pages OK'd and returned to compositor for galleys (1 week); cover comp in for approval (2 weeks)

11/20: Galleys in (1½ weeks)

11/22: Final cover copy to me and comp OK'd (2 weeks)

12/4: Author's and proofreader's galleys to me (2 weeks)

12/6: Final cover mechanical to printer for 3M (2 weeks)

12/11: Collated master galleys back to compositor for pages (1 week)

12/23: Cover 3M in for final OK

12/30: Pages in (2 weeks)

1/6: Pages back to comp for repro (1 week)

1/10: Cover 3M back to printer for final printing (3 weeks)

1/13: Repro in for checking (1 week)

1/20: Corrected repro on hand/repro to printer (1 week)

1/31: Final covers ship to binder (3 weeks)

2/3: First sig blues in for OK (2 weeks)

2/10: First sig blues back to printer for final printing (1 week)

2/28: Finished books available

(A brief explanation: *tissues* are designs using tissue overlays; a *comp* is a composite, a step in the proofing stages; *galleys* are prepublication proofs of typeset copy; *3M* means a color proof; the *mechanical* contains type and shows how artwork will be printed; *repro* means galleys that are ready to be sent to the printer for reproduction; a *sig* is a signature, a section of the book that comes off the press in 8-, 16- or 32-page groupings; *blues* are blueprint proofs of how the book will look when it comes off the press.)

"This is a conservative schedule," Lou added, "but I wanted to give you one you could reasonably count on. I wouldn't advise you to set out to do this much faster or you'll find yourself under pressure to cut corners."

That made sense, but I wasn't nuts about the February 28th delivery date. I could see one trouble-free way to hurry things, however. I could get busy writing the book.

Writing the book was the easy part.

Our furniture arrived July 31st. The following morning I sat down at my desk, plugged in my typewriter, and went to work.

Twelve days later I was done.

I had expected it to go quickly. After all, I could hardly have been more familiar with the material. I had spent the spring months presenting the seminar a dozen times all around the country. While I wasn't sure I could do it in my sleep, I had on one occasion done it in lieu of sleep—I stayed up all night before the June seminar in Chicago. I thought it would be eminently possible to bat out ten pages a day, even with the distractions and disturbances that were a part of relocating to Florida.

As it turned out, I had no trouble turning out 20 pages a day. Understand, please, that those were arduous days. The writing was demanding. I had to turn an oral in-person seminar into something that would work on paper. I had to adapt various processes so that they could be performed by an individual in his own home.

No matter. In less than two weeks I had produced a 250-page manuscript. Since one way I intended to save both time and money was to dispense with the services of a copy editor, I went over the manuscript carefully before sending it off. Lynne gave it a thorough reading and provided me with 11 pages of notes and suggestions. I incorporated some of these and shrugged off the rest with pigheaded abandon, and the manuscript went off to Lou by UPS Next Day Air.

* * *

Lou got back to me by Express Mail the first week in September. He enclosed what he informed me was the first of many bills, this for $350 for the book designer. It was accompanied by the original manuscript, which had gone through the designing process, along with tissue layouts and a complete composition order. A page of type set the way my book would be set was included to show me what my book pages would look like.

First problem. I didn't like the way they looked. The type looked small, was set very tight, and was sans-serif type. **This sentence appears in a sans-serif typeface. See the difference?**

I never had liked sans-serif type for text. It's less readable. Nor did I like the way the pages were going to be so compressed. On the other hand, Lou had anticipated my objections and mentioned in his letter that he had worked with the designer to hold down costs. "The design may look a little tight," he said, "but it will save you money."

I thought this over for a couple of hours. That night I called Lou and told him how I felt. No problem, he said, agreeing that the book would look better set looser and in a face like Bodoni or Baskerville. But that would increase the book's size from 160 to 208 pages, which would boost typesetting costs, paper costs, book production costs, and freight charges as well. The change would probably run me an additional 25¢ a copy, maybe a little more.

Well, I was going to sell the book for ten bucks. What was 25¢ a copy?

A lot, actually. Every penny saved at the cost end makes an enormous difference in the profitability of a venture. And I realized, too, that spending the extra quarter wouldn't increase my sales at all. I was going to sell the book through the mails, so people would be buying it sight unseen. They wouldn't return it because the type was set tight, or because they preferred Baskerville to Optima. Books produced for the mail-order market are typically underproduced. The mail-order book buyer who sends off ten dollars to a self-published author generally receives a small, inexpensively made book or pamphlet with an amateur look to it. If the information within is adequate, he generally overlooks the homemade production job.

But I didn't want this. If I were ever going to get the book into stores, I would have to be able to offer them a professionally produced, attractive book that would look good enough to engender point-of-purchase sales. More important than that, the book was going to have my name on it. I wanted it to look good, and I wanted all my customers to feel they were getting more than their money's worth.

"The hell with it," I said. "Let's do it right."

I returned the manuscript to Lou, along with a copy of a page that he'd noticed was missing. A day or two later I was able to send him the introduction, and an about-the-author blurb for the back cover. On the 10th of the month he sent me revised text layouts, with the body type changed.

It looked beautiful.

So did the cover design, which Lou sent to me on September 19th. I had suggested that the cover be predominantly yellow, since that color gets identified with *Write for Your Life*. (The pens we give out are yellow, the floral arrangement at the head table is yellow, and for a while I was compulsive about wearing yellow neckties.) The proposed cover looked like a yellow legal pad, and I thought it was terrific.

"Things are rolling now," Lou advised. "The manuscript is at the compositor, and the next step will be sample pages set in type. I'll check them to make sure no problems exist and give the typesetter the go-ahead to proceed to galleys. You should see galleys around mid October."

The typesetter's estimate was enclosed, with one half due with the purchase order. I wrote out a check for $900.

The cover layout looked fine, but as I studied it I decided that the title itself was typographically unexciting. Then Lynne or I remembered that we already had an excellent *Write for Your Life* logo. George Sorenson, our good friend and organizer in Minneapolis, had created a logo for a brochure he put together for the Minneapolis seminar, and was going to use it in the ad he was designing for us. Couldn't we use that on the book cover?

We could indeed. I got a repro proof off to Lou, and he had the designer incorporate the change.

Galleys arrived early, the first week of October. Lou wanted them back by the week of the 21st; I proofed them in two days and got them back immediately. "We should have no trouble getting books finished in January," he wrote. "I wouldn't be surprised if you had them quite a bit earlier. Don't count on it, but I'll do all possible to have them before Christmas."

With the galleys, I sent along a check for $122.33 for the cover type.

We still didn't have a photo for the back cover. A session with a local photographer yielded nothing recognizable, let alone usable, and I wound up sending Lou the photo that had run on my short story collection *Like a Lamb to Slaughter*. It was a good picture, but I'd hoped for something newer and with more definition.

In mid October, Lynne and I flew to France to attend a conference in Reims. In Paris I met with the good people at Gallimard, my French publishers. After lunch, one of their photographers took me down alongside the Seine and snapped away. A few days later in Reims someone from Gallimard handed me an envelope full of glossies. Jacques Sassier, the photographer, had done an astonishing job, considering the material he had to work with. I came back from France with the cover photo in hand.

I came back to some bills, too: $350 for cover design, including sketches, comp, mechanical, stats and miscellaneous type; $250 for proofreading; $500 for one half the estimated cost of cover prep, plates, stock, printing and lamination.

It was time, Lou wrote, to finalize quantity. Did I want to print 5,000 right away, which was cheaper but riskier, or 3,000 now and 2,000 when needed, which was more expensive but safer? I bit the bullet and stayed with the decision to run 5,000.

A copy of the cover mechanical was there for my approval. "I tried and tried to work the photo onto the back and it just didn't look right," he wrote. "My suggestion is to drop it. Most paperbacks don't carry authors' photos."

Time, obviously, for another Executive Decision, and this one was easy to make. I have come to believe that all books should carry photographs of their authors, and this looked to be doubly true with *Write for Your Life*, which was such a thoroughly personal book, with the author talking directly to the reader on every page. Besides, I had this great photo I'd just schlepped back from France.

I called Lou and told him a photo had to run, and that I was sending him a new one. The about-the-author blurb could be cut or set tight—that didn't matter—but the photo had to run.

No problem.

About this time, forms arrived from R.R. Bowker. I had to fill them out in order to get an ISBN number assigned. (Lou had tried to handle this for me, but Bowker insists on dealing directly with authors of self-published books.) I filled out the forms and sent them off by return mail.

A couple of weeks later, Lou wrote that he needed the ISBN number. Could I call him as soon as it arrived so that it could be added to the back covers? When the time came to print the covers, I still hadn't heard from Bowker. It was time to make another decision—did we hold off until we had the number or go ahead and print without it? I didn't even have to think about it. At this point we had advertising scheduled and would be getting orders in a matter of weeks. I didn't want to do anything that would delay the books. Every book should have an ISBN—it's hard for stores to order them without it—but I decided I could always add the number when we went back for a second printing. The first printing probably wasn't going to have any store sales anyway.

*   *   *

More bills to pay. The final payment for composition, and the first half to the book manufacturer. Manufacturing costs had originally been estimated at $3,860, but that was for a 160-page book. The new estimate was $5,018, and the difference was right around the 25¢ a book Lou had said it would be, since freight costs would also be increased.

Twenty-five cents doesn't sound like much. $1,250 does.

I sat down and wrote out some checks.

Late in November, a note from Lou advised me that books would be ready December 20th. Then, in mid December, he wrote that the completion date would be a week later than projected. He took some of the sting out of the news by enclosing a copy of the printed cover.

By this time, our first ad for the book had run in *Writer's Digest* and orders were coming in every day. I prepared shipping envelopes, and sat tight.

On the last day of the year, six copies of the book arrived by Express Mail. The bulk shipment left Pennsylvania on Friday, Lou wrote, so I could expect arrival around the sixth of January.

The books looked beautiful. I sent a couple out to reviewers and kept the rest around the house to look at. January 6th came and went. The following week I called Lou, and it turned out that the books had not been shipped; the manufacturer was holding them pending payment, and I was holding his check pending their arrival. A couple of phone calls straightened this out, and on January 20th the books came.

We stacked 106 cartons in the spare room, toted the 107th into the dining room, and went to work. The envelopes were already stamped and labeled. We stuffed and stapled, and first thing next morning I drove down to the Post Office. Even with those delays at the end, we were shipping orders less than six full months after my first lunch with Lou.

*   *   *

What did it cost me?

My total expenditure for the production of 5,000 books came to $8,742.70, exclusive of office overhead. In addition, I paid Lou his fee of 10% of costs, or $874.27, and reimbursed him for $53.75 for five Express Mail shipments to me. Freight added another $440.08, which made the bottom-line figure $10,110.80, or approximately $2.02 per book.

I could not have managed this without Lou's help. I'm sure his expertise in dealing with printers and typesetters saved me considerably more than his fee in dollars alone, not to mention the savings in time and aggravation. The book he produced for me looks perfectly professional, with nothing of the homemade look about it that marks so many self-published volumes. I don't think I could have achieved anything like it on my own.

With the books in hand, I started to find out how different things look from a publisher's standpoint. I'd always been irked when my own publishers failed to send out dozens upon dozens of freebies, thinking it only sound business for them to blanket the globe with review copies.

Why shouldn't I think so? It didn't cost me a dime.

But now it cost me three bucks every time I mailed off a copy—$2.02 manufacturing cost and a dollar's worth of stamps and envelope. I felt myself turning more miserly than any publisher I'd ever been associated with. I managed to realize the folly of being penny wise, but it still stuck in my craw every time I mailed out a comp.

Would I do it again?

I suppose that depends on how this venture pays off, and it's a little too early to tell at this writing. While I have every expectation that I'll sell every copy and reap a handsome profit, the *Literary Digest* was every bit as certain that Alf Landon would swamp Roosevelt in '36. If I wind up using the books to insulate the attic, my enthusiasm for the whole project will very likely wane.

Even if that turns out to be the case, I'll still be glad I had the experience. As I mentioned, the fantasy of self-publishing is one I entertained for years. Relatively few of my long-standing fantasies can be realized without risking public embarrassment or a jail sentence. When I find one that can, my inclination is to go for it.

The work doesn't end when the books arrive, incidentally. My job now is to sell them, and it's at this point that the Rosses' book becomes especially useful. I keep finding new ways to get these books out of the storeroom and into people's hands.

Incidentally, my ISBN arrived from R.R. Bowker just a week after we took delivery on the books. I'm glad I didn't wait, but I'm also glad I've got it now.

We can put it on the cover when we go back to press for a second printing.

• 36 •

Do It Until You Need Glasses
April 1987

WILL CERTAIN TYPES OF WRITING PIGEONHOLE YOU AND HURT YOUR CAREER?

After I'd been writing this monthly column for two years or thereabouts, I found myself waiting for the drought. Sooner or later, I thought, I would run out of things to say about writing. The well would run dry.

But each month something came obligingly to mind, and after a while I came almost to take this coming-to-mind for granted. Somehow or other, a week or a day before my column was due in Cincinnati, the Great Spirit of Ideas would send me an idea and I would bat out the column.

Over the years, this touchingly childlike faith of mine has been rewarded time and time again. Sometimes the Great Spirit of Ideas zings me with an idea while I'm meditating, or playing solitaire, or watching *Cardiology Update* Sunday afternoon on cable. Sometimes the Spirit so arranges things that I come across something in my reading that strikes a chord, rings a bell, or toots a whistle.

When all else fails, the Great Spirit sends me a letter.

This month's letter was postmarked Clute, Texas. "I am writing to you because I admire your work," my correspondent began; then, having won my heart forever, she explained her problem:

"I recently finished a noncredit course at the local college called 'Fiction-Writing for Publication.' I felt that I needed to be around other writers and that four weeks of talking to and being around people interested in writing sounded like heaven. The teacher had just sold her first novel.

"One of the things the instructor said was that she attended as many conferences as possible to make connections with important people. At every one she had gone to, *all* editors agreed they would never read anything if they knew ahead of time that it was written by a porn writer or a creative writing teacher.

"The second secret she let us in on was a revelation from an editor at a leading magazine for writers who said being a romance writer was the kiss of death. It would hurt you far more than anything else, including bad writing."

My correspondent found this news devastating. "I have written and sold four books," she explains, "and they want one a month from me. But they are porn books. In addition, an agent just took me on on the basis of a partially finished romance novel. He has placed more than a hundred books this year, so I thought he knew the score. How can anybody say that any kind of writing is a kiss of death? Is pumping gas or waiting tables better?

"I don't want to write porn the rest of my life. I just want to be able to eat and pay my light bill while I'm learning to write what I really want to write. Every book I write has a plot. Every book I write is practice in dialogue (and not just 'Oooh' and 'Ahhhhh' either). But is it really true that no one will ever take a serious look at my serious work because of the smut?"

Bad Habits

Well, how about it? Is it true? Are editors that strongly disinclined to read anything written by someone who has written fiction appealing to the prurient interest or, more obscene still, taught creative writing?

I'll tell you, it'd be a hell of a thing if it *were* true. Because it seems to me that almost every established professional writer I know has either written porn or taught writing, and a sizable proportion of us have done both, either serially or simultaneously. An editor who steadfastly eschews writers with either of these blots on their résumés will perforce wind up with a very small and highly specialized list.

What, then, can the statement possibly mean? Let's suppose that it's hyperbole, designed merely to suggest emphatically that a writer dabbles in porn or in teaching at his peril, that his serious writing will suffer for it. Is there any truth to that?

Maybe.

And maybe not.

And what of romance? I've known a number of writers who've been ruined by romance—not the ones they've written, but those in which they've participated. Can it hurt you to write romance novels? Or confessions, or action-adventure, or any other type of category fiction?

Maybe.

And maybe not.

The danger, I suppose, is that you can learn bad habits. It has been a quarter of a century since I wrote porn novels, and they were a gentler and rather more innocent sort than the contemporary variety. One could not use certain four-letter words, could not describe activity too graphically, and one learned to cultivate subtlety and nuance. There was rather more in the way of plot and rather less in the way of heavy breathing.

Still, a dirty book is a dirty book, then as now. Writing them, I found it easy to be sloppy in my writing. A plot didn't have to maintain tension, as long as a sex scene every 15 or 20 pages could keep the reader glued to the page. Characters didn't have to be all that well drawn. Indeed, they couldn't really emerge as lifelike beings, because they were all ultimately motivated primarily by their sexual impulses.

And there, finally, is what was probably most detrimental about the books. They were at base unrealistic, reflecting a universe in which the pursuit of sexual gratification was the predominant expression of the life force.

Similarly, much category fiction reflects a simplistic universe. I suspect that what we would point to as the stylistic faults of most romance writing, or most action-adventure writing, or most pornography, is no more than the echo of this false note, this dishonest perception of the world. Life is not like a romance novel, or a porn novel, or an action novel, or any second-rate type of book. When we narrow our vision in order to write such a book, we cramp our own style accordingly.

"The only reason for the existence of a novel," Henry James has written, "is that it does attempt to represent life."

Traces of the Past

When we write categorically inferior work, are we imprinting upon ourselves bad writing habits that we will be hard put to extirpate? Or are we serving a perfectly legitimate apprenticeship?

I suppose it depends. I suppose one person's apprenticeship is another person's life sentence, that what is a stepping stone to one is quicksand to another. I know a number of writers who wrote crap for years and who now write clean, honest work; their sordid past does not seem to have hurt them in the least. And yet I can point to other writers whose current work shows unfortunate traces of the past.

For example, I know of a woman who began writing adult fiction after having achieved great success as a writer of young adult novels. Her books hit the bestseller list, so she's certainly doing something right, but it has taken her a while to slough off some of the simplistic elements of style that are rather less acceptable for an adult audience. She has had to find her way out of the Young Adult Novel mindset.

(Understand, please, that I am not characterizing young adult fiction as trash; my point is merely that it reflects a less profound and realistic view of the world.)

Similarly, there are many writers who have broken in writing romances and have made the move into some more realistic area of novel-writing. Not only their writing style but also their plotting and characterization has to change if they are to succeed, and sometimes these changes don't come all at once. I have read some first mysteries, for example, and have been able to see the romance writer imperfectly concealed in the prose and dialogue.

On the whole, however, I'm inclined to believe that any kind of writing is more help than harm to us, and that what harm shows up in our work is just an indication that we have not yet come out the other side. "If the fool would persist in his folly he would become wise," Blake wrote, and perhaps the way to transcend the inherent weaknesses of porn or romance or any lesser form of fiction is to persist in those forms until we have written our way out of them.

Those Who Can't

And what about that gratuitous slapshot at people who teach writing? Are teachers inherently bad at what they teach? Or is the process of teaching detrimental to one's writing?

No, and no. One can hardly deny that there are people teaching writing who have had little or no success with their own writing. This is perhaps inevitable; there are more writing courses than there are successful professional writers to teach them, and not all professional writers are available for teaching, lacking the time, the inclination, or both. I don't know that one has to be terribly proficient at writing in order to guide other writers, any more than one has to be a star athlete in order to function successfully as a coach.

I think there are dangers in the teaching of writing. In any area, we sometimes teach something in order to avoid learning it ourselves; the writing teacher, invested with authority, can sometimes let his role interfere with his own process of growth as a writer. When you play every day to a roomful of people who assume you have all the answers, it's easy to stop asking questions.

But this doesn't have to happen. In my own teaching, whether in person or through my writing in *WD*, I'm sure I've learned far more than I've taught anyone. My teaching has indisputably been a vehicle of growth, for me if for no one else, and my fiction writing has benefited greatly from it.

Don't Worry

Are there dangers in porn, dangers unknown even to the Meese Commission? Are there pitfalls in romance more to be dreaded than a broken heart? Will they make you a bad writer, a pariah in editorial offices from coast to coast?

I don't think so. Maybe they'll teach you bad habits, but consider another practice occasionally labeled a bad habit, and purported by earlier generations to cause no end of aliments, among them blindness. And remember the youth who, apprised of the dangers, replied that he would do it just until he needed glasses.

And that's my advice to the woman in Clute, Texas, and to anyone hornswoggled by the same dilemma. Don't worry about it, and quit when you need glasses.

Dare to Be Bad
May 1987

TO FIND THE HUMANNESS IN YOUR VILLAINS, YOU MUST HAVE THE COURAGE TO DISCOVER THE VILLAINOUS WITHIN YOURSELF.

Couple of days ago I was wading through the sea of intellectual reading material I'm forced to digest in order to produce my monthly column. In *TV Guide*, I read Mary Murphy's interview with James Garner. The actor was about to appear in *Promise*, a two-hour TV movie, and he had initially turned down the role. "He had serious reservations," I learned, "about what he saw as the unlikable aspects of his character. 'I have always been afraid to be a bad guy onscreen,' says Garner. 'I've been told it's my greatest flaw.'"

Last night I watched *Promise*, and if you missed it, you might want to catch it the next time around. Garner plays a middle-aged bachelor with a schizophrenic brother. Their mother has just died, and he had previously promised her that he would care for his brother in the event of her death. *Promise* shows him attempting to keep his word.

I'll tell you, the character Garner plays is hardly second cousin to Attila the Hun. Maybe he's a tad irresponsible, a poor financial manager, a lad who likes to fish with his buddies and fool around with the ladies, but you've really got to reach to call him a villain. Richard Friedenberg's excellent script presents him as deeply sympathetic, and Garner's performance does nothing to alienate our sympathy.

He's not a bad guy. But he's not *just* a good guy, either. He has strengths and weaknesses. He's human.

Even as you and I.

What does this have to do with writing?

Quite a bit, I suspect. I have long felt that what I do as a writer is not unlike what actors do. I become the characters I create. Each of them is the person I would be if I were to find myself wearing his or her skin. Furthermore, each of them is an aspect of myself, dredged out from beneath my own skin and given expression on the page.

This is most obviously true of those characters whose personalities are similar to the face I show the world, characters whose life experiences echo some of my own. But it is true too of characters who are, on the surface, nothing like me. Even if I deliberately base a character on someone else, some other human being of my acquaintance, the character nevertheless is me in disguise; how can I possibly animate the character other than by contacting within myself that element that is one with him?

"I am Madame Bovary," Flaubert said of his greatest creation. But how? His background, his life experience, his worldview, was nothing like hers. And yet he found her within himself, and found himself within her, to a sufficient extent to make the observation—and to put on the page one of literature's most wholly realized persons.

Hobbled by Fear

It is fear, I suspect, that keeps an actor from playing unsympathetic characters. Fear that the audience will not like him. Fear that he will not like himself.

Writers are hobbled by much the same sort of fear. Our heroes are bloodless because we fear to give them human flaws; our villains are unreal because, afraid to look at what is villainous within ourselves, we are unable to find what is human in them.

The best villains are more than evil. They are also human, and that makes them real, and that in turn makes their menace more than the stuff comic books are made of.

Consider *Firestarter*, by Stephen King, who certainly has strong ideas in his fiction about good and evil. One of the bad guys in *Firestarter* is a hired killer whose assignment it is to murder the charming child who is the book's heroine. King makes of this character a very evil person indeed, but while doing so he gets under the character's skin and tells us that this villain prefers to gaze into his victim's eyes as they die. Not, as we might suppose, out of sadistic glee, but rather out of an abiding curiosity. He hopes each time to get some clue at the moment of death, to learn where the soul goes when it flees the body. He kills, not out of blood lust, not out of hatred, but in a never-satisfied quest for knowledge.

When you know that, you feel different about this villain. You still want him to fail. More than ever, you want him to die and the girl to live. He is nonetheless menacing for being human. But, as a reader, you touch the part of him that is human, and touch within yourself (if you are as courageous as the author) that part of you that *could be* (in another time, another life, another universe) just that sort of thoughtful, dispassionate killer.

It is worth noting, I think, that writing of this sort demands courage on the part of the reader as well as the writer. Not every reader wants to identify with the bad guy. Some readers strongly prefer characterization to be a clear-cut matter, with heroes to cheer and villains to hiss and no shades of gray to cloud the issue. And less ambitious fiction generally fits itself to the wants of these less adventurous readers.

In the very best work, on the other hand, that work we find ourselves calling Art and Literature, there are no heroes and there are no villains. There are only human beings. Some of them behave heroically. Some of them do terrible things. We may well wish for one to prevail over the other, but we don't quite cheer and we don't quite hiss.

I can recall a personal epiphany in this area. When I first read *From the Terrace*, I was astonished to realize that none of John O'Hara's characters was bad. I started off by identifying with Alfred Eaton, the protagonist, and thus was fully prepared to hate and despise his enemies, at least for as long as it took me to read the novel. But there was no one to hate. Various characters were good to Alfred in one chapter and did him ill in another, but there were no actual villains. I was struck by this, and the thought quickly came to me that life itself was probably rather like that, with no villains to be found, just a whole lot of human beings, each the protagonist of his own real-life novel.

I was 20 at the time, and while my life may have been sheltered my reading was not; you'd have thought I'd have managed this epiphany earlier. I'd read any number of books that could have delivered the same message, but evidently I wasn't ready to hear it until then.

The Killer Inside

A couple of years ago I tried writing a novel from the viewpoint of a clever and likable fellow who would be revealed, perhaps a third of the way into the novel, to be a serial thrill-killer. The reader would already have grown to like him before learning this.

I found it impossible to complete the book, for reasons not limited to its nature; it was one of several books that went unfinished that year until I was able to accept the fact that I needed a year away from novel-writing. But I do know that I was made uncomfortable by the character I was creating. I had written from the viewpoint of killers before on more than one occasion; here, though, I was working closer to the bone, looking for a killer within myself to transfer to the page. I was uncomfortable, and I had the feeling that anyone who read the book would be similarly uncomfortable.

The late Jim Thompson did much the same thing in a novel called, appropriately enough, *The Killer Inside Me*. The book has become an underground classic, and is just beginning to get critical recognition. I'm sure that it won less of an audience at the time of publication than it would seem to deserve because it made most readers uncomfortable. The very element that has allowed the book to endure kept it from finding a wider audience earlier.

I don't know if I'll ever go back and write my book, in one form or another. Commercial considerations aside, I'm not altogether certain I'm willing to spend that much time poking around in that particular chamber of my self. My guess is that I'll incorporate the character in a third-person multiple-viewpoint novel; I think he'd be easier to take that way, for writer and reader alike.

In *Silent Terror*, recently published as an original paperback by Avon Books, James Ellroy uses a serial killer as narrator, and makes his protagonist quite terrible and wholly human; one finds oneself, against one's will, wanting him to get away with it. Reading the book, I admired Jim enormously, not just for the considerable skill with which he had brought it all off but for the inestimable artistic courage it must have required. I found myself, too, at once envious and grateful; now that he's written his book, I may no longer need to write mine.

To know all is to forgive all, according to Madame de Staël. According to Socrates, all knowledge begins with knowledge of oneself.

We write for no end of reasons, but surely discovery of self ranks high among them. We discover ourselves by writing, and we write by discovering ourselves in our characters. When we are successful, we facilitate a similar process of self-discovery for our readers.

I believe, incidentally, that the process is the same in nonfiction as in fiction. (Nonfiction about people, that is; I don't really think there's much self-discovery for reader or writer in an instruction manual on operating a Cuisinart, or a stockholder's report.) Even when the writer sticks strictly to the facts, even when he keeps his own ego well out of the picture, he plumbs his own depths to create a real-life character in cold print.

And, when he does everything right, he can produce characters that are at once sympathetic and terrible. The example that comes to mind for me is Norman Mailer's *The Executioner's Song*. I felt for Gary Gilmore even as I prayed for them to shoot him and get it over with. That's a perfect example, but so is any really good piece of writing about a villain. To know all is to forgive all.

Are there ultimately no truly bad people? Perhaps we'll be best off leaving that one to the moral philosophers among us. We might safely say, though, that there are no truly bad characters—only writers who have not dared to gaze fully upon them.

Looking for Madame Bovary
June 1987

CREATING BELIEVABLE CHARACTERS DEPENDS MORE ON INNER IDENTIFICATION THAN OUTER SIMILARITIES.

With *Suspects*, his fine second novel, perching comfortably on the bestseller list, my friend William Caunitz was doing what writers do. He was working away at Novel #3.

And having problems. Then one day he called his agent (who also happens to be my agent) to report. "I figured out what was wrong," he said. "In the first book, *One Police Plaza*, my hero was a lieutenant. In *Suspects* the hero's also a lieutenant. But in the new book he was a detective, and I couldn't get a handle on him, and then I realized I can't remember what it's like to be a detective, a part of a squad. I'm used to being in command."

Bill Caunitz, I should mention, served for many years as a lieutenant in the New York Police Department until his success with *One Police Plaza* led him to retire to fulltime writing.

"So I went back to the beginning," he went on, "and I changed it and made my guy the head of the detective squad instead of just one of the detectives, and it's like night and day. It's going fine now."

"That's wonderful," our agent said, as who would not when a bestselling client says that a new book is proceeding apace?

"I suppose so," said Caunitz, "but it bothers me. I mean, what kind of a writer am I that I can only write about one kind of character? It seems to me that I must be very limited. Oh, I'm glad I'm on the track and the book's going well, but it bothers me."

Finding the Characters

Last month, if you recall, we considered tarnished heroes and human villains. I suggested we create characters most effectively when we become willing and able to find them within ourselves. To do this, I observed, may require courage.

This month I'd like to look at another aspect of that same overall topic—an aspect that calls not so much for courage as for versatility. How do we manage to write convincingly from the point of view of characters with whom we have rather little in common?

I wrote earlier of Flaubert. "I am Madame Bovary," he said, proclaiming his inner identification with a character to whom he would seem to have been altogether dissimilar. But how does one achieve this? How does one become Madame Bovary, how does one find the unfortunate lady within one's own self?

First, I think it's useful to recognize that the process involved is not an intellectual one. You can't "figure out" a character and by so doing create an individual who will come to life on the page. You may be able to produce an android that way (and much fiction is peopled by androids, and some of it does well enough in the marketplace) but you won't create a human being.

It is useful, certainly, to know things about your character. In the book version of Write for Your Life, I explain a character-creation process that involves observing a stranger on a bus or at a restaurant and subsequently inventing facts about him or her, jotting down a slew of one-liners loaded with data about the person's background or present life. Then, having done this, you put the list aside and meditate on the character. Finally, without referring to your list, you write a character sketch of one sort or another.

This is just an exercise, but one does something similar when developing a character for a book. You know a little about your character, and you think about him, and you turn him over to the unconscious portion of your mind. Some of the "facts" you knew about him drop away. Others come to you. Then you sit down at the typewriter and allow the character to emerge from within you.

Last month I noted that what I do sometimes seems to me not unlike what actors do. You might want to look at *An Actor Prepares*, by Constantin Stanislavski (Theatre Arts Books); a writer of my acquaintance has called it the most useful book for a writer that he had ever read. (Perhaps I should point out, however, that he made this observation before he had the opportunity to read *Write for Your Life*.)

Intuitive Casting

Writers have one clear advantage over actors. We are less limited in our choice of roles.

Helen Hayes can't play a teenager. Don Knotts can't play a middle linebacker. An albino can't play Othello. Clear-cut considerations of age and physique and gender and race put some roles out of bounds for some actors. (I say this in spite of the fact that Whoopi Goldberg is starring as Bernie Rhodenbarr in *Burglar*, a film based on a novel of mine. My character is a white male, but the screenwriter had already given Bernie a sex-change operation before Ms. Goldberg was called to bring him—her?—to life on the screen.)

Because we have more range, because we are less obviously limited by our own circumstances of age and gender and body type, because Flaubert could indeed *be* Emma Bovary, we may assume that we can create any character we want, that no role is closed to us.

That may be true in theory, but it's something else in practice. Most of us can do some characters well and others poorly, and the determinant often has nothing to do with outside appearances or life experience. And, while it is good to be able to extend one's range, it is also essential to recognize and acknowledge one's limitations.

When I first began to develop the character of Matthew Scudder, I intended for him to be a working New York cop. Long before I began plotting the first book, I had transformed Scudder into an ex-cop. I realized that I would not be at ease writing from the point of view of a character who was a part of a system, even though I knew from the beginning that Scudder would do most of his work outside normal channels. I wanted him to be even more of an outsider.

More to the point, I didn't know what it was like to be a cop. But I did—somehow—know what it was like to be an ex-cop. Not because I had spent great amounts of time with ex-cops. Not because I had amassed a great deal of data about them. Not because my own life experience contained something equivalent. All the same, I knew. Not factually, not experientially, but intuitively, as one must know things in order to produce convincing fiction.

Some writers have trouble with characters of the opposite sex. It has always been quite natural for me to write from a female viewpoint. I don't know that I can be said to understand women any better than the next man, but I seem to be comfortable writing from a woman's point of view. My first novel featured a female lead character and was published under a female pseudonym. I made some curious mistakes—I never thought to give the lady a purse, and had her carrying keys and money in her pockets, for example. But I had no trouble bringing the character to life.

Once, years and years ago, I tried to write a book about a black private eye. After 30 or 40 pages it was clear to me that I couldn't make it work. I felt fraudulent, and the character seemed wholly unconvincing.

Now, it is certainly possible for a writer to cross racial lines successfully. It was also by no means impossible for a white writer to bring off a book about a black private detective; a couple of years after my attempt, Ernest Tidyman made a very nice thing out of *Shaft*. And, sometime later, I proved to be capable of writing from a black point of view. Simmons, one of the lead characters of *The Specialists*, was a black man, and it was no more awkward to write about him than any of the others.

What made the difference? I'm not really sure. Looking back, it seems to me that in the first instance all I knew about my private detective was that he was black. When I looked at him, all I saw was his color. I couldn't see the person. When I wrote about Simmons, I didn't have that problem. I don't know what had originally caused it, and I don't know why it went away.

Finding the Right Shoe

A Florida writer who has attended two of my Write for Your Life seminars has published a couple of dozen confession stories all written from a black female viewpoint. His explanation is that a black confession magazine gave him his first acceptance, and that he's continued to write for that market out of a combination of loyalty and inertia.

I suspect there's more to it than that. For one reason or another, this white male writer finds it easiest to express himself fictionally through the eyes of a black woman. Perhaps he feels less exposed by having adopted a persona so circumstantially different from himself. I'm not sure the reason matters much.

An observer might urge him to do otherwise. "Quit hiding behind a mask," one might advise him. "Put your own self into your work. Write about what you know."

One is always well advised to put oneself into one's work, to write about what one knows. But it's my hunch that the man has been doing just that, that the mask he has taken up allows him to put himself into his work, that he is indeed writing about what he knows. If Flaubert could be Madame Bovary, why can't he be black and female in his fictional heart?

And does this mean he should properly aspire to nothing higher than the rather ill-paying and inglorious confession market for which he has been writing? Not necessarily. I should think he can grow artistically and commercially to whatever level his talent and drive can take him—and without necessarily writing from other than the point of view he has found comfortable. He could write romance novels, he could write mainstream fiction, he could write the contemporary black equivalent of *Madame Bovary*. The possibilities are vast.

Is Bill Caunitz limited because his heroes have to be take-charge guys?

I don't think so. If anything, it seems to me that he can congratulate himself for having found out what wasn't working and correcting it. That makes far more sense than trying to force life into a lifeless husk. If the shoe fits, wear it—but if it doesn't, toss it and find one that does. This fiction dodge is tough enough as it stands. There's no point looking for ways to make it tougher.

A curious business, this lunatic calling of ours. It lets us masquerade as all sorts of different people leading all manner of lives. By so doing, we find ourselves.

Go figure.

Turnabout Is Fair Play
July 1987

CAN CHARACTERS TAKE OVER A STORY?

"I had certain ideas about what was going to happen in the book, and then the characters just took over. They simply insisted on altering the course of the plot, and I couldn't control the little darlings."

Ah, yes. We've all heard versions of the above remark. Hopeful authors gunning for the bestseller list are forever saying something of the sort to Merv or Johnny or Oprah. There seems to be something self-serving in the ingenuousness of the statement. If you don't like my story, the author is saying, don't blame me. It's not my fault, it's all the fault of the little darlings, who simply wouldn't do what I wanted them to do.

One thinks of Humpty Dumpty. "When I use a word," he tells Alice, "it means precisely what I want it to mean, neither more nor less." It is, he explains, a question of who's to be in charge.

By the same token, I would think the writer ultimately remains in charge of the story he's writing. If he chooses to delegate authority to his characters, to give them free rein, well, he can do so secure in the knowledge that they're only carrying out his wishes. What are they, after all, but aspects of his own self, figments and fragments of his creative imagination? To blame them for doing what he has created them to do is to blame one's hand for acting as one's brain has willed it to act.

Yet one's characters do take over—I think everyone who writes fiction has that experience sooner or later. And sometimes these characters are not primarily aspects of oneself.

Sometimes they are other people.

Travels with Mr. Weber

What the hell is he talking about?

Ahem. Let me explain. As I write these lines, I am in a rented house in Key West. The day before yesterday I finished work on a book entitled *Turnabout*. In the ordinary course of things, I would not be slaving at my typewriter so soon after having completed a major project. I would be out for a walk, or getting a massage, or resting my damaged brain in front of the television set.

But I had an unusual experience writing *Turnabout*, with implications concerning both fiction and nonfiction, and I'd like to share them with you while they're still fresh.

Most of my writing, as most of you know, is fiction. *Turnabout* is not. It is a joint venture, written in collaboration with a gentleman named Richard Weber. Mr. Weber left home at the usually tender age of 13, and in his first month on his own he found employment as a long-haul trucker's helper, drank a great quantity of whiskey, slept with several women, committed his first armed robbery, and commenced what was to be a lifelong study of the oriental martial arts. Over the next several decades Mr. Weber had careers as a truck driver, as a criminal, as a mercenary, and as a drug dealer.

Ten years ago Mr. Weber's life began to turn itself around. (And I think I'll stop calling him Mr. Weber and start calling him Richie, because he is a friend of mine in addition to being my collaborator, and that is what I do in fact call him.) Richie works as a freelance confidential informant for the Drug Enforcement Administration and other law enforcement organizations, operating undercover, winning the confidence of narcotics dealers, setting up large drug transactions, and assisting in the arrest and conviction of these dealers. He is, I should add, exceptionally good at what he does.

Turnabout is his autobiography. It tells his story, in his own words, from the beginning to the present. It is, to begin with, an absolutely astonishing story of adventure and violence, but that's the least of it. Ultimately, it is a story of human redemption unique in my experience.

Had it been otherwise, I would never have undertaken to write it. I don't much like writing nonfiction, except for these monthly love letters to my profession, and I hate collaborating with anyone; as a child, they never wrote "Works and plays well with others" on my report card. But when I heard Richie's story, I knew that it deserved—nay, cried out—to be told. And, to my considerable surprise, I realized that I wanted to be a part of its telling.

Our collaboration had a lengthy pre-collaborative stage, a period of more than a year between the time we decided to do the book and the day we actually began work on it. Early on I taped several hours of conversation with Richie and wrote an 11-page, single-spaced book proposal. It took a while to place the book; every publisher who saw it was interested, but months passed before we got the deal we wanted with St. Martin's Press.

During this time, Richie and I became close friends. My wife Lynne and I spent a great deal of time with him, and we spoke daily. Richie became my instructor in Tai Chi. He assisted at Write for Your Life seminars in Fort Myers, Atlanta, and Cincinnati. Together we watched the Chinese acrobats perform in Orlando. Finally, I went along to Miami Beach a couple of times to observe as he set a dope deal in motion, and I got to meet some of the players on both sides.

Meanwhile, I was clearing up my other writing commitments. In September Richie went out west to work with the Reno office of the DEA, and when he came back we got down to work on the book. Every day for eight or ten days we got together and set the tape recorder spinning, and Richie told me the story of his life. For the most part, all I did was sit there. Every once in a while I would ask for more detail on a point, or toss in a question. We mailed the tapes to a typist he knew in San Francisco, requesting a verbatim transcript. I told the typist not to be concerned about niceties of spelling and punctuation, or to worry about dividing the text properly into paragraphs. Accordingly, we received some 400 pages of double-spaced transcript from her, all in a single stupefying paragraph.

Now I had to figure out what to do with all this. From the beginning I had been uncertain as to the best form for the narrative. I had any number of options. I could write the entire book in the third person, so that Lawrence Block would be reporting on Richard Weber's life. I could write the book in the first person, telling it in Richie's voice. I could combine these two approaches, with sections of third-person narrative intercut with passages in Richie's voice. I could even splice in sections in question-and-answer interview form.

Earlier, one prospective publisher had tried to talk me into presenting the material in the form of the novel. While the subject matter was certainly rich enough for fiction, I felt that a lot of the book's impact lay in the fact that it was a true story. Similarly, I came to believe that any artifice that stood between Richie and the reader would work to the book's detriment. I could best serve the book by becoming invisible, channeling Richie's words to the reader.

In order to introduce Richie and to provide some initial perspective and dimension, I decided to begin with a first-person present-tense chapter by Lawrence Block, reporting on the Miami Beach dope deal I'd observed directly. Then I would turn it over to Richie. He could begin with his initial decision to go to work for the DEA, then could go back and start his story with running away from home at age 13, and could then proceed chronologically through his life story. I wrote a couple of drafts of that first chapter—I am, after all, unused to functioning as a reporter—and then I groped my way through some 30 pages of first draft, and then I bundled up everything, the transcript and the tapes and my notes, and ran off to isolate myself in Key West.

And wrote the book.

I was uniquely well prepared to do this. Besides having the transcript with me, I had heard all the material at the time it was recorded. In addition, I had heard most of the stories on the tape several times over on other occasions; not as specific preparation for the book but in the course of the exchange of life stories that is part of the establishment of a friendship. I had also heard dozens of stories that didn't get on the transcript. In short, I know Richie as few people have known him, and this certainly made it easier for me to write in his voice.

When I did, something curious happened.

When I get profoundly involved in the writing of a book, when I immerse myself in it, its reality is at least as great as the external reality of my life during that period. If I am to get into a book, I can only do so by getting out of myself to a corresponding extent.

Similarly, I tend to become my viewpoint characters. This is especially true when I write in the first person, as I have done in the greater portion of my novels in recent years. During the hours that I spend at the typewriter, and to a lesser extent during other hours as well, I am seeing through the character's eyes, filtering my perceptions through the character's world view, and, of course, speaking in the character's voice.

Don't get the wrong idea. When I'm writing about Bernie Rhodenbarr, my crime-solving burglar, I don't go around breaking into other people's houses. Like Humpty Dumpty, I'm quite clear as to who's in charge here. But while I'm writing, though I may not entirely cease being Lawrence Block, I definitely do become Bernie Rhodenbarr or Matthew Scudder or Evan Tanner or Chip Harrison. Some transformational process occurs, and when I write a scene, I don't stop and figure out what Bernie or Matt or whoever would say in that situation. I *am* the character, and I react accordingly.

I should point out that I can do this without entirely ceasing to be myself, because these characters are creations of mine, and out of what other than my own self could I have conceivably created them? When I become Bernie, I am merely becoming that portion of myself from which Bernie evolved. This may make the process no less mysterious, but it does enable me to fit comfortably in the character's skin.

This, of course, was not the case with *Turnabout*. For one thing, the book was not fiction, and I did not have the leeway one has as a novelist. I was attempting to produce a factual account, and aside from changing some names I did not intend to take any liberties with the facts. In addition, I already had been exposed to the material in Richie's own words, and I had those words present on the transcript and in my own memory.

At the same time, I had a lot of left-brain decisions to make while writing the book. I had to determine which incidents to include and which to omit, and I had to decide in how much detail certain incidents ought to be recorded. It was Lawrence Block who had to make those decisions.

All the same, writing the book, I became the character, and this time the character was not altogether of my own making. I could write the book only by seeing the world through Richie's eyes and reliving the story from inside Richie's skin. Sometimes in the course of the narrative it would seem to me that a comment would be called for, and it might be that Richie had not commented on that particular topic in my hearing. I found myself making the comment for him, and acting with much the same assurance that I would possess in doing the same thing for Matt or Bernie or Evan or Chip.

The end of a day's work would find me exhausted. This in itself was unremarkable; I was putting in long hours and getting a lot of work done each day, and I'd have felt strung out whatever I was writing. But I felt specifically undone by the effort involved in being another person all day.

I mentioned as much late one night to Lynne. I called her every night, and she was the only person with whom I was in contact while I worked on the book, and indeed the only person who knew how to get hold of me. (When you don't even let your agent have your telephone number, *that's* isolation.) The following night, she reported that the process I was engaged in seemed to be a two-way street.

"Richie said something funny today," she said. "He said he's been feeling weird the past few days, as though there's somebody crawling around inside his head. And he finally figured out that it must be you. So I told him what you said last night, and I said, 'Rich, quit fighting! Let Larry get in there. He won't hurt anything.'"

The Alchemic Miracle

Before I wrote *Turnabout*, I had trouble swallowing Truman Capote's definition of *In Cold Blood* as a nonfiction novel. The phrase seemed a contradiction in terms and nothing more. Similarly, I figured that Norman Mailer had elected to call *The Executioner's Song* a novel chiefly because fewer sales will carry you to the top of the fiction bestseller list than the nonfiction list.

Now I'm a little closer to knowing what they meant. When a novelist writes factual material from the point of view of a real person, he is performing the same alchemic miracle as when his characters are imaginary and his incidents invented. Fiction, it seems to me, is not simply any piece of prose that lacks veracity. It is, I submit, an account of real or imagined events filtered through the inner truth of a fictioneer's vision.

If that sounds mysterious, well, I should hope so. Fiction-writing is a mystery, and the longer I participate in it the more utterly mysterious it appears to me. I can only give thanks that I don't have to understand what I'm doing in order to do it.

Pieces of String Too Small to Save
August 1987

POTPOURRI FROM A COLUMNIST'S MAILBAG

Ever since this column's inception in the Jurassic Era, one its shaggiest fringe benefits has been the response it has generated from you its readers. *WD* subscribers are, after all, writers, and one of the things they write is letters. (*Are* letters? *Some* of the things they write are letters? Never mind.)

I always enjoy reading mail from readers, except for the occasional letter with an adverse comment on my lineage or personal behavior, and more often than not I reply. (Years ago I answered absolutely everything, but consider how much lower postal rates were then.) Answered or not, reader mail lets me know that you're out there and helps me get my energy up for the next column. And, in more than a few instances, it suggests a topic or avenue of approach for a column somewhere down the line.

Now and then someone raises a point of general interest, but one that's just not a stout enough peg to hang a whole column on. "I'll have to write about that some time," I tell myself, and toss the letter in a file.

A frugal New Englander was supposed to have had a drawer marked "Pieces of string too small to save," and I once caught myself sorting hardware, with some items going into a jar I'd mentally labeled "Bent nails not worth straightening." Here, then, are some bent nails and short strings, all strung together and hammered into a column:

Abstract Questions

Last year I met an artist and asked him what type of art he collected. As he was of the abstract school, I figured he would collect abstract art. I was surprised to learn he collected Japanese art. He explained that abstract was too close to home for him. He would be too critical toward other abstract paintings, and might lose some of his own style.

It made sense, and I began to wonder if authors were similarly inclined. Is there anything you don't like to read when writing? I recall that Georges Simenon reads nothing but biographies and history to avoid being influenced by other writers. Do you agree?

I understand the artist's position. It can be a conflict to create and collect in the same area, just as coin and antique dealers frequently find it a conflict to collect the same kind of material in which they trade.

Quite a few writers avoid reading other people's fiction while writing their own. Some are concerned that their own style will be eroded by exposure to another's style. Others find themselves comparing their work to what they're reading, seeing only those ways in which the other person's work is superior to their own; this saps their confidence and inhibits them.

In my own case, I often have difficulty reading anybody's fiction when I'm hard at work on my own. Even if I'm done for the day, even if my own work has been exiled from my conscious mind and consigned to my subconscious, I am nevertheless too much caught up in my own imaginary world to immerse myself in someone else's. When my typewriter is really smoking, I don't have enough energy at the day's end to follow somebody's storyline, let alone get lost in it. It's all I can do to stare at something brainless on television.

In more ordinary times, I certainly don't avoid any kind of writing because I'm afraid of its influence. Some of my favorite writers are stylistically and categorically far different from me, while other favorites are quite close. Donald E. Westlake and I are frequently mentioned in the same breath, and our pseudonymous work is occasionally misattributed, yet each of us is an enthusiastic reader of the other's work.

It's worth noting, I think, that many writers of fiction read progressively less fiction with the passage of time. Most (but not all) fictioneers start out as heavy readers, but we don't all remain so. I know several long-time pros who claim to avoid reading fiction altogether, except for corporate reports and Presidential press releases.

I'm not sure why this happens. It may be that fiction loses its power to draw one in when one knows how it's made, just as a butcher will lose his taste for sausage. Similarly, writing sharpens one's critical senses, and one becomes increasingly sensitive to amateurishness and clumsiness in what one reads.

I still read a great deal, and when I find something I truly like, I enjoy it as much as I ever enjoyed anything. But it seems to me that each year I leave a greater proportion of books unfinished, and I read less in my own field not for fear of influence but because I find less in that field engaging.

Prevailing Customs

I've just finished a novel. Could I possibly prevail upon you to read the manuscript?

No.

No way.

Every professional writer gets asked this question a lot, and most of us learn to say no. Many of us wind up saying it in a loud voice, because the people we say it to don't want to take it for an answer.

Reading something one has not oneself chosen to read is work. Reading critically, with an eye toward telling the author what is right and wrong with it, is *hard* work. It is, furthermore, work that one is more often than not expected to perform for free, out of some professional obligation to encourage the development of new talent.

It is work, too, for which one is not necessarily qualified. Whatever ability I may have as a writer does not necessarily qualify me as an editor, and it certainly does not certify me as a judge. I am far too sensitive to matters of style to read manuscripts objectively; if all of the books on the current bestseller list were submitted to me anonymously and in manuscript form, I don't doubt that I would reject more than half of them out of hand as unworthy of publication.

William Faulkner is supposed to have asked Sherwood Anderson to read his first novel in manuscript. "I'll get someone to publish it," Anderson replied, "but please don't ask me to *read* it."

Please don't ask me to get your book published, either. And that, I might add, is what most new writers are really after when they ask another writer to read their work. Not criticism, not even praise and acknowledgment, but a little help on the road to publication.

I can't provide that help. My own agent is not open to new clients. I can't recommend any other agents, or provide any introductions to editors or publishers. I won't deny for a minute that introductions and referrals and recommendations go a long way toward getting a manuscript some useful editorial attention, and I would advise you to exploit whatever friendships and acquaintances might prove useful. But leave me out of it.

Film Mistreatments

What control do you have over the treatment of your work in films? How do you feel about letting filmmakers change and reinterpret your books?

I've been asked this question a lot since *Eight Million Ways to Die* was filmed, with the locale shifted from New York to Los Angeles and the plot reworked beyond all recognition. When *Burglar* came out, with Whoopi Goldberg playing Bernie Rhodenbarr, the question came up again.

I don't have any control over the treatment of my work in films, and I think that's the way it ought to be.

This is not to say that I don't wish *Eight Million Ways to Die* had been a better film than it was. I do, and I think it would have been better if the producers had stayed closer to the original material. But it's really none of my business. They bought the right to make a picture and to make it any way they wanted, and I agreed to that when I took the money.

Some writers go nuts about this sort of thing. When *The French Lieutenant's Woman* was released as a film, John Fowles said he regretted having allowed it, that forever after people would envision the film rather than his book when they thought of the story. Many writers have written screenplays in order to have some control over what winds up on the screen, and that doesn't always work; they can always bring in another writer to make late changes, and, failing that, a willful director can always screw things up all by himself. Joseph Wambaugh was sufficiently incensed at the treatment his books got not only to write but also to direct.

Even then your control's limited. A book, after all, is one person's work, one writer's vision set down on the page in that writer's own words. A film is always a collective effort, the product of the artistic abilities of a great many different people. Actors, editors, cameramen, the second unit crew—everybody has something to do with what winds up on the screen.

The people who make films spend an extraordinary amount of money. Their primary concern, understandably enough, is to get something made that will bring enough people into enough theaters to earn back that sum of money—and, God willing, more. It's nice if they can be true to the author's vision of the material while they're at it, but if not, tough.

A writer gets a lot of money for film rights to a property. He also picks up a good deal in the way of publicity, and his book sales go up if a film based on his work does any business at all. He can legitimately decide it's not worth it; J.D. Salinger, dismayed at an adaptation of "Uncle Wiggily in Connecticut," did just that, refusing ever after to sell film rights to anything else of his. That strikes me as a wholly unassailable artistic position, but it's not one I myself have been inclined to take. I'm profoundly grateful that a couple of my literary properties have been purchased for filming and that a couple of films have actually been made and released. I can like or dislike the finished product, but where do I get off feeling betrayed?

James M. Cain had the best word on the subject. Someone asked him, author of *Mildred Pierce* and *The Postman Always Rings Twice*, how he felt about what the movie industry had done to his books. "But they haven't done *anything* to my books," he said, with a gesture. "They're right over there on the shelf, exactly as I wrote them."

On-the-Job Training

My job is stifling my creativity and I've been thinking of getting something less demanding. What are the best jobs for a writer-in-training?

That depends on who you are and what you're looking for. There are three things a job can provide—life experience, technical training, and money to live on. Your ideal job is the one that best supplies what you most need.

Will Adler, a young mystery writer, has what strikes me as an ideal job. He's a desk clerk at a fleabag hotel in Manhattan. That's a great source of life experience—but only if that particular world and the people in it will nourish the kind of fiction you want to write. Another writer might be more likely to draw inspiration from a job as a forest ranger, or a niche in the corporate world, or a hitch in the Navy.

For technical training, my own belief is that the best job involves reading the manuscripts of amateur writers. I had this job myself in a literary agency, but one could have about the same experience as a first reader at a publishing house. Seeing what does and doesn't work in somebody else's fiction is invaluable, and one can see this more easily in less polished work, and more readily in manuscript than in printed form.

Finally, if you know what you want to write and how you want to write it, the best job is that which pays the rent and puts food on the table with the least wear and tear on your body-mind-spirit. Some kind of boring assembly-line work may be ideal.

My Newsletter: I get out an email newsletter at unpredictable intervals, but rarely more often than every other week. I'll be happy to add you to the distribution list.

A blank email to lawbloc@gmail.com with "newsletter" in the subject line will get you on the list, and a click of the "Unsubscribe" link will get you off it, should you ultimately decide you're happier without it.

Lawrence Block has been writing award-winning mystery and suspense fiction for half a century. His newest book is *In Sunlight or in Shadow*, an anthology with 17 new stories, each inspired by an Edward Hopper painting; contributors include Stephen King, Joyce Carol Oates, Lee Child, Megan Abbott, Michael Connelly, Jeffery Deaver, and Joe Lansdale. His most recent novel, pitched by his Hollywood agent as "James M. Cain on Viagra," is *The Girl with the Deep Blue Eyes*. Other recent works of fiction include *The Burglar Who Counted The Spoons*, featuring Bernie Rhodenbarr; *Keller's Fedora*, featuring philatelist and assassin Keller; and *A Drop Of The Hard Stuff*, featuring Matthew Scudder, brilliantly embodied by Liam Neeson in the new film, *A Walk Among The Tombstones*. Several of his other books have also been filmed, although not terribly well. He's well known for his books for writers, including the classic *Telling Lies For Fun & Profit* and *Write For Your Life*, and has recently published a collection of his writings about the mystery genre and its practitioners, *The Crime Of Our Lives*. In addition to prose works, he has written episodic television (*Tilt!*) and the Wong Kar-wai film, *My Blueberry Nights*. He is a modest and humble fellow, although you would never guess as much from this biographical note.

Email: lawbloc@gmail.com
Twitter: @LawrenceBlock
Facebook: lawrence.block
Website: lawrenceblock.com

www.ingramcontent.com/pod-product-compliance
Lightning Source LLC
Chambersburg PA
CBHW060459090426
42735CB00011B/2039